FLY IDAHO!

A Guide to Adventure in the Idaho Backcountry

Idaho Airport Facilities Directory
Idaho Div. Aeronautics
  208/334 - 8775

Bob Plummers 3 day Mtn flying
Seminar. Challis Idaho
May-June-July
  208/879-2364

Galen L. Hanselman

Q.E.I. Publishing, Box 1236, Hailey, Idaho 83333

Authored by: Galen L. Hanselman
Edited by: Shannon Besoyan
Copy Edited by: Mary L. Hanselman, Bob Doyle

Production by Peak Media, Inc.
P.O. Box 925 Hailey, ID 83333
Creative Director Mark Kashino
Art Director Judy Guryan

Photo Credits: all color by John Plummer
Cover: Bob Hannah airplane photo by John Plummer
black & white by author or as otherwise noted

Published by:
Q.E.I. Publishing
Box 1236, Hailey, Idaho 83333
(208)788-5176, (800)-574-9702

Printing History: First published in 1994.
LC# 94-92030
ISBN# 1-884915-05-1

Printed in Korea

DEDICATION

Captain Ben Hurtig,
U.S.M.C. retired

"Good judgment comes from experience; experience comes from bad judgement." Unknown quote taken from Ben Hurtig's log book.

This book is dedicated to my long-time friend Ben Hurtig. Ben has been instrumental in teaching literally thousands of "kids" the virtues of shooting straight, telling the truth, and riding tall in the saddle.

When I was 13, Ben introduced me to a lifelong appreciation and responsibility associated with firearms and hunting. At the age of 29, Ben and his wife Peggy, gave me the self confidence I needed to leave a full time job and start my own business (with a wife, a two year old son, and a hundred dollars in the bank).

In spite of my efforts, the business grew and prospered. Ben then sparked in me an interest in aviation as he brought broken headsets and flakey intercoms for me to repair. When he took me flying in his Super Cub, I was fascinated by the instrumentation, the discipline, and learning required to become a good pilot. The hook was set! I soon learned how to fly and discovered that airplanes and business were a natural mix.

While listening to Ben tell stories of flying the Idaho Backcountry, my interest piqued. Ben directed me to getting some backcountry flying instruction from the best pilots in the business. The more I learned, the more questions I had for Ben concerning where an airstrip was, what the approach was like, or how the fishing was. It was at this point I decided to document this information, not only for my own use, but for the adventure and safety of others in *FLY-IDAHO!*

I'm not sure where this fork in my life will lead but I do know how I got to this juncture. Without the confidence and encouragement from my friend, I would never have gotten off the ground.

For this I remain forever grateful, and, while I look forward to my next adventure, I know it will be influenced by the fine gentleman to whom this book is dedicated: Ben Hurtig.

WARNING & DISCLAIMER

The information in *Fly-Idaho! a guide to Adventure in the Idaho Backcountry,* has been compiled from many sources, including but not limited to, the Idaho Division of Aeronautics, U.S. Forest Service, Idaho Fish and Game, and personal on-scene visits by the author. Although every effort has been made to assure accuracy, no warrant is made and no responsibility is assumed to any person or persons in connection with the use of this information contained herein or later made a part of this book adding to, or deleting, or otherwise affecting those contents.

The procedures for each airport are advisory in nature and represent recommendations from experienced pilots, but do not substitute for sound judgement necessary for safety. Pay particular attention to the Airport Caution section of each airport: here you'll find rules of good practice where conditions or features call for something other than normal procedures.

Fly Idaho! a guide to Adventure in the Idaho Backcountry, begins where other books leave off. Ten of the airstrips in this book have never before been published in a directory. None of the airstrips in this book have paved surfaces, and in fact the surfaces run the gamut from undefinable brush covered hill sides, to mine tailings, to golf course-like turf.

Generally, with exceptions noted, there is no fuel available, no runway lighting, no aircraft maintenance, no beacons, no emergency services, no radio communications, no towns, and no people at any of these airstrips. Quite often, windsocks, runway markings, and tiedowns are non-existent.

The Relative Hazard Index (RHI) should not be used as a substitute for qualified instruction in visiting a "new" airstrip. The RHI is simply an objective rating of the number of known current physical hazards associated with an airstrip with which some comparisons can be made to the RHI of other airstrips. The RHI does not factor in airplane performance, pilot performance/experience, isolation, lack of communication, nor potential hazards such as adverse weather and threat of big animal collisions.

Elk, deer, moose, bear, bighorn sheep, mountain goats, badgers, ground squirrels, cattle, horses, and domestic sheep all claim these airstrips as their own. Expect to see big game animals grazing on the runway while on short final. Expect moose to affectionately rub against your airplane while it is tied down and fighting bull moose to stumble through your new Stits. Expect stone chips on your prop and in that new paint job. Expect those cute little beavers to have dammed up the nearby creek and flooded the runway (or dropped some trees on it).

This book is sold with the understanding that the author and publisher are not engaged in providing a navigational information update service. The author and publisher assume no responsibility in the accuracy of the navigational information contained within nor in the interpolation or interpretation of the value of the RHI numbers.

The purpose of this book is neither to encourage nor to discourage a pilot from utilizing the Idaho Backcountry airstrips. Rather it is to provide as much objective information with which the pilot can use to intelligently and safely pursue adventure in Idaho's most beautiful, historic, and remote areas. If you purchased this guide for any other reason or feel that it does not meet your needs, please return it with sales slip for a full refund.

ACKNOWLEDGMENTS

Tom Allegrezza, Don Atkinson, Backeddy Press, Darell Bentz, Rusty Bentz, Shannon Besoyan, Barry Bryant, Cort Conley, William S. Cooper, Bob Danner, Bill Dorris, Mike Dorris, Ray Glidden, John Goostrey, Judy Guryan, Bob Hannah, Marc Hanselman, Mary Hanselman, Diana Haynes, Ken Hessel, Hank Hill, Larry Hippler, Ben Hurtig, Idaho County Free Press, Idaho State Historical Society, Idaho State Library, Pete Johnson, Mark Kashino, Art Lazzarini, Bonnie Lazzarini, Dennis Loosli, Andrew J. McNab, John Maakestad, Russell Munson, Guy Pere, Bob Plummer, Gridley Rowles, E. Lee Schlender, State of Idaho Division of Aeronautics, Pam Staton, Sterling Stoll, Steve Tubbs, Lita West, Jim White.

Thanks to Bob "Buckwheat" Hannah, aka "Hurricane Hannah", for his help in locating the unknown airstrips of Big Creek and Hells Canyon, as well as his assistance as subject for the cover shot of *FLY IDAHO!* While Bob is best known for his precision, intelligence, endurance, and athletic ability riding motorcycles, he has carried those same attributes into his flying. When he isn't flying warbirds, or performing aerobatics in his Pitts, he is busy flying (as well as anyone I know) the Idaho Backcountry in his Super Cub.

Thanks to professional photographer John Plummer who made this project feasible. John spent innumerable hours flying right seat (actually the seat was missing - as well as his door) photographing the Idaho Backcountry airstrips. His enthusiasm for the project has never wavered - even when we lost Loran coverage in Northern Idaho and were proceeding hell bent for leather (read: lost) towards the Canadian border or when our only chart blew out the open door of the airplane somewhere over Hells Canyon - I think.

A special thanks goes to my wife Mary, who has been exceedingly tolerant in my never-ending pursuit of dreams and adventure. And now it appears as if our son, Marc, has heard the same call to adventure as his father, as he travels the world searching for new rock to climb. I suspect, if men came with warranties, Mary would have gotten a full refund long ago.

HOW TO USE THIS BOOK

QUICK START - Use the quick start procedure if you are choosing a destination you are familiar with and simply want to refamiliarize yourself with the airport environment and navigation information.

a. Turn to the color air section for aerial views of your destination airstrip. Review the RHI number.

JUMP START - If you are familiar with the different regions of Idaho and simply want to find out more about specific airstrips.

a. Turn to the ground section for airport descriptions, services and lodging, camping, exploring, history, hunting and fishing, hikes, and mountain bike rides to each of the airstrips within the region.

b. Turn to the color air section for aerial views of each of the airstrips. Use the photos to familiarize yourself with the location of the airstrip relative to the surrounding terrain. Use the RHI number (review the RHI derivation under General Information) to help determine the known physical hazards associated with this strip.

KICK START - Use this procedure for trip planning and are unfamiliar with the different geographical regions of Idaho.

a. Use the geographical index map to locate specific regions. Read the regional descriptions and associated list of airstrips.

b. Turn to the ground section for airport descriptions, services and lodging, camping, exploring, history, hunting and fishing, hikes, and mountain bike rides to each of the airstrips within the region.

c. Turn to the color air section for aerial views of each of the airstrips. Use the photos to familiarize yourself with the location of the airstrip relative to the surrounding terrain. Use the RHI number (review the RHI derivation under General Information) to help determine the known physical hazards associated with this strip.

ABOUT THE AUTHOR

The author of *FLY-IDAHO!* seems like a pleasant, unassuming and forthright fellow at first meeting; but scratch the surface and you will continue to become engaged with the multifaceted personality and talents of Galen L. Hanselman.

A physicist by education, he has seemingly, quite effortlessly, gone about the pursuit of a multitude of interests and pasttimes, turning each and every one of them into a success story.

FLY-IDAHO! happens to be his most recent adventure, which evolved from a love for flying and a love for the State of Idaho, where he has lived for most of his life.

An anniversary present from his wife Mary, his first flying lesson ultimately evolved into the much needed escape mechanism from his thriving electronics business.

In 1989, he was able to achieve what most men (and women) dream of...an early retirement at the age of 41. After selling his business, he collared his co-pilot, a golden retriever named Dusty, and began flying Idaho in earnest.

In between Idaho adventures, he has pursued his love for hunting in Argentina (ducks, geese, and upland game), Mexico (whitewings and ducks), Alaska (caribou and salmon), and South Dakota (pheasants). But he soon learned that there really is no place like home (especially if you live in Idaho), and set about recording his tracks up and down the state that boasts more wilderness than any other in the lower 48.

When you're in the Backcountry, look around for a jolly, bearded fellow under a well-travelled fedora. He'll probably be chatting with another good old boy, listening for more tales that otherwise would be lost in time...like the ones you will find as you enjoy reading *FLY-IDAHO!*

Shannon Besoyan

SYMBOLS/ABBREVIATIONS

Air Section

RHI ... Relative Hazard Index
AE ... Airport Environment
A/D ... Approach/Departure
RSH ... Runway Surface Hazards
IAFD ... Idaho Airport Flight Directory
W ... Wilderness Airport, special rules apply

	19	RHI
11	07	01
AE	A/D	RSH

For derivation of the RHI number see page I-xx.

Airport Layout Legend

- Building
- City or town
- Fence
- Paved Road
- Unpaved Road

- Railroad
- River or stream
- Swamp or Marsh
- Trees
- Forest or Woodland

- Lake or Reservoir
- Power Line
- Paved Surface
- Windcone
- Beacon
- Airport Location

Ground Section

Lodging Information

R: Restaurant on premises, CU: Cooking Units, P: Pets Allowed, TV: TV in rooms, C/M: Cable TV/Movies, SP: Swimming Pool, Ph: Phone in room, MR: Meeting Room, AB: Alcoholic Beverages, SH: Showers, L: Laundry Facilities, HU: R.V. Hookups, LP: LP Gas, DS: Dump Station, CC: Major Credit Cards accepted, HT: Spa/Hot Tub, HA: Handicap Access Facilities

Camping Information

* primitive camping, no facilities
** improved camp sites with tables, fire rings, and toilet
*** deluxe camp sites with tables, fire rings, toilets, showers, and often recreational facilities such as horse shoes, boat dock, community fire ring, etc.

SYMBOLS/ABBREVIATIONS

Explanation of symbols
used in the Ground Section

 Mountains

 Camping

 Desert

 Dining

 Canyon

 Restrooms

 Trees

 Lodging

 Lakes & Rivers

 Telephone

 Potable Water

 Courtesy Car

 Boating

 Hunting

 Bicycling

 Fishing

GEOGRAPHICAL INDEX

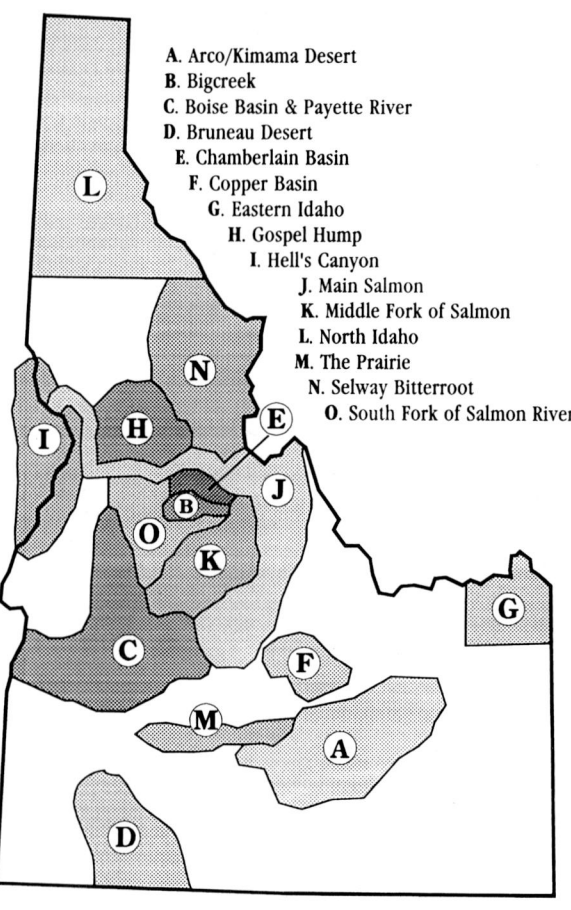

TABLE OF CONTENTS

ARCO/KIMAMA DESERT

The Arco/Kimama Desert is mysteriously haunting and downright eerie. Its rugged lunar-like surface of volcanic rock is forbidding and does not beckon the foot traveler. Early trappers and wagon trains could not traverse the region, but today, meandering two-track roads cross scattered areas of vegetation. However, the hundreds of square miles of lava flows remain largely unknown and could very well be the least explored region of the state.

BIG CREEK

Big Creek is a major tributary of the legendary Middle Fork of the Salmon River Country. This region contains all the superlatives of the Idaho Backcountry. Rich in history, it was the battle ground of the Sheepeater War of 1879.

The late 1800s saw lucrative gold strikes, the 1900s hosted hardy pioneer ranching families, and the 1940s and 1950s welcomed dude ranching. Today, the Forest Service and Fish and Game have acquired most of these private parcels and returned the region to its natural state.

BOISE BASIN & PAYETTE RIVER

Only remnants remain of the Boise Basin's earlier days of boomtowns and the gold rushes of the 1860s. But exist they do...isolated from the outside world by hundreds of miles of mountain wilderness. Tucked far away in this rugged and beautiful country, the lure of "hitting it big" continues to drive a few men to endure the hardships of this region. Current-day visitors are lured to the area, not by hardships but the rich recreational opportunities... fly-fishing, whitewater rafting, and excellent elk hunting. But after the sportsmen return home to the comforts of civilization, the solitude of the Boise Basin is broken only by the occasional sound of a prospector's pick.

BRUNEAU DESERT

Just when you think you have a grasp of Idaho's vast and varied geography, the Gem State throws you a curve...as in great sand dunes, the highest in North America! The Bruneau State Park's sand dunes are bordered to the south by the spectacular Bruneau Canyon, home of bighorn sheep and antelope. As you fly over the canyon, the gorge appears so quickly that the desert flats seem to split apart in front of you.

The Paiute Indians discovered this hidden canyon long ago, and their elaborate drawings can be found on rock slabs across the desert. Today, the remaining Paiutes live on the Duck Valley Indian Reservation where a fishing permits can be purchased for trophy rainbow trout.

CHAMBERLAIN BASIN

Pristine and quiet is this high country wilderness basin, until the fall of the year, when it becomes a very busy drop-off point for elk hunters from around the world. For privacy seek spring or summer, and you will share this beautiful basin only with the moose. And, it appears they enjoy your company. It is not uncommon to see a moose meandering toward an airplane to give it a friendly little moosey nudge. Some say they even get downright amorous.

COPPER BASIN

When you visit Copper Basin, you will understand why fishermen have discreetly chosen to keep it a secret. A haunt of Idaho's famous outdoor writer Ted Trueblood, the basin used to provide an abundance of small mountain streams filled with scrappy rainbows and brook trout. However, for the time being, the seven-year drought has taken its toll on the fishing. The rugged and diverse terrain is certainly worth visiting in the meantime, and, when the fishing does come back, you won't hear a word about it.

EASTERN IDAHO

Eastern Idaho rises with mountain splendor, out of fertile agricultural valleys to the snow-capped peaks of the Grand Tetons. Vast forests rise out of a giant caldera - a land of towering pines, colorful aspen and abundant wildflowers - a land of thundering waterfalls, glistening lakes and free running rivers. Trumpeter swans, bald eagles, elk and moose all call this home. This wild land of challenge is where mountain men and Indians rendezvoused in the early years. Uncrowded still, it beckons to be rediscovered.

GOSPEL HUMP

The friendly folk of this area, nestled contentedly in the heart of Idaho, have found themselves in the midst of a hornet's nest as radical environmentalists and the U.S. Forest Service take their stands on the controversial issue of logging. The otherwise enviable peace and tranquility of life, way off the beaten path, has got the woods buzzing with controversy. The summer of 1993 saw the town of Dixie in turmoil with arrests when members of the Earth First group allegedly spiked and chained themselves to trees, and destroyed roads. Meanwhile the Forest Service opened new areas for clear cut logging.

HELLS CANYON

Although Idaho truly is a paradise found for sportsmen and outdoor enthusiasts, Hells Canyon takes the honors as the "deepest gorge in North America" providing limitless recreational opportunities. Seventy miles of rugged river country is lined with crumbling black basalt walls thrust high over head, twisting across the deep blue skyline. The deep canyon offers jet boating, river rafting, fishing and hunting, and hiking. And, to complete the picture, the Seven Devils peaks hide 30 alpine lakes and many miles of hiking trails.

MAIN SALMON

The legendary Salmon River, called the "River of No Return", by Lewis and Clark, has its humble beginning near the Smiley Creek Airstrip. A modest stream at this point, gives no suggestion of what's to come. Gaining power and force, as it takes a mighty plunge to its confluence with the Snake River some 400 miles downstream, the Salmon takes on the attitude of its status as a "Wild and Scenic River". This great roaring river with its white sandy beaches and great canyon wilderness is a must to see.

MIDDLE FORK OF SALMON

Accessible only by trail, whitewater raft, or airplane, the Middle Fork Country sums up what Idaho Backcountry is all about. History, as we know it, began with the Sheepeater Indians. Mining and ranching followed. Today it is held in great esteem as protected wilderness, preserved as a treasure for the future of mankind. Steep and awesome canyon walls meet crystal clear water that nurture a bounty of elk, bighorn sheep, and wild trout. Once visited, the Middle Fork will never leave you.

NORTH IDAHO

North Idaho boast a greater concentration of lakes than any other western state. Home of the osprey and the great

American bald eagle, this land of fishing boats and rain-washed docks holds the key to trophy trout and kokanee salmon fishing. A much wetter climate than the southern portion of the state, this region provides all the lushness that only comes with and abundance of precipitation. North Idaho is a land of mossy cascades, giant cedars and forest flowers. Taste the sweetness of wild huckleberries, smell the aroma of fresh cut timber, and bask in the friendliness of a casual and relaxed countryside.

The Prairie: The gently rolling hills of the Prairie separate the agricultural lands of the Snake River Basin from the rugged mountain terrain of central Idaho. Both migrating Indians and early settlers took this easier route through this portion of Idaho. The bountiful prairie provided Indians with camas bulbs, hunting, and fishing. A branch of the Oregon trail brought settlers to the Prairie in the 1860s followed by an influx of men seeking asylum from the ravages of the Civil War and fortunes in gold.

Selway Bitterroot: The Selway-Bitterroot Country has deep cut canyons which provide dramatic slashes through the mountains. The Selway, Lochsa, and Clearwater Rivers provide miles of tumbling whitewater interspersed with quiet pools for migratory and resident fish. The excellent wildlife habitat of these mountains produces large herds of elk, moose, and other big game. The ridges between the deep canyons have provided travel corridors across the mountains for centuries of mankind, including Nez Perce Indians and, in 1805, the Lewis and Clark expedition.

South Fork of Salmon: Time stopped here at just about the right moment. Largely undiscovered by the tourist industry, the quaint towns of Warren and Yellowpine are living museums of days gone by. The South Fork country lies outside the western border of the Frank Church River of No Return Wilderness. Once the focus of frenzied gold seekers, it is heavily timbered mountainous country. In these parts, Thunder Mountain buried the boom town of Roosevelt under a murky lake and found its way into print as the subject of a Zane Gray novel of the same name. The past 100 years really haven't left much of a mark on these little hamlets, due to the area's remoteness. Long dusty wagon roads still wind their way through the mountains...with no telephone lines overhead.

Geographical & Historical Information

Flying Information

General Information

Appendix

* note: location of airstrips indicated by (*) are not commonly shown on aeronautical charts but have been shown on portions of remarked Great Falls sectional chart in *FLY IDAHO!*

These remarked charts are FOR INFORMATION ONLY and are NOT TO BE USED FOR NAVIGATION!

LET'S GO!

AIR

AIR NOTES

_____

_____

_____

_____

_____

_____

_____

_____

_____

_____

_____

_____

_____

_____

_____

ANTELOPE VALLEY

ANTELOPE VALLEY   U92

Lat: N43-40.56
Long: W113-36.10

Class: State REC EM
Chart: Salt Lake

CTAF: 122.9
FSS: 123.6

AIRPORT LAYOUT

TIEDOWNS

3450 X 50 TURF

ANTELOPE G.S.

N

5

23

ELEVATION 6180

AIRPORT CAUTION • The IAFD recommends "**landing RWY 5, depart RWY 23** when wind conditions allow. • Airport located in high mountain valley surrounded by high terrain. • Close flight plan prior to landing. • No winter maintenance." • Info: **(208)334-8775** Div. of Aeronautics.

ATLANTA

ATLANTA

55H

CTAF: 122.9
FSS: 122.6

Lat: N43-49.49
Long: W115-19.91

Class: CA REC EM
Chart: Salt Lake

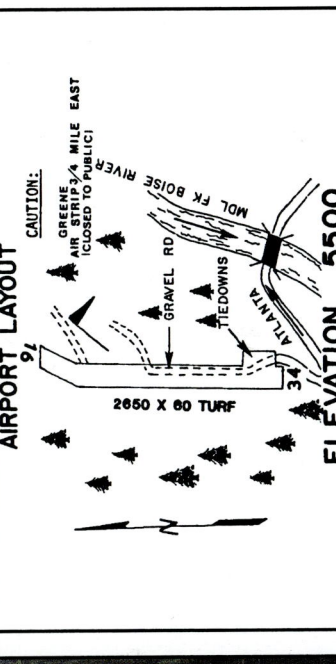

AIRPORT LAYOUT

CAUTION:

GREENE
AIR STRIP 3/4 MILE EAST
(CLOSED TO PUBLIC)

MDL FK BOISE RIVER

GRAVEL RD

TIEDOWNS

ATLANTA

16

2650 X 60 TURF

34

N

ELEVATION 5500

16

34

AIRPORT CAUTION • High-timbered ridges limit the maneuvering area. • **CAUTION:** Due to close proximity of Greene Airport, monitor-announce intentions on 122.9. • High-timbered ridges limit the maneuvering area. • The IAFD recommends: **Land-RWY34. Depart-RWY 16.** Approach up Boise River — making right circling pattern over valley to check traffic at Greene Airport. Depart with a right turn-out down Boise River. • Close flight plan with Boise FSS prior to landing. • No winter maintenance. • Info: **(208)336-0606.**

BEAR TRAP

BEAR TRAP 1UØ

CTAF: 122.9
FSS: 122.4

Lat: N42-58.49
Long: W113-21.03

Class: State EM
Chart: Salt Lake

AIRPORT LAYOUT

SAGE BRUSH

SAGE BRUSH

2250 X 120 TURF

TIEDOWNS

ARCO

MINIDOKA

N

24

6

ELEVATION 4716

AIRPORT CAUTION • The IAFD advises: **"No line of sight between RWY ends. RWY 6-24 subject to ongoing damange by livestock,** grounds vehicles, and rodents. • Close flight plan prior to landing. • No winter maintenance."
• Info: (208)334-8775 Div. of Aeronautics.

BERNARD

17

35

22	RHI
10	02
AE	A/D	RSH

BERNARD (W)

U54

CTAF: 122.9   Lat: N44-58.78   Class: USFS REC W
FSS: 122.1T 113.5R   Long: W114-44.09   Chart: Great Falls

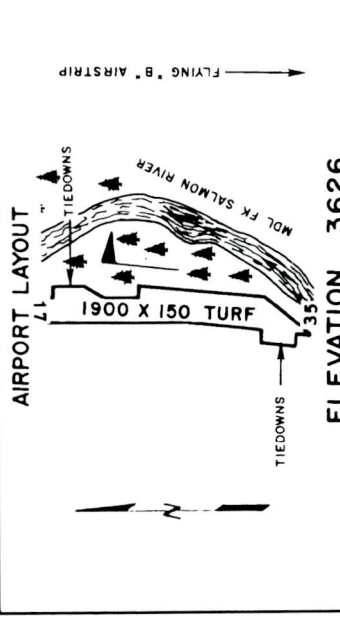

AIRPORT CAUTION • The IAFD cautions that "Flying B Airport located 1/2 mile upstream. Operates on CTAF 122.9. **Land RWY 35, take off RWY 17**, go arounds not recommended due to steep rising terrain north of RWY. • Close flight plan prior to landing. • No winter maintenance." • The approach to RWY 35 is directly over the Flying B. • Trees obstruct the approach. • The terrain rises at the north end. • Info: **(208)756-2215** Salmon National Forest.

BIG BAR

35

17

BIG BAR

CTAF: 122.9
FSS: 122.6

Lat: N45-32.2
Long: W116-31.5

Class: USFS REC EM
Chart: USGS Topo
Temperance Cr. OR-ID

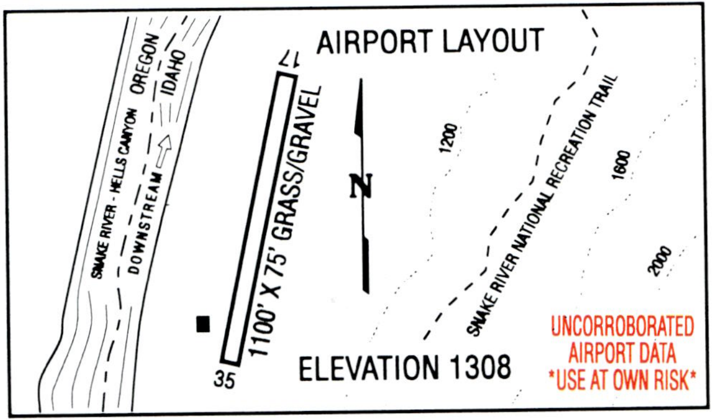

AIRPORT LAYOUT

N

1100' X 75' GRASS/GRAVEL

17

35

ELEVATION 1308

UNCORROBORATED
AIRPORT DATA
USE AT OWN RISK

2000

1600

SNAKE RIVER NATIONAL RECREATION TRAIL

1200

SNAKE RIVER - HELLS CANYON
OREGON
IDAHO
DOWNSTREAM

35 17

AIRPORT CAUTION · USE AT YOUR OWN RISK. This strip is suitable for Super Cub, 180, and 206 type aircraft. · Airport located in narrow river canyon subject to local turbulence and very high summer temperatures. · Not recommended for inexperienced pilots. · Close flight plan prior to landing. · No winter maintenance. · Info: **(509)758-0616** Hells Canyon NRA.

BIG CREEK

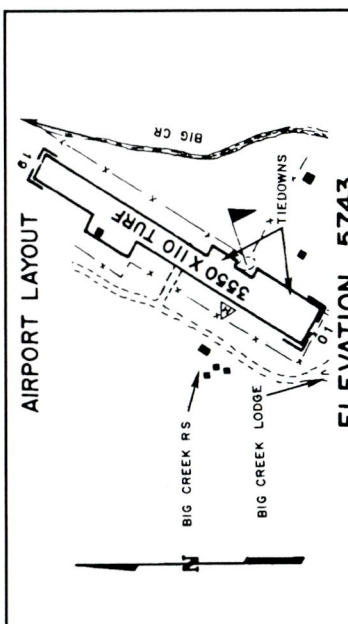

BIG CREEK

CTAF: 122.9   Lat: N45-07.99   Class: USFS REC
FSS: 122.1T 116.2R   Long: W115-19.31   Chart: Great Falls

AIRPORT LAYOUT

3550 X 110 TURF

TIEDOWNS

BIG CR

ELEVATION 5743

BIG CREEK RS

BIG CREEK LODGE

N

AIRPORT CAUTION • The IAFD recommends **"land RWY 19, take off RWY 01** when wind permits. Pilots should be experienced in high density altitude and turbulent air. • Be alert for sprinklers on RWY. • Open to ski equipped aircraft in winter: Aircraft use sides of strip during ski operations. • Close flight plan prior to landing. • No winter maintenance." • Be alert for moose, deer, and elk on or near the strip. • The runway has a large dip at the north end. • Info: **(208)334-8775** Div. of Aeronautics.

BIG SOUTHERN BUTTE

BIG SOUTHERN BUTTE   U46

Lat: N43-25.8
Long: W113-03.5

Class: State EM
Chart: Salt Lake

CTAF: 122.9
FSS: 122.4

AIRPORT LAYOUT

N

2600 X 110 DIRT

19

ARCO

TIEDOWNS

1

ELEVATION 5073

"Livestock on and in vicinity of airport. Runway 1/19 subject to ongoing damage by livestock, rodents, and ground vehicles. • Close flight plan prior to landing. • No winter maintenance."

AIRPORT CAUTION • The IAFD cautions: • Info: **(208)334-8775** Div. of Aeronautics.

BRUCE MEADOWS

23

5

A-16

9	RHI
08	00	01
AE	A/D	RSH

BRUCE MEADOWS   U63

	Lat: N44-24.93	Class: State REC
	Long: W115-19.01	Chart: Salt Lake

CTAF:122.9
FSS: 122.6

AIRPORT LAYOUT

STANLEY

TIEDOWNS

U63

5000 X 110

LOWMAN

5

ELEVATION 6370

23

5

AIRPORT CAUTION • The IAFD recommends "Land RWY 5, take off RWY 23 when wind conditions permit. • Airport is located in a high mountain valley surrounded by high terrain. Very high density altitudes in summer. • Aircraft tiedown area is rough. • Close flight plan prior to landing. • No winter maintenance." • Info: (208)334-8775 Div. of Aeronautics.

CABIN CREEK

11	13	28	RHI
AE	A/D	04	RSH

20

2

CABIN CREEK (W)

IØ8

Lat: N45-08.0   Class: USFS REC W
Long: W114-56.0   Chart: Great Falls

CTAF:122.9
FSS: 122.1T 113.5R

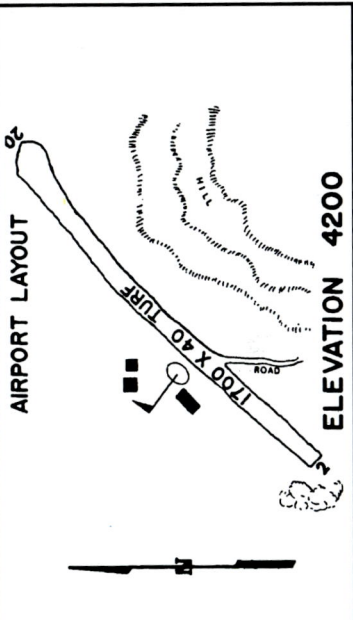

AIRPORT LAYOUT

1700 X 40 TURF

ROAD

HILL

ELEVATION 4200

AIRPORT CAUTION • The IAFD recommends "Before using this airport, special consideration should be given to density altitude, mountain flying proficiency. •Land **RWY 20**, take off **RWY 2**. •No go-around. •Close flight plan prior to landing. •No winter maintenance." • Info: **(208)634-8151.**

CAVANAUGH BAY

CAVANAUGH BAY   66S

Lat: N48-31.25
Long: W116-49.81

Class: State REC
Chart: Great Falls

CTAF: 122.9
FSS: 122.65

AIRPORT LAYOUT

3100 X 120 TURF

33

2484

ELEVATION

TIEDOWNS

CAMP GROUND

COOLIN

N

33

15

AIRPORT CAUTION • The IAFD cautions "Watch for sprinklers on RWY. • No line of sight between rwy ends. • Right hand traffic pattern for RWY 15. • Recommend land RWY 15, depart RWY 33, when wind conditions permit. • No winter maintenance."
• Info: (208)334-8775.

CAYUSE CREEK

2

20

22

CAYUSE CREEK

CTAF: 122.9
FSS: 122.1 122.8R

Lat: N46-40
Long: W115-04

Class: USFS EM
Chart: Great Falls

AIRPORT LAYOUT

RUNWAY
1800 X 100
TURF

CAYUSE CREEK AIRPORT

1800 X 100 TURF

N

20

2

AIRPORT CAUTION • The IAFD recommends: "Before using this airport special consideration should be give to density altitude, turbulence, and mountain flying proficiency. • Terrain elevation rises to south. • Recommend **take-off RWY 2**. • Airport not maintained." • Info: **(208)942-3113**, Powell Ranger District Clearwater National Forest.

CHAMBERLAIN

07	03	12
AE	A/D	RHI
	02	
	RSH	

CHAMBERLAIN (W)   U79

CTAF: 122.9   Lat: N45-22.74   Class: USFS REC
FSS: 122.1T 116.2R   Long: W115-11.81   Chart: Great Falls

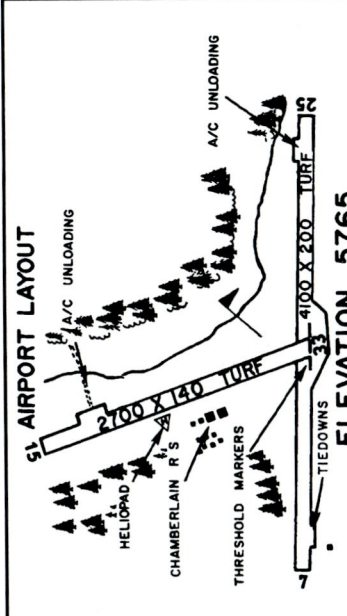

AIRPORT LAYOUT

A/C UNLOADING

A/C UNLOADING

4100 X 200 TURF

2700 X 140 TURF

HELIOPAD

CHAMBERLAIN R S

THRESHOLD MARKERS

TIEDOWNS

ELEVATION 5765

33

7

15

AIRPORT CAUTION • The IAFD cautions "Runways soft early spring. • Caution: High density altitudes during summer. • Close flight plan prior to landing. • No winter maintenance." • Be alert for downdrafts over Chamberlain Creek early morning and late afternoon. • Info: (208)634-0700 USFS Krassel District, Payette National Forest.

COLD MEADOWS

COLD MEADOWS (W)   U81

CTAF: 122.9   Lat: N45-17.49   Class: USFS REC W
FSS: 122.1T 116.2R   Long: W114-56.97   Chart: Great Falls

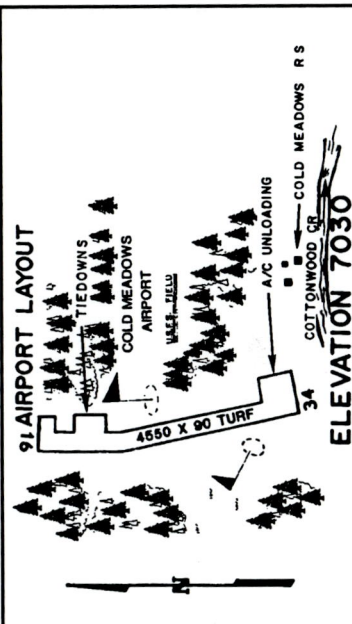

AIRPORT CAUTION • The IAFD cautions "Rodent activity on and in vicinity of airport. • US Forest Service recommends left turn down Cottonwood Creek after departing RWY 16. • **Caution: high density altitude airport. Recommend land RWY 34, takeoff RWY 16 when wind conditions allow.** • No winter maintenance." • Recommended for experienced pilots; close flight plan prior to landing. • Close flight plan prior to landing. • Water diversions installed across field to stop surface erosion and visible from air. • Info: (208)634-0746 Payette Forest Air Officer.

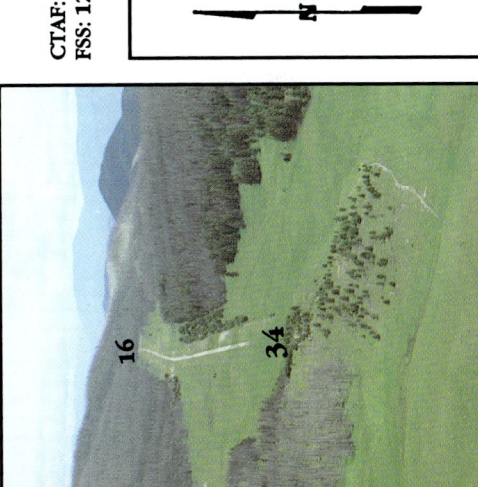

COPPER BASIN

30

12

COPPER BASIN

ØU2

| CTAF: 122.9 | Lat: N43-48.11 | Class: State REC |
| FSS: 123.6 | Long: W113-49.89 | Chart: Salt Lake |

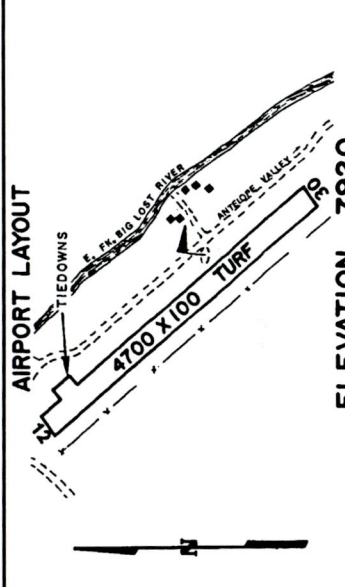

AIRPORT LAYOUT

TIEDOWNS

E. FK. BIG LOST RIVER

ANTELOPE VALLEY

4700 X 100 TURF

ELEVATION 7920

N

AIRPORT CAUTION • The IAFD cautions "Livestock on and in vicinity of airport. • Airport located in high mountain valley surrounded by high mountains. • Extremely high density altitude airport. • Close flight plan prior to landing. • No winter maintenance." • Fences do not enclose the airstrip. Be alert for hoof prints and rodent holes. • Info: **(208)334-8775 Div. of Aeronautics.**

COX'S WELL

COX'S WELL

CTAF: 122.9
FSS: 122.55

Lat: N43-13.1
Long: W113-13.6

Class: State EM
Chart: Salt Lake

AIRPORT LAYOUT

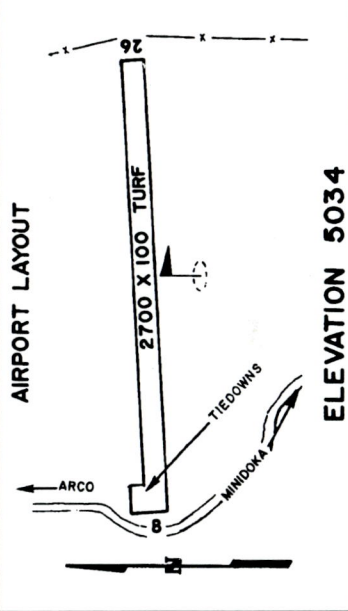

2700 X 100 TURF

ARCO

TIEDOWNS

MINIDOKA

8

26

N

ELEVATION 5034

AIRPORT CAUTION • The IAFD cautions: "airport subject to ongoing damage by livestock, ground vehicles, and rodents. • Close flight plan prior to landing. • No winter maintenance." • Info: (208)334-8775 Div. of Aeronautics.

DEADWOOD RESERVOIR

DEADWOOD RESERVOIR

NO ID

CTAF: 122.9   Lat: N44-20   Class: B.R. REC EM
FSS: 122.1T 116.2R   Long: W115-40   Chart: Salt Lake

AIRPORT LAYOUT

UNCORROBORATED
AIRPORT DATA
USE AT OWN RISK

N

PARKING

24

ROAD

WIND
SOCK

1800' X 300' GRASS/DIRT

HEAVY TIMBER

UPHILL

HEAVY TIMBER

ELEVATION 5400

HEAVY TIMBER

6

ROAD

DEADWOOD RESERVOIR

AIRPORT CAUTION • The IAFD notes "approach is from out over the reservoir. • Normally landing uphill and taking off downhill. • 5% grade to the east." • Info: (208)382-4258 Bureau of Reclamation.

DEWEY MOORE

10

28

DEWEY MOORE (W)   NO ID

CTAF: 122.9   Lat: N45-09.00   Class: EM USFS
FSS: 122.1T 116.2R   Long: W115-04.29   Chart: USGS Topo
                                        Acorn Butte

AIRPORT LAYOUT

STEEP RISE

28

700' x 30' GRAVEL

UNCORROBORATED
AIRPORT DATA
USE AT OWN RISK

10

STEEP RISE

PACK TRAIL

N

DOWNSTREAM

STEEP RISE FROM RIVER

ELEVATION 4494

BIG CREEK

STEEP RISE FROM RIVER

AIRPORT CAUTION · NOT MAINTAINED. USE AT YOUR OWN RISK. · This strip is suitable for Super Cub type aircraft. · Runway surface conditions subject to ongoing deterioration. · Special consideration should be given to density altitude, turbulence, and mountain flying proficiency. · Usage limited to highly experienced mountain pilots. · Close flight plan prior to landing. · No winter maintenance. · Information: (208)634-0746 Payette Forest Air Officer.

DIXIE TOWN

DIXIE TOWN

Lat: N45-33   Class: Private
Long: W115-27.5   Chart: Great Falls

CTAF: 122.9
FSS: 122.1T 113.5R

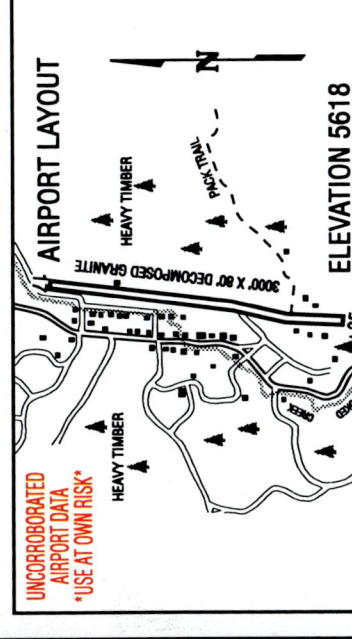

AIRPORT LAYOUT

N

HEAVY TIMBER

PACK TRAIL

3000' X 80' DECOMPOSED GRANITE

35

HEAVY TIMBER

CREEK

ORCHARD

ELEVATION 5618

UNCORROBORATED
AIRPORT DATA
"USE AT OWN RISK"

The IAFD recommends "Land north, take off south." • Info: (208)842-2467 John Wenzel, 103 Airway Dr., Dixie, ID 83525.

AIRPORT CAUTION • RWY HDG N/S, RWY Length 3000', RWY Width 80', decomposed granite. • The IAFD recommends "Land north, take off south. • Snow covered November - May."

DIXIE USFS

DIXIE USFS

ID05

Lat: N45-31.3 Class: USFS REC
CTAF: 122.9
FSS: 122.1T 113.5R Long: W115-31.0 Chart: Great Falls

AIRPORT LAYOUT

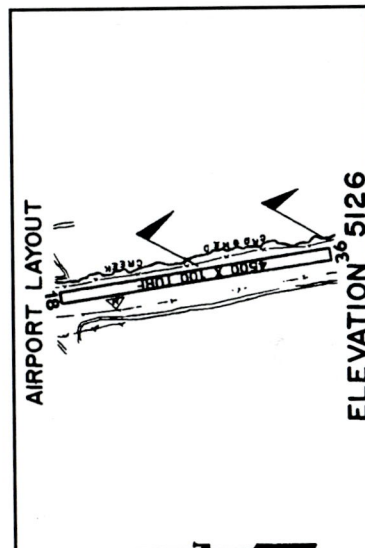

ELEVATION 5126

AIRPORT CAUTION · The IAFD recommends **"Land RWY 36, depart RWY 18** right turn down Crooked Creek. · Extensive helicopter activity in summer months. · Close flight plan prior to landing. · No winter maintenance." · Info: (208)842-2255 USFS.

DUG BAR

27	RHI
07 AE	13 A/D
	07 RSH

32

14

A-40

DUG BAR

CTAF: 122.9 Lat: N45-48.5 Class: USFS REC EM
FSS: 122.6 Long: W116-41.3 Chart: USGS Topo
Cactus MTN ID

AIRPORT LAYOUT

UNCORROBORATED
AIRPORT DATA
"USE AT OWN RISK"

1600
1400
1200

IDAHO/OREGON
BORDER

CREEK

DOWNSTREAM SNAKE RIVER

1900' - 75' TURF

32
14

UNCORROBORATED
AIRPORT DATA
"USE AT OWN RISK"

FENCE

ROAD

UNDERGROUND
IRRIGATION
PIPE MARKERS

1200

ELEVATION 1120

CREEK
1400
1600

N

AIRPORT CAUTION · USE AT YOUR OWN RISK. This strip is suitable for Super Cub, 180, and 206 type aircraft. · Airport located in narrow river canyon subject to local turbulence and very high summer temperatures. · Be alert for sprinkler pipes on RWY and possible ditches. · Not recommended for inexperienced pilots. · Close flight plan prior to landing. · No winter maintenance. · Info: (509)758-0616 Hells Canyon NRA.

ELK CITY

ELK CITY

S9Ø

CTAF: 122.9   Lat: N45-49.36   Class: CA REC
FSS: 122.1T 113.5R   Long: W115-26.39   Chart: Great Falls

AIRPORT LAYOUT

2600 X 150 DIRT

16

34

TIEDOWNS

N

ELEVATION 4097

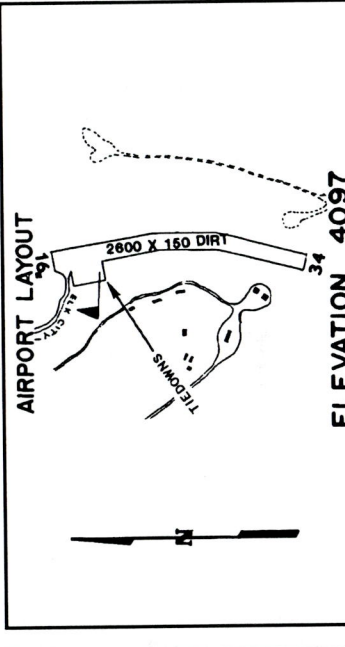

AIRPORT CAUTION • The IAFD recommends "Land RWY 16, depart RWY 34, when wind conditions allow. RWY 16/34 is a curved RWY and has 40' wide dirt - gravel strip down RWY centerline. • No winter maintenance."
• Info: (208)842-2275 Trent Wood, Airport Manager.

FAIRFIELD

25

7

	6	RHI
06	00	00
AE	A/D	RSH

A-44

FAIRFIELD

CTAF: 122.9	Lat: N43-20.24	Class: CA
FSS: 122.4	Long: W114-47.80	Chart: Salt Lake

AIRPORT LAYOUT

TO US 93

MTN HOME ← US 20

2950 X 40 DIRT

25

7

A/C PARKING

SEWAGE POND

N

ELEVATION 5058

AIRPORT CAUTION • The IAFD recommends: "Irregular winter maintenance and snow removal. Check RWY condition with airport manager before using." • Info: **(208)764-2261** Camas County Sheriff.

FISH LAKE

26	RHI	
11	10	05
AE	A/D	RSH

FISH LAKE (W)   S92

CTAF: 122.9 Lat: N46-19.81 Class: USFS REC
FSS: 122.1T 112.8R Long: W115-03.79 Chart: Great Falls

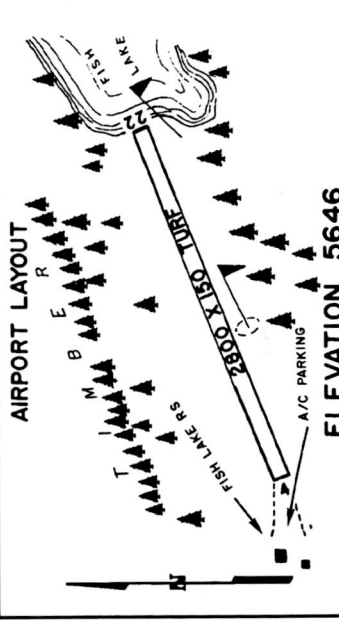

AIRPORT LAYOUT

2800 X 150 TURF

FISH LAKE RS

A/C PARKING

ELEVATION 5646

AIRPORT CAUTION • The IAFD recommends: "**Land RWY 22, take off RWY 04.** Go arounds not recommended due to steep rising terrain off west end of RWY. Down drafts prevalent over lake. Recommend early morning and late evening operations during summer months. • **Caution: High density altitude airport.** • Contact airport manager (208)476-4541 for briefing and RWY conditions. • An additional 400' is available for takeoff on RWY 4 by taxing all the way to the Forest Service Guard Station.

FLYING B RANCH

16

34

FLYING B RANCH (W)　　NO ID

CTAF: 122.9　　**Lat:** N44-58　　**Class:** Private
FSS: 122.1T 113.5R　　**Long:** W114-44　　**Chart:** USGS Topo
　　　　　　　　　　　　　　　　　　　　　　Aparejo Point

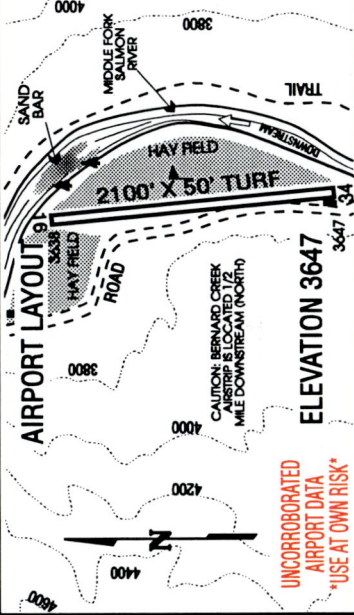

AIRPORT LAYOUT

MIDDLE FORK SALMON RIVER

SAND BAR

HAY FIELD

2100' X 50' TURF

HAY FIELD

ROAD

TRAIL

DOWNSTREAM

3638

3647

16 / 34

4000 3800 3800 4000 4200 4400 4600

CAUTION: BERNARD CREEK AIRSTRIP IS LOCATED 1/2 MILE DOWNSTREAM (NORTH)

ELEVATION 3647

UNCORROBORATED AIRPORT DATA *"USE AT OWN RISK"*

N

16

34

AIRPORT CAUTION • This is a private airstrip and requires prior permission by owner to land here. A landing fee is required. Announce landing/departure on 122.9. • Caution: Bernard Creek Airstrip is located 1/2 mile downstream (north). • Info: **(208)756-6295.**

GARDEN VALLEY

28

10

GARDEN VALLEY   U88

CTAF: 122.9
FSS: 122.6

Lat: N44-04.08
Long: W115-55.89

Class: State REC
Chart: Salt Lake

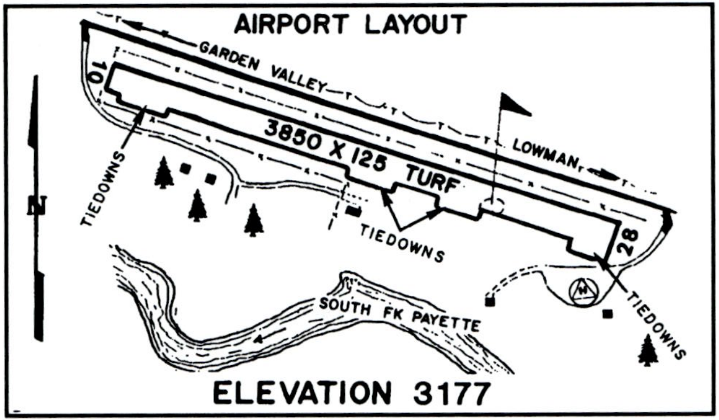

AIRPORT LAYOUT

3850 X 125 TURF

GARDEN VALLEY

LOWMAN.

28

TIEDOWNS

TIEDOWNS

10

TIEDOWNS

SOUTH FK PAYETTE

N

ELEVATION 3177

AIRPORT CAUTION • The IAFD cautions "USFS heliport operations adjacent to southeast end of airport. • Sprinkler pipes may be in place on RWY 10-28. • Recommend landing RWY 10, depart RWY 28 when wind conditions allow. • Close flight plan prior to landing. • No winter maintenance." • Info: (208)334-8775 Div. of Aeronautics.

GRAHAM

18

36

GRAHAM

U45

Lat: N43-57.31
Long: W115-16.36

Class: USFS REC
Chart: Salt Lake

CTAF: 122.9
FSS: 122.6

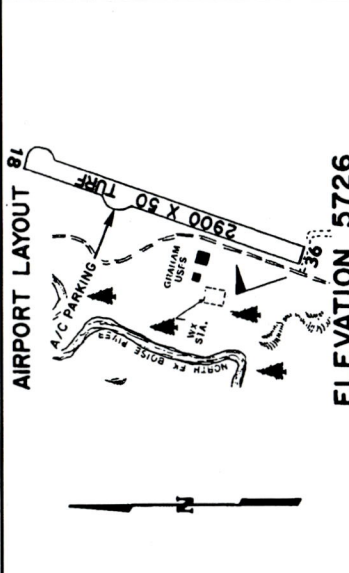

AIRPORT LAYOUT

2900 X 50 TURF

A/C PARKING

GRAHAM USFS

WX STA.

NORTH FK BOISE RIVER

ELEVATION 5726

N

AIRPORT CAUTION • The IAFD recommends "landing RWY 36; depart RWY 18 when wind conditions allow. No line of sight between RWY ends. First 500' of RWY 36 is rough. • Close flight plan prior to landing. • No winter maintenance."
• Info: (208)334-1516 Boise Forest Air Officer.

GRASMERE

GRASMERE

U91

CTAF: 122.9   Lat: N42-21.99   Class: State EM
FSS: BOI 122.6   Long: W115-53.06 Chart: Salt Lake

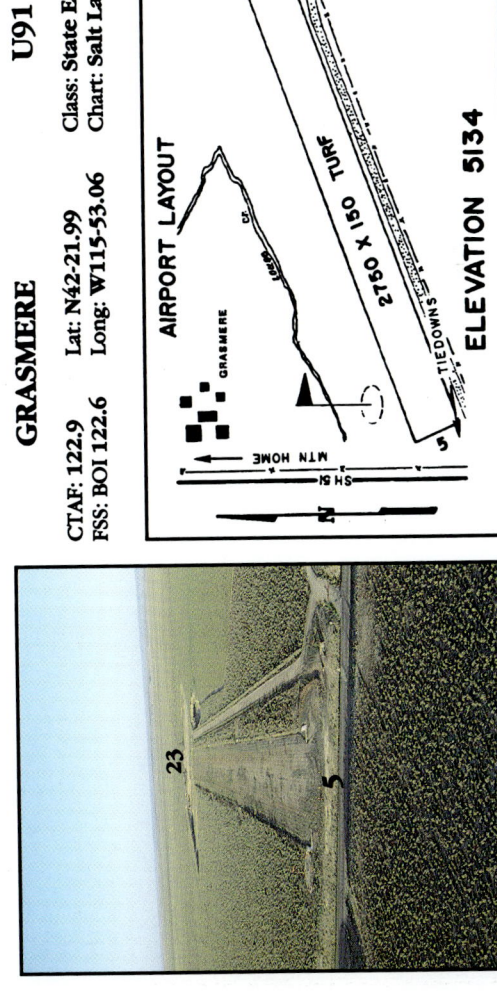

AIRPORT LAYOUT

GRASMERE

MTN HOME ←

SH 51

23

2750 X 150 TURF

TIEDOWNS

5

ELEVATION 5134

AIRPORT CAUTION • The IAFD cautions: "Runway subject to ongoing damage by livestock, rodents, and ground vehicles. • No winter maintenance." • Info: (208)334-8775 Div. of Aeronautics.

HENRY'S LAKE

24

<u>6</u>

08	00	01
AE	A/D	RSH
9		RHI

A-56

HENRY'S LAKE

Lat: N44-37.75
Long: W111-21.05

Class: State REC
Chart: Great Falls

CTAF: 122.9
FSS: 122.45

AIRPORT LAYOUT

TO HWY 20

24 ← TIEDOWNS

4800 X 170 TURF

6

N

ELEVATION 6596

AIRPORT CAUTION • The IAFD cautions "Livestock has access to the airport from September to June annually. Do not leave aircraft unattended during this time period. June to September, an electric fence surrounds airport. • Recommend land **RWY 6**, takeoff **RWY 24** when wind conditions allow. • Close flight plan prior to landing. • North - South RWY closed. • No winter maintenance." • Be alert for antelope and cattle on or near the field and badger holes. • Info: (208)334-8775 Div. of Aeronautics.

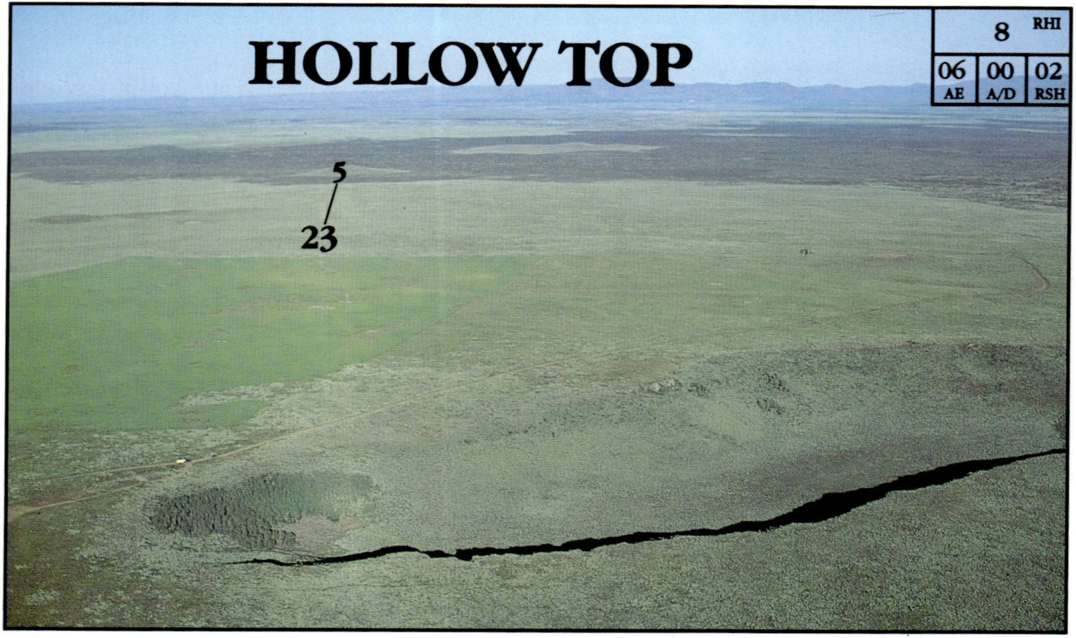
HOLLOW TOP
8
RHI
06
AE
00
A/D
02
RSH
5
23

HOLLOW TOP   ØU7

CTAF: 122.9	Lat: N43-19.5	Class: State EM
FSS: 122.4	Long: W113-35.3	Chart: Salt Lake

AIRPORT LAYOUT

MARTIN

23

TIEDOWNS

2500 X 140 TURF

5

N

ELEVATION 5359

AIRPORT CAUTION • The IAFD cautions: "No line of sight between RWY ends. Rwy surface subject to ongoing damage by livestock, ground vehicles, and rodents. • Close flight plan prior to landing. • No winter maintenance."
• Info: (208)334-8775 Div. of Aeronautics.

IDAHO CITY

IDAHO CITY

Lat: N43-49.24
Long: W115-51.06

Class: USFS REC
Chart: Salt Lake

CTAF: 122.9
FSS: 122.6

AIRPORT LAYOUT

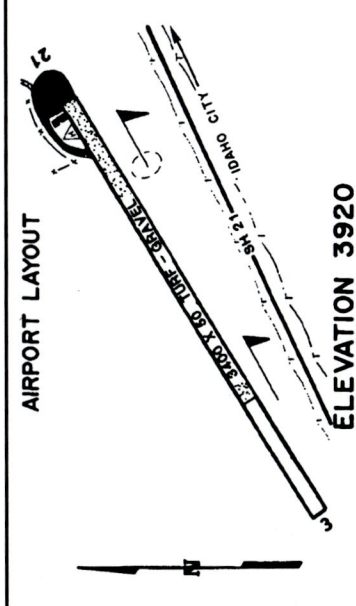

TURF – GRAVEL
3400 X 90

SH 21 — IDAHO CITY

ELEVATION 3920

N

AIRPORT CAUTION • The IAFD recommends **"Land RWY 21 when wind conditions permit.** • Close flight plan prior to landing.
• No winter maintenance." • Info: **(208)392-6681.**

INDIAN CREEK

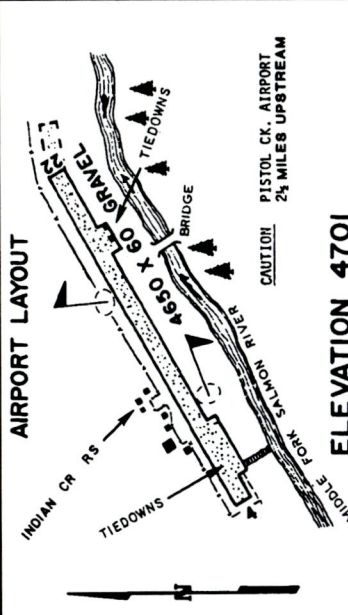

INDIAN CREEK (W)   S81

CTAF: 122.9   Lat: N44-45.68   Class: USFS REC W
FSS: 122.1T 116.2R   Long: W115-06.44   Chart: Great Falls

AIRPORT LAYOUT

INDIAN CR RS

TIEDOWNS

60 GRAVEL

4650 X

MIDDLE FORK SALMON RIVER

N

TIEDOWNS

BRIDGE

CAUTION

PISTOL CK. AIRPORT
2½ MILES UPSTREAM

ELEVATION 4701

AIRPORT CAUTION · The IAFD cautions: "Other traffic confined to same canyon area. Special consideration should be given to density altitude, turbulence, and mountain flying proficiency. Pistol Creek airport located 2.5 miles upstream. · USFS recommends remain in main canyon when departing up or downstream. · Do not attempt to climb out side canyons. · Close flight plan prior to landing. · No winter maintenance." · Info: (208)879-5204 USFS Middle Fork District, Challis, Idaho.

JOHNSON CREEK

35

17

14 RHI
09 05 00
AE A/D RSH

JOHNSON CREEK 3U2

CTAF: 122.9   Lat: N44-54.2   Class: State REC
FSS: 122.1T 116.2R   Long: W115-29.1   Chart: Great Falls

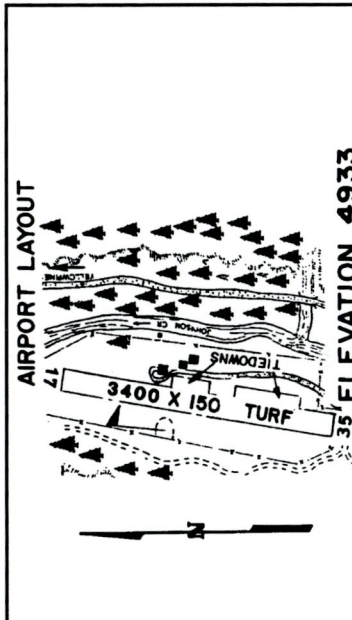

AIRPORT LAYOUT

3400 X 150   TURF

TIEDOWNS

ELEVATION 4933

AIRPORT CAUTION • The IAFD recommends **"Land RWY 17, takeoff RWY 35** when wind conditions permit. • Be alert for sprinklers on RWY. • Special consideration should be given to density altitude, turbulence, and mountain flying proficiency. • Close flight plan prior to landing. • No winter maintenance." • Info: (208)334-8775 Div. of Aeronautics.

Camping/Toilets

KRASSEL

35

17

A-66

KRASSEL

CTAF: 122.9   Lat: N44-58.7   Class: USFS REC
FSS: 122.1T 116.2R Long: W115-43.2   Chart: Great Falls

AIRPORT LAYOUT

75' USABLE WIDTH

HELIPAD

1600 X 150 TURF

17   35

SALMON RIVER

ELEVATION 3852

AIRPORT CAUTION • The IAFD cautions: "Airport located in steep canyon with walls 1000' or more above airport. • Not recommended for inexperienced pilots. • Extensive USFS helicopter operations during summer months. • Recommend land RWY 17, depart RWY 35 when wind conditions permit. • No winter maintenance." •Info: (208)634-0600.

LAIDLAW CORRALS

7

25

LAIDLAW CORRALS   U99

CTAF: 122.9	Lat: N43-02.2	Class: State EM
FSS: 122.4	Long: W113-44.0	Chart: Salt Lake

AIRPORT LAYOUT

2250 X 130 TURF

TIEDOWNS

CAREY

25
7

ELEVATION 4427

AIRPORT CAUTION • The IAFD cautions: • "Animals on and in vicinity of airport. • Rwy surface subject to ongoing damage by livestock, ground vehicles, and rodents. • Close flight plan prior to landing. • No winter maintenance."
• Info: **(208)334-8775** Div. of Aeronautics.

LANDMARK

09	00	01
AE	A/D	RSH

10 RHI

LANDMARK

ØUØ

CTAF: 122.9   Lat: N44-38.54   Class: USFS REC
FSS: 122.1T 116.2R   Long: W115-32.01   Chart: Great Falls

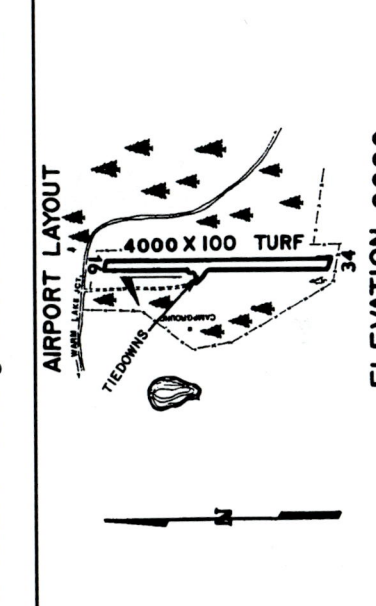

AIRPORT LAYOUT

4000 X 100 TURF

34

TIEDOWNS

CAMP-GROUND

N

ELEVATION 6680

AIRPORT CAUTION • The IAFD cautions "No line of sight between RWY ends. • Airport located in high mountain valley surrounded by high terrain. • Before using this airport special consideration should be given to density altitude, turbulence, and mountain flying proficiency. • Close flight plan prior to landing. • No winter maintenance". • Info: (208)334-1516 Boise Forest Air Officer.

LORD FLAT

33

15

LORD FLAT

CTAF: 122.9
FSS: 122.6

Lat: N45-40.2
Long: W116-37.1

Class: USFS REC EM
Chart: USGS Topo
Lord Flat OR-ID

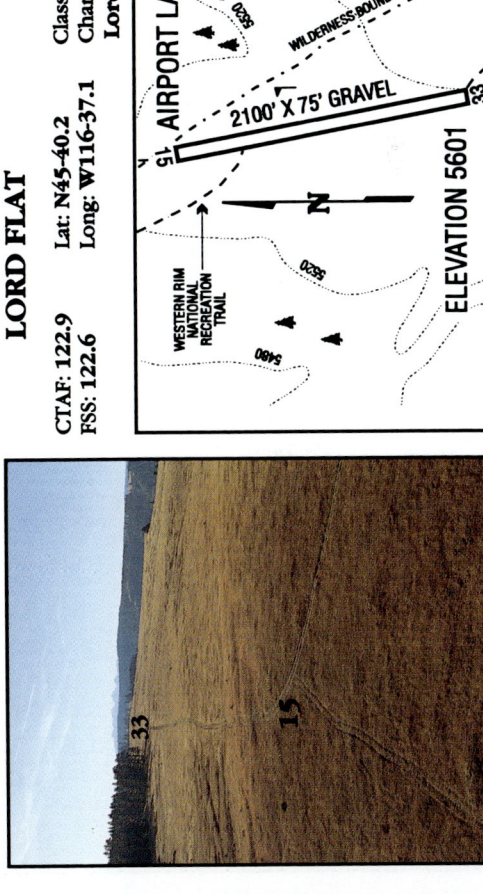

AIRPORT LAYOUT

UNCORROBORATED
AIRPORT DATA
USE AT OWN RISK

WILDERNESS BOUNDARY

2100' X 75' GRAVEL

33

16

WESTERN RIM
NATIONAL
RECREATION
TRAIL

N

ELEVATION 5601

5580

5560

5600

5580

5480

AIRPORT CAUTION • USE AT YOUR OWN RISK. • This strip is suitable for Super Cub, 180, and 206 type aircraft. • Not recommended for inexperienced pilots. • Close flight plan prior to landing. • No winter maintenance.
• Info: **(503)426-4978** Wallowa-Whitman Nat'l. Forest.

33

15

LOWER LOON

42 **RHI**

12 **AE** | 25 **A/D** | 05 **RSH**

31

13

▲ 74

LOWER LOON

CTAF: 122.9   Lat: N44-48.15   Class: IDF&G REC EM
FSS: 122.1T 113.5R   Long: W114-48.45   Chart: Great Falls

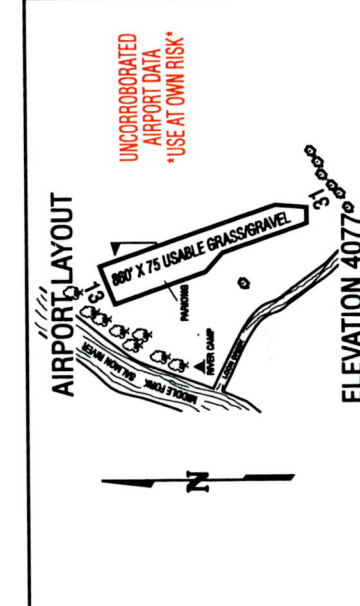

AIRPORT LAYOUT

UNCORROBORATED
AIRPORT DATA
USE AT OWN RISK

860' X 75 USABLE GRASS/GRAVEL

PARKING

RIVER CAMP

MIDDLE FORK SALMON RIVER

LOON CREEK

31

ELEVATION 4077'

N

13

31

AIRPORT CAUTION • The Fish & Game cautions: "The airstrip is HAZARDOUS and use should be limited to emergency and ideal conditions only; use at your own risk." • Recommended for proficient mountain pilots and high performance aircraft only. • Special consideration should be given to density altitude, turbulence and mountain flying proficiency. • Approach and departure requires abrupt low level turn over river. • Runway surface subject to flooding from irrigation. • Info: (208)756-2271 Idaho Fish & Game.

MACKAY BAR

MACKAY BAR

CTAF: 122.9
FSS: 122.1T, 116.2R

Lat: N45-23
Long: W115-30

Class: Private
Chart: Great Falls

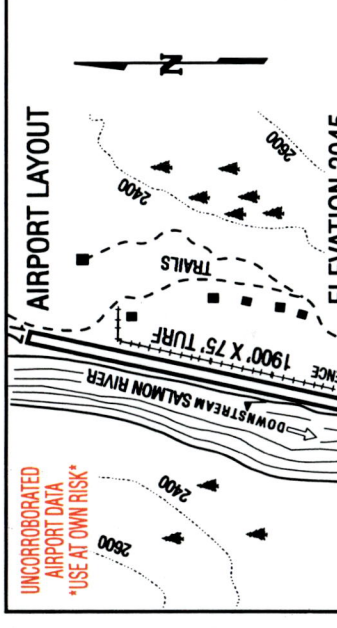

AIRPORT LAYOUT

N

2400

2600

TRAILS

FENCE

1900' X 75' TURF

DOWNSTREAM SALMON RIVER

ELEVATION 2045

2400

2600

UNCORROBORATED AIRPORT DATA *USE AT OWN RISK*

35

17

AIRPORT CAUTION • Recommend landing downstream and departing upstream. Pilots should be experienced in high density altitude and turbulent air. • Be alert for animals on runway. • Close flight plan prior to landing. • No winter maintenance. • Info: (800)854-9904.

MAGEE

36

18

MAGEE

CTAF: 122.9
FSS: 122.65

Lat: N47-50.24
Long: W116-15.81

Class: State REC EM
Chart: Great Falls

S77

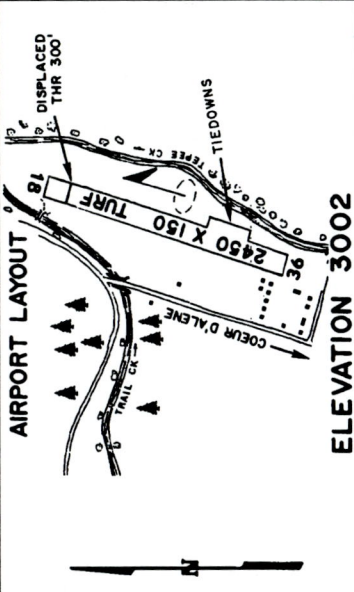

AIRPORT LAYOUT

DISPLACED THR 300'

TIEDOWNS

TEPEE CK

18

2450 X 150 TURF

36

COEUR D'ALENE

TRAIL CK

N

ELEVATION 3002

AIRPORT CAUTION • The IAFD cautions: "Special consideration should be given to density altitude, turbulence, and mountain flying proficiency. • Watch for big game animals on RWY. • Recommend land RWY 18, take off RWY 36 when wind conditions permit. • YCC Youth Camp located adjacent SW. • Close flight plan prior to landing. • No winter maintenance." • Loran signals are unreliable in this part of Idaho. • Info: **(208)334-8775** Div. of Aeronautics.

MAGIC RESERVOIR

MAGIC RESERVOIR U93

Lat: N43-16.94	Class: State REC	
Long: W114.23-72	Chart: Salt Lake	

CTAF: 122.9
FSS: 122.4

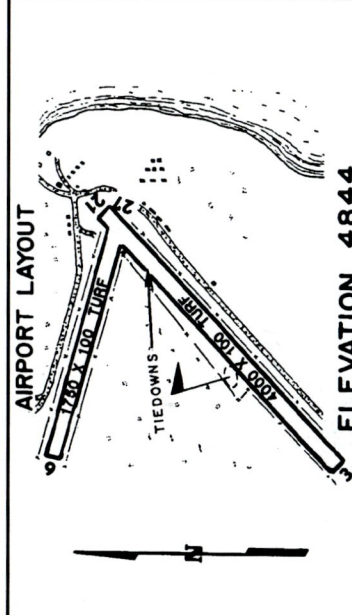

AIRPORT LAYOUT

1260 X 100 TUBE

1000 X 100 TURF

TIEDOWNS

N

ELEVATION 4844

21 27

9

3

AIRPORT CAUTION • The IAFD recommends "When wind conditions allow, land RWY 3 or RWY 9, depart RWY 21 or RWY 27 to avoid flying over resort area. • RYW 9-27, no line of sight between RWY ends. • No winter maintenance". • Watch for antenna and trees at approach end of RWY 21. • Info: (208)334-8775 Div. of Aeronautics.

MAHONEY CREEK

28	RHI
10	15	03
AE	A/D	RSH

3

21

MAHONEY CREEK (W)   ØU3

Lat: N44-44.68
Long: W114-55.29

Class: USFS REC
Chart: Great Falls

CTAF: 122.9
FSS: 122.6

AIRPORT LAYOUT

TIEDOWNS

2150 X 30 DIRT

21

3

TO BIG
CREEK
200'

BLUFF

MIDDLE FK SALMON RIVER

ELEVATION 4618

N

3

21

AIRPORT CAUTION • The IAFD recommends "special consideration should be given to density altitude, turbulence, and mountain flying proficiency. • Other airport traffic confined to same canyon area. • RWY elevation rises to SW. • Recommend land **RWY 21**, **depart RWY 3** when wind conditions allow. • Close flight plan prior to landing. • No winter maintenance."
• Info: (208)879-5204 Middle Fork Ranger District.

MEMALOOSE

18

36

MEMALOOSE 25U

CTAF: 122.9
FSS: 122.6

Lat: N-45-25.66
Long: W-116-41.63

Class: USFS REC
Chart: Great Falls

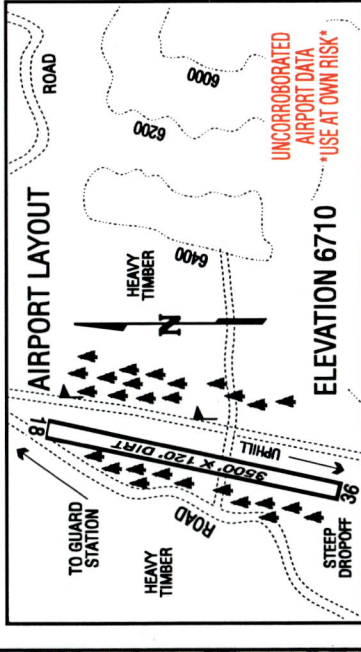

AIRPORT LAYOUT

TO GUARD STATION

HEAVY TIMBER

ROAD

STEEP DROPOFF

18

36

3500' X 120' DIRT

UPHILL

HEAVY TIMBER

N

ROAD

6400

6200

6000

ROAD

ELEVATION 6710

UNCORROBORATED AIRPORT DATA "USE AT OWN RISK"

AIRPORT CAUTION • Use right traffic for RWY 18 and RWY 36. • Runway surface has loose rocks and is rough. • Expect downdrafts on short final landing RWY 36. • North end wet in spring, if landing RWY 18 land long. • Livestock on and in vicinity of airport. • Pilots should be experienced in high density altitude and turbulent air. • Close flight plan prior to landing. • No winter maintenance. • Information: (503)963-7171.

MIDWAY

2

20

MIDWAY

U37

CTAF: 122.9
FSS: 122.55

Lat: N43-27.5
Long: W112-48.5

Class: State EM
Chart: Salt Lake

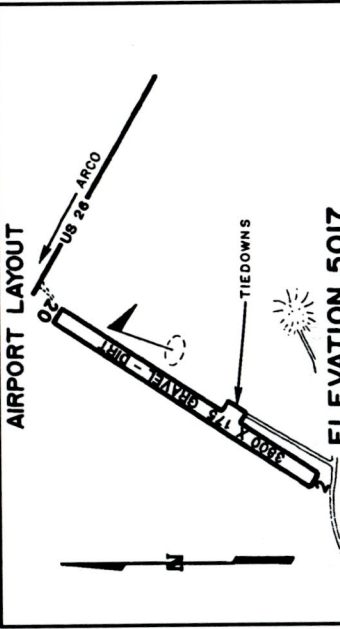

AIRPORT LAYOUT

US 26 ARCO

02

3400 X 175 GRAVEL — DIRT

TIEDOWNS

ELEVATION 5017

N

AIRPORT CAUTION · The IAFD cautions: "First 1500' of RWY 2 is dirt, remainder is gravel. · Close flight plan prior to landing. · No winter maintenance." · Info: (208)334-8775 Div. of Aeronautics.

MILE HI

CTAF: 122.9   Lat: N45-09.08   Class: USFS EM
FSS: 122.1T 116.2R   Long: W114-59.54   Chart: USGS TOPO
                                                 Vinegar Hill

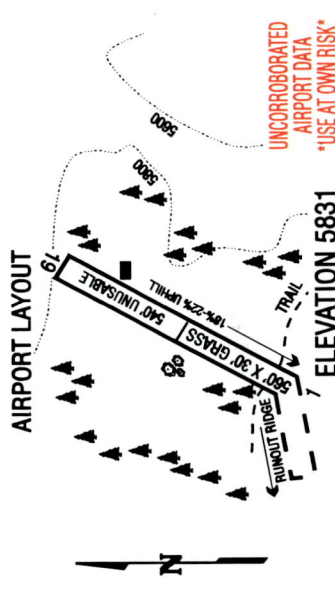

AIRPORT LAYOUT

540' UNUSABLE

560' X 30' GRASS

18%-22% UPHILL

RUNOUT RIDGE

TRAIL

ELEVATION 5831

UNCORROBORATED
AIRPORT DATA
USE AT OWN RISK

AIRPORT CAUTION • NOT MAINTAINED. USE AT YOUR OWN RISK. Recommend landing RWY 19, takeoff RWY 1. First 540' of runway unusab¹ᵉ for landing, 18% to 22% upslope on usable end of runway. • **Caution:** On takeoff the runway is not fully visible. Careful alignme…_ritical. • This strip is suitable for Super Cub type aircraft. Runway surface conditions subject to ongoing deterioration. Special consideration should be given to density altitude, turbulence, and mountain flying proficiency. • Info: (208)634-0746.

MOOSE CREEK

24 RHI	
06 AE	18 A/D	00 RSH

MOOSE CREEK (W)   1U1

CTAF: 122.9   Lat: N46-07.25   Class: USFS REC
FSS: 122.1T 112.8R   Long: W114-55.64   Chart: Great Falls

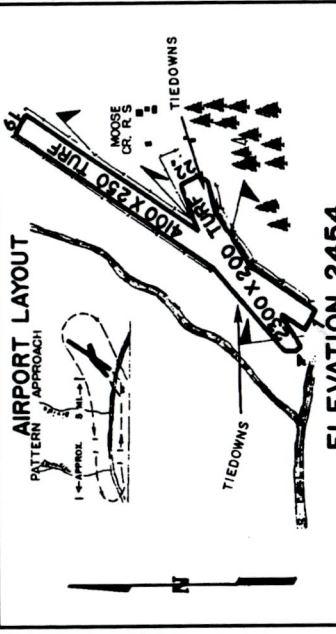

AIRPORT LAYOUT

PATTERN | APPROACH

1←APPROX. | 8 MI. |

TIEDOWNS

MOOSE
CR. R.S.

TIEDOWNS

4100 x 250 TURF

2200 x 200

TURF

ELEVATION 2454

N

AIRPORT CAUTION • The IAFD recommends "Contact airport manager for briefing and RWY conditions. Recommend landing runway 1 or 4 and depart runways 19 or 22 when runway conditions allow. Runway 1-19 soft spring and winter. Use runway 4-22 early spring and late fall/winter when possible. • Close flight plan prior to landing. • No winter maintenance."
• Info: (208)983-1964 Airport Manager for Nez Perce National Forest.

MURPHY HOT SPRINGS

4		RHI
03	00	01
AE	A/D	RSH

MURPHY HOT SPRINGS 3U0

CTAF: 122.9	Lat: N42-01.24	Class: State REC EM
FSS: 122.6	Long: W115-20.30	Chart: Salt Lake

AIRPORT LAYOUT

5250 X 120 TURF

19

1

TIEDOWNS

THREE CREEK

MURPHY HOT SPRINGS

FAA 3751

ELEVATION 5829

N

1

19

AIRPORT CAUTION • The IAFD cautions: (Airport)... "unattended. No line of sight between RWY ends. • Close flight plan prior to landing. • RWY soft when wet. Murphy Hot Springs Resort 1 mile SW of airport. • Caution: Extensive military traffic operating in Bruneau MOA's and R-3202 NW of airport. Contact Mountain Home Approach Control on 124.8 for traffic advisories. • No winter maintenance." Info: **(208)334-8775.**

OROGRANDE

OROGRANDE

CTAF: 122.9   **Lat: N45.43**
FSS: 122.1T 116.2R   **Long: W115.32**

NO ID

Class: USFS REC EM
Chart: USGS TOPO
    Orogrande

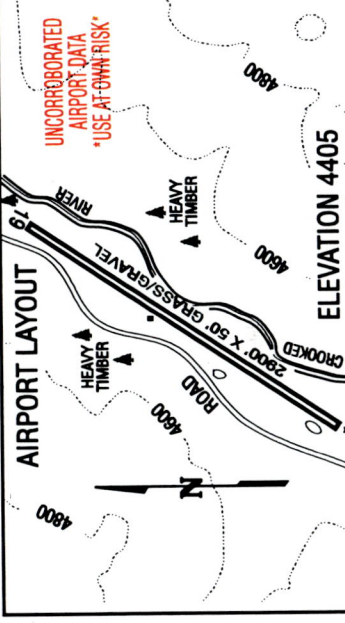

AIRPORT LAYOUT

UNCORROBORATED
AIRPORT DATA
"USE AT OWN RISK"

HEAVY
TIMBER

HEAVY
TIMBER

RIVER

CROOKED

ROAD

2900' X 50' GRASS/GRAVEL

4800

4800

4600

4600

19

7

N

ELEVATION 4405

AIRPORT CAUTION • CONDITION UNCERTAIN - USE AT YOUR OWN RISK. Call (208)842-2245 for present conditions. • New tree growth on sides of runway limit usable width to 50'. • Special consideration should be given to density altitude, turbulence, and mountain flying proficiency. • Close flight plan prior to landing. • No winter maintenance. • Information: (208)842-2245 Elk City Ranger Station.

PINE

16

34

PINE

CTAF: 122.9
FSS: 122.6

Lat: N43-27.74
Long: W115-18.55

Class: State REC EM
Chart: Salt Lake

AIRPORT LAYOUT

TIEDOWNS

ANDERSON
RANCH RESERVOIR

2300 X 125 TURF

16

34

PINE

MOUNTAINS AND SCATTERED TIMBER

ELEVATION 4232

N

AIRPORT CAUTION • The IAFD advises "Runway and terrain elevation rises to the north. Recommend land RWY 34, depart RWY 16 when wind conditions permit. RWY 34 right traffic. • Close flight plan prior to landing. • No winter maintenance." • Runway surface subject to ongoing damage; no line of sight between runway ends. • Info: (208)334-8775 Div. of Aeronautics.

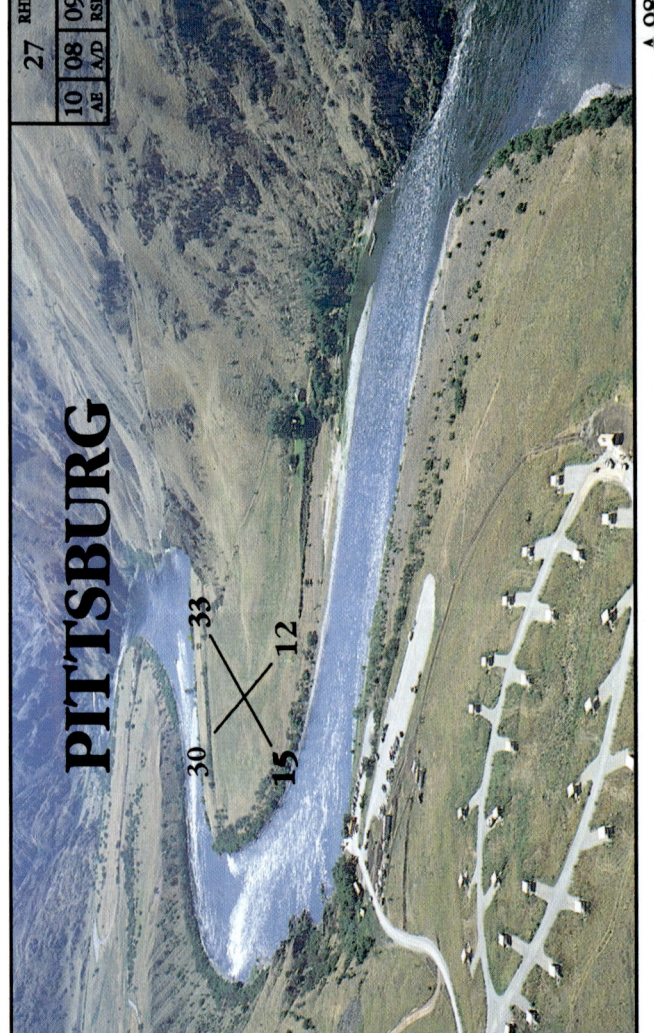

PITTSBURG

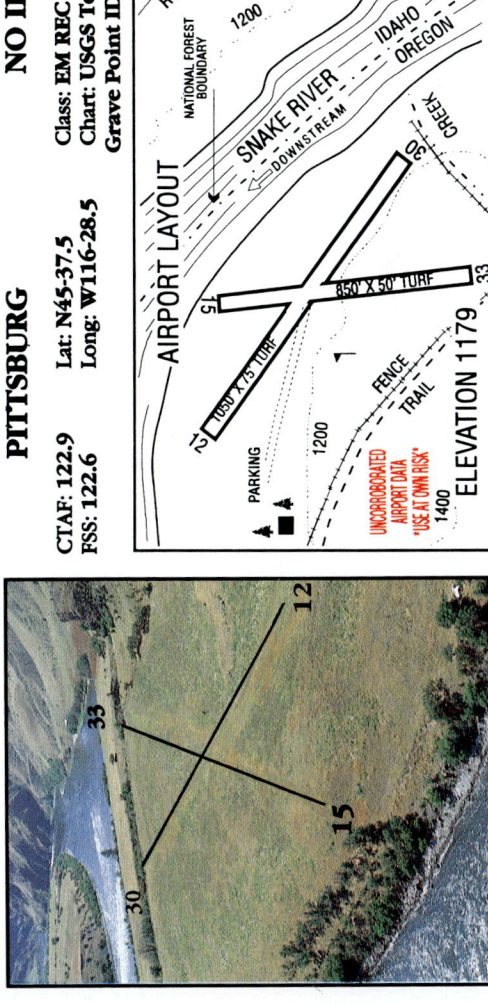

A-99
NO ID

PITTSBURG

CTAF: 122.9
FSS: 122.6

Lat: N45-37.5
Long: W116-28.5

Class: EM REC USFS
Chart: USGS Topo
Grave Point ID-OR

AIRPORT LAYOUT

ROAD

1200

SNAKE RIVER

DOWNSTREAM

IDAHO
OREGON

NATIONAL FOREST BOUNDARY

N

CREEK

850' X 50' TURF

33

15

1050 X 75' TURF

21

PARKING

1200

FENCE

TRAIL

ELEVATION 1179

1400

**UNCORROBORATED
AIRPORT DATA
"USE AT OWN RISK"**

AIRPORT CAUTION · **USE AT YOUR OWN RISK**. This strip is suitable for Super Cub, 180, and 206 type aircraft. · Airport located in narrow river canyon subject to local turbulence and very high summer temperatures. · Not recommended for inexperienced pilots. · Close flight plan prior to landing. · No winter maintenance. · Info: **(509)758-0616** Hells Canyon NRA.

PRIEST LAKE

14

32

PRIEST LAKE

Lat: N48-34.50	Class: USFS REC	
Long: W116-57.81	Chart: Great Falls	

CTAF: 122.9
FSS: 122.65

AIRPORT LAYOUT

NORDMAN

RANGER STATION

TIEDOWNS

PRIEST RIVER

14   4600 X 175   TURF   32

ELEVATION 2611

N

14

32

AIRPORT CAUTION • No winter maintenance. • Full length of runway may not be mowed.
• Info: (208)772-3283 Coeur d'Alene Dispatch.

SALMON BAR

15

33

31   Rib

10   11   10
AB   AD   RSH

SALMON BAR

CTAF: 122.9
FSS: 122.6

Lat: N45-51.9
Long: W116-48.3

Class: USFS REC EM
Chart: USGS Topo
Deadhorse Ridge OR-ID

AIRPORT LAYOUT

ELEVATION 916

UNCORROBORATED
AIRPORT DATA
USE AT OWN RISK

DANGER!
TWO FOOT
DEPRESSION

700' X 60' UNIMPROVED GRASS

SNAKE RIVER

IDAHO
OREGON

DOWNSTREAM

TRAIL

CREEK

AIRPORT CAUTION · USE AT YOUR OWN RISK. This strip is suitable for Super Cub, 180, and 206 type aircraft. · Airport located in narrow river canyon subject to local turbulence and very high summer temperatures. · Not recommended for inexperienced pilots. · Close flight plan prior to landing. · No winter maintenance. · Information: **(503)426-4978** Wallowa-Whitman National Forest.

SHEARER

36

18

SHEARER (W)

2U5

CTAF: 122.9
FSS: 122.1T 113.5R

Lat: N45-59.50
Long: W114-50.46

Class: USFS REC
Chart: Great Falls

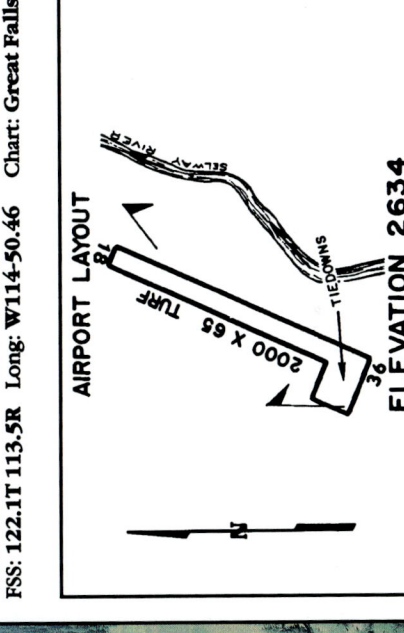

AIRPORT LAYOUT

2000 X 65 TURF

18

36

ELEVATION 2634

TIEDOWNS

SELWAY RIVER

N

AIRPORT CAUTION • The IAFD recommends "Inexperienced pilots should use for emergencies only. Recommend early morning or late evening operations during summer. First 400' of RWY 18 is rough. • Land RWY 18. Depart RWY 36. Blind approach to RWY 18. • Avoid overflying Selway Lodge located downstream from airport. • Close flight plan prior to landing. • Closed during winter months." • Info: (208)983-2712 Moose Creek Ranger District.

SIMONDS

SIMONDS (W)

CTAF: 122.9
FSS: 122.1T 116.2R

Lat: N45-04.50
Long: W115-07.23

Class: USFS EM
Chart: USGS TOPO
Ctr. Mt. & Monument

UNCORROBORATED
AIRPORT DATA
USE AT OWN RISK

AIRPORT LAYOUT

STEEP RISE

HEAVY FOREST
ALL AROUND
LANDING STRIP

900' X 37' GRAVEL

4% TO 9% UPHILL

STEEP DROP
TO STREAM

ELEVATION 5243

28

10

N

AIRPORT CAUTION • NOT MAINTAINED. USE AT YOUR OWN RISK. Recommend landing downstream RWY 28, departing upstream RWY 10. RWY 28 located on 6% uphill slope, with 23% side slope above and below runway. • Tall trees on approach end. • This strip is suitable for Super Cub type aircraft. • Runway surface conditions subject to ongoing deterioration. Special consideration should be given to density altitude, turbulence, and mountain flying proficiency. **Caution:** When grass is wet, side slope will cause plane to slide during turnaround. Doval Ranch Airstrip located 1 mile upstream. • Info: (208)634-0746.

SLATE CREEK

10	RHI
03	06	01
AE	A/D	RSH

A-108

SLATE CREEK 1S7

CTAF: 122.9   Lat: N45-40.5   Class: State REC EM
FSS: 122.1T 116.2R   Long: W116-18.5   Chart: Great Falls

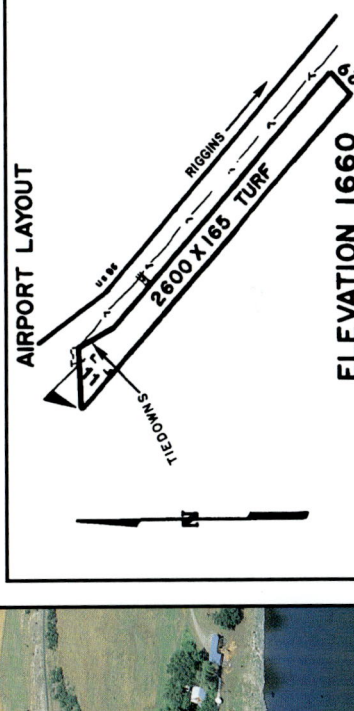

AIRPORT LAYOUT

RIGGINS

2600 × 165 TURF

TIEDOWNS

ELEVATION 1660

N

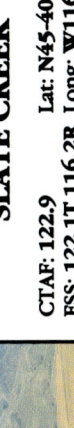

11

29

AIRPORT CAUTION • The IAFD cautions: "Soft when wet. 30' powerline along east boundary of airport. No line of sight between RWY ends. • Close flight plan prior to landing. • No winter maintenance." • Info: (208)334-8775.

SMILEY CREEK

32

14

7 RHI

07 AE | 00 A/D | 00 RSH

A-110

SMILEY CREEK

U87

CTAF: 122.9
FSS: 122.6

Lat: N43-54.91
Long: W114-47.84

Class: State REC
Chart: Salt Lake

AIRPORT LAYOUT

4900 X 150 TURF

32

SALMON RIVER

TIEDOWNS

STANLEY

US 93

N

ELEVATION 7160

14   32

AIRPORT CAUTION • The IAFD recommends **"Land RWY 14, depart RWY 32** when wind conditions permit. Special consideration should be given to density altitude before using this airport. • Close flight plan prior to landing. • No winter maintenance." • The runway slopes uphill to the south. • Use caution for sprinkler pipes on the runway. • The turf extends takeoff roll.
• Info: (208)334-8775, Div. of Aeronautics.

SMITH'S PRAIRIE

23

5

| 03 AE | 00 A/D | 01 RSH | 4 RHI |

SMITH'S PRAIRIE

CTAF: 122.9
FSS: 122.6

Lat: N43-29.91
Long: W115-32.89

Class: State REC EM
Chart: Salt Lake

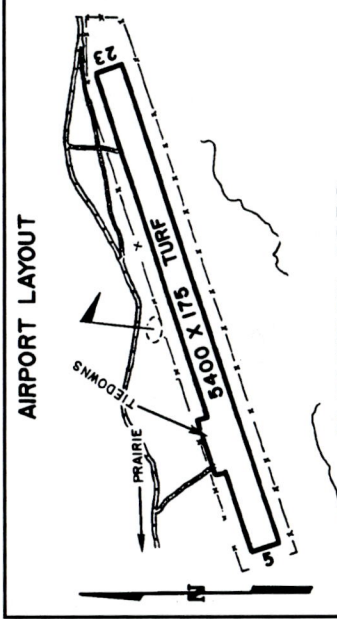

AIRPORT LAYOUT

PRAIRIE

TIEDOWNS

5400 x 175 TURF

23

5

N

ELEVATION 4958

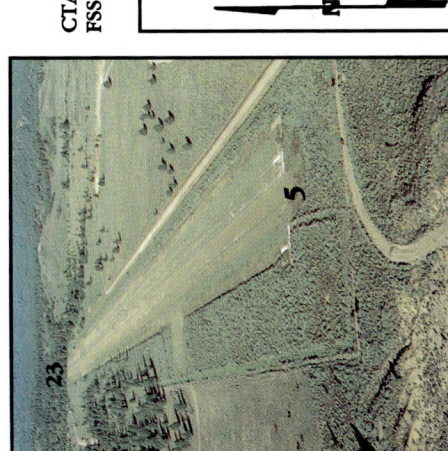

AIRPORT CAUTION · The IAFD recommends **"Land RWY 5, depart RWY 23 when conditions permit.** · Close flight plan prior to landing. · No winter maintenance." · Info: **(208)334-8775** Div. of Aeronautics.

SOLDIER BAR

7

25

32	RHI
11 AE	12 A/D	09 RSH

SOLDIER BAR (W)   85U

CTAF: 122.9   Lat: N45-06.0   Class: USFS REC W
FSS: 122.1T 113.5R   Long: W114-48.0   Chart: Great Falls

AIRPORT LAYOUT

STEEP RISE

BUMP 450'   DIRT

1600 x 20

BUMP 303'

HIGHEST END

25

7

N

ELEVATION 4190

AIRPORT CAUTION • The IAFD recommends **"land RWY 25, depart RWY 07.** Recommended for proficient mountain pilots and high performance aircraft only." • No winter maintenance." • Info: (208)879-2285 Challis Forest Air Officer.

STANLEY

17

35

7	RHI
06 AE	00 A/D	01 RSH

STANLEY

2U7

CTAF: 122.9
FSS: 122.6

Lat: N44-12.51
Long: W114-56.07

Class: CA REC
Chart: Salt Lake

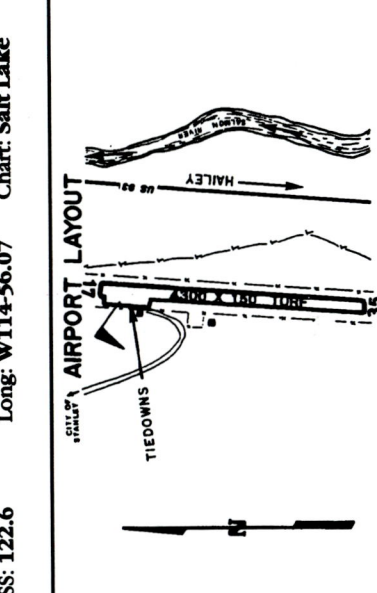

AIRPORT LAYOUT

CITY OF STANLEY

TIEDOWNS

5100 X 150 TURF

41

35

US 93

HAILEY →

SALMON RIVER

N

ELEVATION 6403

AIRPORT CAUTION • The IAFD cautions "Airport located in valley surrounded by high mountainous terrain. • Recommend land 35, take off 17, wind permitting. • Numerous air taxi operations during summer months. • No winter maintenance." • Trees obstruct the approach end of RWY 17. • Info: (208)334-8775 Div. of Aeronautics.

SULPHUR CREEK

8

26

15	RHI
08	04	03
AE	A/D	RSH

SULPHUR CREEK RANCH (W) NO ID

CTAF: 122.9
FSS: 122.6

Lat: N44-32
Long: W115-21

Class: Private
Chart: USGS Topo
Big Soldier Mtn. ID

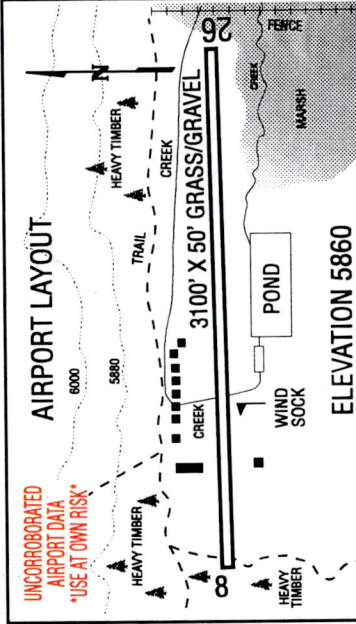

AIRPORT LAYOUT

UNCORROBORATED AIRPORT DATA "USE AT OWN RISK"

3100' X 50' GRASS/GRAVEL

ELEVATION 5860

N

HEAVY TIMBER

CREEK

TRAIL

6000

5880

CREEK

POND

WIND SOCK

HEAVY TIMBER

HEAVY TIMBER

26

8

FENCE

CREEK

MARSH

AIRPORT CAUTION • The IAFD recommends "land RWY 26 (upstream) take off RWY 8 (downstream); one way strip."
• Information: (208)377-1188.

THOMAS CREEK

3

21

10 AE	12 A/D	02 RSH
24 RHI		

A-120

THOMAS CREEK (W) 2U8

CTAF: 122.9   Lat: N44-43.58   Class: State REC
FSS: 122.6 116.2R   Long: W115-00.21   Chart: Great Falls

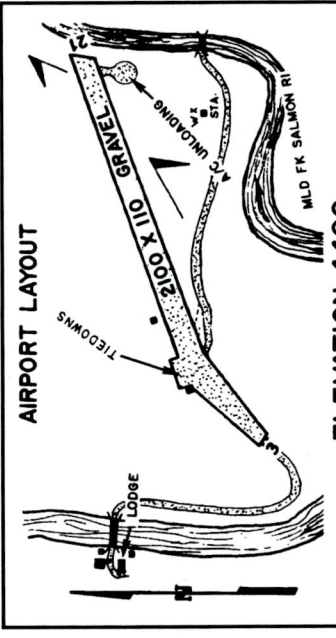

AIRPORT LAYOUT

ELEVATION 4400

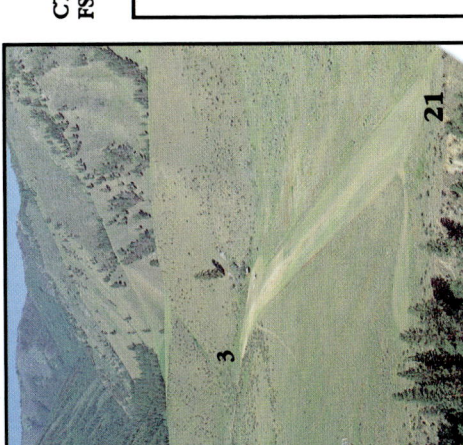

AIRPORT CAUTION • The IAFD recommends "Land RWY 21, takeoff RWY 3. • Caution: Special consideration should be given to mountain flying proficiency. • Close flight plan prior to landing. • No winter maintenance."
• Info: **(208)334-8775** Div. of Aeronautics.

TWIN BRIDGES

21

3

TWIN BRIDGES

U61

CTAF: 122.9   Lat: N43-56.79   Class: State REC
FSS: 122.1T 113.5R   Long: W114-06.59   Chart: Salt Lake

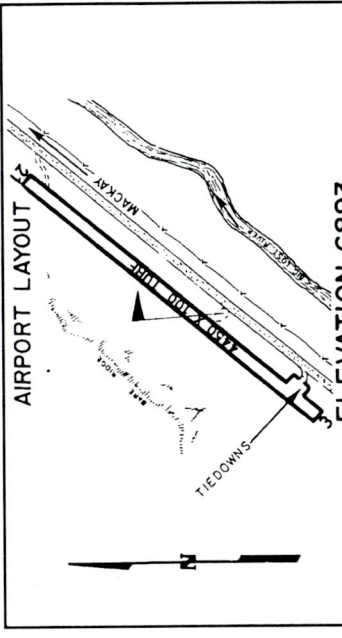

AIRPORT LAYOUT

MACKAY

TIEDOWNS

ELEVATION 6893

N

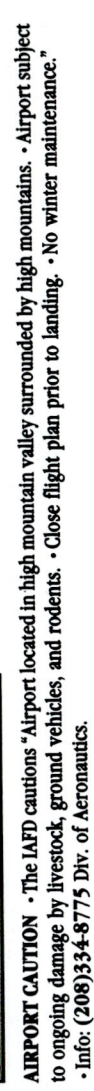

AIRPORT CAUTION • The IAFD cautions "Airport located in high mountain valley surrounded by high mountains. • Airport subject to ongoing damage by livestock, ground vehicles, and rodents. • Close flight plan prior to landing. • No winter maintenance."
• Info: (208)334-8775 Div. of Aeronautics.

UPPER LOON CREEK

4

22

UPPER LOON CREEK

CTAF: 122.9
FSS: 122.1T 113.5R

Lat: N44-35.49
Long: W114-49.39

Class: USFS REC
Chart: Great Falls

AIRPORT LAYOUT

ELEVATION 5500

2350 X 20 GRAVEL

LOON CK 69

LOON CK 24

22

TIEDOWNS

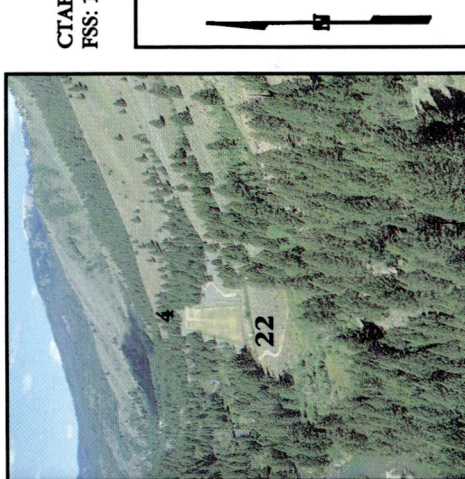

4

22

AIRPORT CAUTION • The IAFD recommends **"Land RWY 22, depart RWY 4 when wind conditions permit.** • Recommended for experienced mountain pilots only. • Close flight plan prior to landing. • No winter maintenance." • Info: (208)879-5204.

VINES

9

27

36 RHI
11 AE | 17 A/D | 08 KSH

A-126

VINES (W)

Lat: N45-07.86 Class: USFS EM
Long: W114-59.85 Chart: USGS TOPO
Vinegar Hill

CTAF: 122.9
FSS: 122.1T 116.2R

AIRPORT LAYOUT

UNCORROBORATED
AIRPORT DATA
"USE AT OWN RISK"

GARDEN CREEK

BIG CREEK

DOWNSTREAM

N

ROCKS

27

1100' X 30' GRAVEL/BUNCH GRASS

9

STEEP RISE
WITH HEAVY TIMBER

ELEVATION 4110

AIRPORT CAUTION • NOT MAINTAINED. USE AT YOUR OWN RISK. • Recommend landing upstream RWY 27, takeoff downstream RWY 9 . • On approach follow river to avoid trees. • Caution: Large rocks on edge of runway. • Rough runway surface. • Morning sun blinds pilot on takeoff. This strip is suitable for Super Cub type aircraft. • Runway surface conditions subject to ongoing deterioration. • Special consideration should be give to density altitude, turbulence, and mountain flying proficiency. • Usage limited to highly experienced mountain pilots. • Info: **(208)634-0746** Payette Forest Air Officer.

WARM SPRINGS

20

2

WARM SPRINGS

ØU1

CTAF: 122.9
FSS: 122.6

Lat: N44-08.53
Long: W115-18.86

Class: REC
Chart: Salt Lake

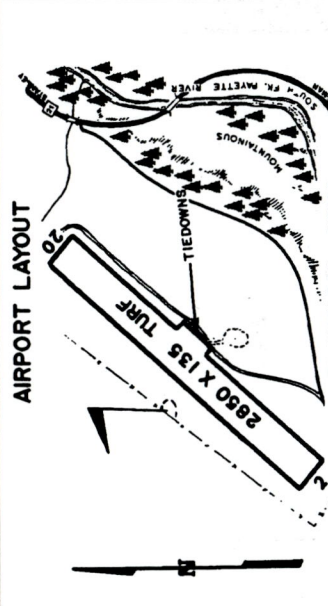

AIRPORT LAYOUT

2850 X 135 TURF

TIEDOWNS

SOUTH FK. PAYETTE RIVER

MOUNTAINOUS

ELEVATION 4831

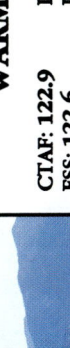

AIRPORT CAUTION · The IAFD recommends **"Land RWY 2, depart 20 when wind conditions permit.** · Close flight plan prior to landing. · No winter maintenance." · Info: **(208)334-8775** Div. of Aeronautics.

WARREN

WARREN

3U1

CTAF: 122.9
FSS: 122.6

Lat: N45-16.09
Long: W115-41.01

Class: USFS
Chart: Great Falls

AIRPORT LAYOUT

2765' X 75' GRAVEL

TIEDOWNS

WARREN ½ MI.

ELEVATION 5912

AIRPORT CAUTION · The IAFD cautions: "Threshold markers have been relocated from RWY 29 end. RWY width varies from 65' to 85'. Recommend land RWY 11, depart RWY 29 when wind conditions permit. · Down drafts prevalent RWY 11 during summer months. · Recommend use early morning and late evening. · Not recommended for inexperienced pilots. · Close flight plan prior to landing. · No winter maintenance." · Info: (208)634-0700.

WEATHERBY

21

3

WEATHERBY

52U

CTAF: 122.9
FSS: 122.6

Lat: N43-49.49
Long: W115-19.91

Class: USFS REC
Chart: Salt Lake

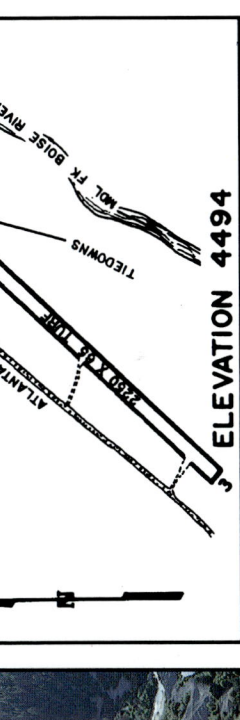

AIRPORT LAYOUT

BOISE RIVER

MDL FK

TIEDOWNS

ELEVATION 4494

ATLANTA

3280 X 75 TURF

3

21

AIRPORT CAUTION · The IAFD cautions: "Airport located in narrow river canyon subject to local turbulence. · Recommend land RWY 3, depart RWY 21 when wind conditions permit. · Close flight plan prior to landing. · No winter maintenance." · Info: (208)334-9800 Boise Forest Air Officer.

NOTES

NOTES

NOTES

GROUND

ANTELOPE VALLEY

HIGHLIGHT ✈ *Antelope Valley is unspoiled high desert cow country surrounded by high mountains. Indian Rock-Art documents an ancient peace treaty.*

· · · · ·

AIRPORT DESCRIPTION: Antelope is often listed as being located 1 mile west of the "city" or "town" of Grouse but this is a little misleading. Nothing exists in the area but a few scattered ranch houses. The Grouse School listed on Forest Service maps has been remodeled into a ranch house.

The well maintained airstrip, surrounded by private ranch land, has a gravel/ turf surface, and one tiedown near the windsock.

This airport could best be used to supply a hunting camp and shuttle hunters in and out of the area.

CAMPING: If you really want to, you could camp most anywhere - and you'd really have to want to - there's no facilities. The runway terminates essentially in a barnyard and most of the surrounding valley floor is privately owned. But if you wish to taste, smell, and listen to the quiet of the Old West, this is the spot.

It has been reported that someone did camp in the area up in the sagebrush, along the way to Graveyard Canyon...for just one night.

The ****Antelope Creek Guard Station Camp** is 4.7 miles west of the airport. The gravel road climbs 330' over the distance - a nice mountain bike ride and a real coaster on the return. Three camp sites with picnic tables and a pit toilet are situated along the cottonwood lined creek.

EXPLORING ANTELOPE VALLEY: I landed on RWY 5 and taxied to the tiedown area near a corral and ranch house, where I was first greeted by a big whiff of "Corral #9". The big wide open spaces of real Idaho Cowboy Country are on all sides; an open valley of meadow grass, a meandering stream leading to sage and cheat grass covered foothills.

To the west, rising snow-capped mountains have patches of quaking aspen

below and majestic stands of fir and lodgepole higher up. That's about it, but some people like it that way. Humans are far outnumbered by the bawling calves in the nearby corral.

Above their mournful cry, floating high on the desert breeze, I could almost hear the famous Eddy Arnold ballad, "Cattle Call". After singing an imaginary verse, "Hear that l-o-n-e-some c-a-t-tle c-a-ll...," I snapped back to the realization I was 50 miles from civilization and could not possibly be standing in the middle of nowhere singing along with cowboys in the sky.

Antelope Valley Airstrip.

After a 1.3 mile hike to Antelope Pioneer Cemetery (see hikes below), my illusions were replaced by the harsh reality of how the pioneers and present day inhabitants endured this harsh, mysterious and yet beautiful country.

And then, as if out of nowhere, an amiable young fellow on his tractor pulled up beside me. Casey Bitton said "howdy" and told about living in the valley most of his life. His grandmother's house was perched up on the hill to the south. I tried to no avail to casually slip into the conversation a question about my earlier encounter with cowboy music in the sky. But just then, Casey remarked about other pilots flying into the valley and hearing mysterious music.

Relieved, I listened to his tale. It is the country western station on the radio, he keeps it on 24 hours a day in the corral that the calves love most. It seems to settle them after their mothers have been removed.

HIKES: The 1.3 mile roundtrip hike to **Antelope Pioneer Cemetery** is easy and a worthwhile step back in time. There is no trailhead or trail, but from the tiedown area go to the northeast end, climb the fence, and follow the road to the south for about 1/4 mile. The road takes a hard turn to the left.

At this point, open the gate on the right (be sure to close it-remember this is cattle country and private property), then follow the old road up Graveyard Canyon 0.6 miles and you will see the cemetery in a small fenced area on your left. There is no gate in the fence. You will find eight to 10 graves, overgrown with sagebrush and tumbleweeds. All are unmarked except the grave of two-year-old Ruth Richardson, who died in 1889. Another grave has a broken down headstone put together with horseshoe nails.

As you explore the cemetery, please show as much respect for those who are buried here as they did for the surrounding untamed wilderness.

MOUNTAIN BIKE RIDE TO SHOSHONI ROCK WRITING: This is an easy 6.8 mile roundtrip hike or mountain bike ride to the unmarked **Antelope Valley Indian Writings**.

From the airstrip, follow the Antelope Road 3.1 miles east to its intersection with Cherry Creek Road. Turn left and continue 0.3 miles. Immediately adjacent to the road, on the right hand side, is a large outcropping of gray rocks. The writings are primarily on the largest vertical sheer cliff wall. The Indian artists used their mixture of red paints to record a sacred and binding peace ceremony.

The writings are not immediately visible, but once you first spot one of them, the others may slowly and cautiously reveal themselves. As they share their ancient secrets, revere and guard them, for these spiritualists had great powers.

Site of the Antelope Valley Indian rock writing.

HISTORY: As early as 1914, **Antelope Valley Airstrip** was indicated on maps, but was named **Scott Airstrip**. The current name, Antelope Valley, was influenced by nearby **Shoshoni Indian rock writing** (see Exploring Antelope Valley).

The pictograph was interpreted in 1937 as a peace treaty between two warring bands of Indians. The drawing on the eastern side of the writings designated this as antelope country and gave the name Antelope Creek to the stream flowing though the eastern plain.

It consists of a Shoshoni Chief, giving a sacred speech to a council of Indians, represented by a chief from a tribe of antelope hunters to the east, whose food and clothing were derived from the antelope, the principal animal of the plains; and a chief of a tribe of goat and bear hunters from the mountains to the west.

The chief from the mountains is fitted out with a war-bonnet and other war paraphernalia hanging down the back. His escutcheon breast piece notes a preparedness for war.

War paraphernalia scattered or removed from the Indians, indicates that both this council and this treaty of peace have resulted from some manner of fighting between these two tribes. However, a discarded spear affirms that the conflict is concluding, despite the display of armament.

The thunderbird depicted is the go-between for the Sun-Father and the Earth-Mother, making the compact a sacred and binding obligation. An Indian's oath, which he considers the most binding obligation, is made by pointing, with his pipe, to the sun and then to the earth.

The golden eagle is depicted, to whom the Indian is indebted for feathers and claws with which to adorn his headdress, and other war paraphernalia. He is one of the Indian's most loved friends and in this writing is the symbol of friendship, denoting that this treaty brought to the members of these tribes friendship and they henceforth separate as friends.

The coyote is the common tribal progenitor, who, being impartial to any of his progeny, is stationed between these signatories to see that the treaty is not evaded but is executed and enforced in an equitable manner.

MAPS, LOCAL CONDITIONS, AND INFORMATION:

Nearby forest information: Challis National Forest, Lost River Ranger District Box 507, Mackay, Idaho 83521 (208)588-2224.

Airport information: Division of Aeronautics: 3483 Rickenbacker St., Boise, Idaho 83705, (208)334-8775 (800)346-9134 in state.

Antelope, Idaho. Circa: March 1899.
Courtesy: Idaho Historical Society.

ATLANTA

HIGHLIGHT ✈ *Two wonderful natural hot springs, lodging, a restaurant, and an historic mining community in one of Idaho's most beautiful mountain settings.*

- - - - -

AIRPORT DESCRIPTION: This strip is located on the western edge of the beautiful Sawtooth Wilderness Area and sits on a bench above the Middle Fork of the Boise River. Towering Ponderosa Pines and wildflowers surround the site. Bordering the airstrip is the crystal clear Middle Fork of the Boise River with

Main Street, Atlanta 1993.

the historic and friendly town of Atlanta just one (easy walking) mile to the west.

Majestic Greylock Mountain dominates the view to the north with an elevation of 9,317 feet.

On your way to town, you will pass the USFS Riverside Campground about a half mile from the end of RWY 34.

TRANSPORTATION: A courtesy car is not provided. However, it is not particularly necessary. Easy walking, mountain biking, and ATVs will get you where you want to go. Atlanta can be reached by car, but it takes some determination and an affinity for dust to do it.

SERVICES AND LODGING: The Beaver Lodge, located on Main Street, Atlanta, offers breakfast, lunch, and dinner. The proprietors, Lois and her son Russ, share good food and warm

hospitality. They are happy to give suggestions and directions to nearby explorations.

For rent by the night ($40), or by the week ($150), is a new and roomy cabin behind the lodge. For information and reservations, call (208)864-2132.

The Beaver Lodge offers down home hospitality and good food.

CAMPING: The ***Riverside Campground has 7 improved campsites tucked along the banks of the Middle Fork of the Boise River. Open from June 1 to October 1, the campground has picnic tables, fireplaces, bbq grills, and pit toilets. With the exception of the spring run-off when the water turns off-color, you'll find very good fly fishing for rainbow and cutthroat trout. A daily camping fee is charged.

EXPLORING ATLANTA: You will be greeted by the alpine aroma of ponderosa pine, and quite possibly a deer running by as you walk to town. A lilac bush in late spring, bursting with bloom in the middle of a meadow, typifies the wild and untamed nature of Atlanta.

WALKING TOUR: A handy, mini-history and walking tour of the historic mining town of 37 friendly folks, is printed on the back of the Beaver Lodge menu. A self-guided tour with menu in hand seems to be the logical next step to locating the jail, schoolhouse (five grades for five students), cemetery, barber shop, and various historic homes and hotels.

Before you leave the lodge, ask about their world famous "Beer Sponge Sandwich", an alleged miracle cure for hangovers.

SUPPLIES: The tiny "Whistle Stop" store sits just about in the middle of town and provides the bare necessities. Mary leaves a quarter and her phone number taped to the door so customers can call her if she happens not to be in.

HOT SPRINGS: It is not uncommon for locals to keep the directions to hot springs to themselves, but this is not the case in Atlanta. The residents are glad to share the good life, so ask at the Beaver Lodge how to find Atlanta and Chattanooga Hot

Springs, two of the most beautiful natural hot springs you will ever see.

Atlanta Hot Springs is about a two-mile walk from town, along the road to the Power Plant Campground. The luxurious rock bathtub, complete with its own wooden stopper, fills with crystal clear water and beckons a relaxing soak. A split log sitting bench adds to the idyllic setting. Run-off from the springs leads to a pond which doubles as a popular swimming hole.

Chattanooga Hot Springs is easy to overlook but a must to visit. This pool looks as if it should grace the cover of a home and garden magazine. A 50-foot cliff is alive with cascading springs, which fill the tub below. Again, the water is crystal clear and guarantees a memorable soak. Sound effects are provided by Mother Nature, with hot water bubbling from the rock toward the river roaring beneath the pool.

To find this treasure, look for a left turn marked by a tree bisecting the road just before the pond on the way to Atlanta Hot Springs. Follow a short spur to an unofficial camping area. Pass a "No Camping" sign and directly ahead you will find a steep path down a bank leading to the hot springs.

Janet Kellam tests the inviting warm water at Atlanta Hot Springs.

HISTORY: Atlanta is a gold mine for history buffs, would-be prospectors and ghost busters. In 1864, about 400 people lived here. In November of that year, an astonishing quartz discovery was made and aptly named the "Atlanta Lode" by confederate miners in Yuba. The lode was reputed to be 1.5 miles in length and ranged from 15 to 30 feet wide...depending on the optimism of the prospector.

In 1867, the need arose for a large stamp mill to replace the existing arastras and a couple of smaller mills. The Alturas Mining Company found a mill site and prepared to erect a building, and had a 20-ton mill well on the way to the lode.

Unfortunately, the president of the company, an Easterner with no knowledge of mining, reached Rocky Bar by the time the mill had arrived at Junction Bar (modern Featherville) eight miles below. The last half-gallon of whiskey in Rocky Bar rendered his trip to Yuba impossible. He then declared the country "worthless" and disastrously instructed that the teams and hauling wagons be sold on the spot. The mill was left to rust at Junction Bar. The lumber for the buildings at Yuba City was also abandoned to ruin during the hard winter.

Due to the inaccessibility of the area, developing mineral potential of the area was exceedingly slow. However, by 1930, $16 million of mineral wealth finally was extracted from Atlanta, established as a gold mining town 66 years earlier.

Another venture got off to a much faster start in Atlanta. Two prostitutes, Peg Leg (Anne McIntire) and her friend Emma "Dutch Em" Von Losch, were living here in the late 1890s. They took off on foot to a dance at Rocky Bar in the spring of 1896 or 1898, depending on who's telling the story, and were ambushed by a blizzard. Only after the two-day storm, did a search party set out to find them. Annie was found deranged and crawling in the snow with frozen feet, while Dutch Em was found frozen to death clad in Annie's garments.

The doctor, summoned from Mountain Home 80 miles away, amputated Annie's feet. Even though a fund was started to provide Annie with artificial legs,

Atlanta Views from a Lithograph by Britton & Rey, San Francisco. Circa 1880-1881. Courtesy Idaho State Historical Society.

she preferred pegs, and acquired the name Peg Leg Annie. She lived with Henry Longhene for 22 years supporting herself by selling whiskey and taking in laundry. Longhene left Annie, and used her $10,000 life savings to return to Italy. Peg Leg Annie died in 1934, and is buried at Morris Hill in Boise.

Greylock Mountain - This spectacular mountain to the north of Atlanta, was named by the early Chinese miners. If you look at the mountain from town, you see that it is mostly gray rock...the Chinese couldn't pronounce the "r" in rock. The rest is history.

HUNTING & FISHING: Sawtooth Wilderness Outfitters provides guided pack trips for elk, deer cougar, bear, and fish in Units 35 & 39. For information, call Darl Allred, Box 81, Garden Valley, Idaho 83622. Summer phone (208)259-3408, winter phone (208)462-3416.

ANNUAL EVENTS & ACTIVITIES: Atlanta Days is held the first full weekend in August, with a street dance and all the small town fun you would expect. It is rumored a golf cart drag race between two ladies in town could be on the schedule of events.

MAPS, LOCAL CONDITIONS, INFORMATION:

For maps and local information, stop in the Atlanta Forest Service Guard Station, on the road leading from the airport into town. Open summer and fall - no telephone.

The Forest Service District Office is located in Idaho City and is open all year with maps, camping and forest information. Idaho City Ranger District, Box 129, Idaho City, Idaho 83631 (208)364-4330.

Airport Conditions: Richard Cooke, the Airport Manager, is very knowledge-able on the airport and the non-standard approach needed to land here. For your first arrival, talking to Mr. Cooke is well worth the phone call. Richard Cooke, Airport Manager, Box 1702, Boise, Idaho 83701 (208)383-7797.

BEAR TRAP

HIGHLIGHT ✈ *An isolated desert airstrip with a nearby cave to explore.*

- - - - -

AIRPORT DESCRIPTION: The dirt and turf runway is well maintained. The runway markers are well defined and the grass in kept mowed. The one tiedown is overgrown with weeds but would work. The strip appears to be well used.

Because of its close proximity to a relatively good desert road and its remote location, the airstrip has long been suspected of being used by drug smugglers (yes-even in Idaho). Report any suspicious activities to the Power County Sheriff in American Falls (208)226-2319.

EXPLORING BEAR TRAP: HIKE TO BEAR TRAP CAVE - This is an easy two mile round trip hike from the west end of the airstrip. As I stepped out of my airplane, I was greeted by a rattlesnake skin shed by its previous owner. I would advise leaving Fido in the plane or at home.

Follow the road west 100 yards to where it junctions with the Minidoka desert road. Turn right and stay on the road for about a mile. The cave is on the left side of the road and is well marked. It is a collapsed lava vent tube leading from a nearby volcanic cone.

For the inexperienced desert explorer, it is wise to stay on the roads, as distant landmarks are non-existent and it's easy to get turned around. Lots of spent cartridges and empty beer cans along the road indicate this area is probably used at night by "hunters" spotlighting jackrabbits, coyotes, and rattlers out of the back end of their Ford pickups.

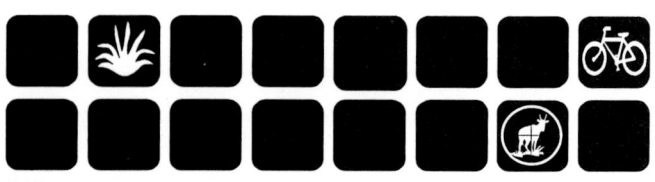

MAPS, LOCAL CONDITIONS, AND INFORMATION:

Maps and area recreational information:
    Bureau of Land Management
    U.S. Department of the Interior
    Shoshone District Office
    400 West F Street
    Shoshone, Idaho 83352
    (208)886-2206

Airport information:
    Division of Aeronautics
    3483 Rickenbacker
    Boise, Idaho 83705
    (208)334-8775

For more information, refer to Arco-Kimama overview on page I-1.

*"The way I figure it, three weeks at a good trot
and I can be home chasing joggers!"*

BERNARD

HIGHLIGHT ✦ *Historic river bar on the lower Middle Fork of the Salmon. Wonderful microenvironments in close proximity.*

· · · · ·

AIRPORT DESCRIPTION: Bernard is not an airstrip for an inexperienced pilot. Swallow your pride and hire a backcountry pilot to show you the ropes, fly an airplane with appropriate performance, and stay light. During a late spring afternoon the temperatures can hover around 85 and in August you'll see 100 degrees and more.

Bernard is the last strip on the Middle Fork before it meets with the Main Salmon River, 28 miles downstream. Sagebrush covered hills begin to grow steeper as the river proceeds toward the mouth of Impassable Canyon. Drastically different than the upstream terrain, this lower stretch turns into sheer vertical rock walls. The river becomes shadowed by high slanting peaks and 1500 ft. high dark walls; natural skyscrapers if you will.

Tiedowns are located at both ends of the turf runway which has a well defined track down the middle. The decomposed granite is soft and has a tendency to extend the take-off roll. We noted two soft spots during a spring visit.

CAMPING: The ***Bernard Camp** is located at the north end of the airstrip along the river. There are no facilities here other than one pit toilet. The scenery here is very stark. Scattered douglas fir and a few big bitterbrush line the river bank. In May, the numerous small cacti along the river were in bloom. Their beautiful bright pink flowers were in contrast to the tan decomposed granite. Rattlesnakes inhabit this lower section of the river, so between the cactus and snakes · watch your step.

EXPLORING BERNARD: The Flying B Ranch is a mile upstream from Bernard Creek and sells beer, soft drinks, and candy. This private resort also serves breakfast, lunch, and dinner and provides lodging. Please re-pay your privilege of patronizing with consideration and courtesy. Watch your litter. The Flying B currently charges a $25 non-member landing fee.

HIKES: BERNARD CREEK TRAIL There is an excellent hike here along Bernard Creek. It will show you the sharp contrast between the arid desert of the airstrip and the lush and humid micro-environment deep down in the narrow confines of the creek bottom.

However, you must travel six miles uphill to the **Short Creek Lookout**. Since there is a 4,000 ft. ascent, you may want to elect to take in just two or three miles as I did. The creek bottom is an oasis for forest grouse, mule deer, elk, and a nice variety of mushrooms are at home in the decaying humus.

The warm moist air is sweet with the smell of sap flowing in the douglas firs. Quaking aspen, dogwood, wild roses, choke cherries, elderberries and ferns are alive and well in the 50-ft. wide wet corridor. If you look up the hillsides only a few yards, you will see again the desert-like environment of the airstrip.

Finding the trailhead: The trail begins directly uphill from the Guard Station. The trail immediately splits, with the left fork crossing Bernard Creek and heading for the Flying B, and the right fork following Bernard Creek uphill.

Bernard Creek waterfalls.

The Middle Fork swells from the spring runoff.

The Hike: The well defined trail follows the north side of the stream for about 1.5 miles, climbing about 1000 feet. Deer like to bed down in the cool shadows of the creek bottom. After the trail crosses the stream, a series of cascading waterfalls begin. Beyond 2 miles, you are on your own. The adventurous can continue 4 miles to the lookout. The casual hiker can enjoy a picnic lunch near a private water falls and look for mushrooms on the return trip.

HISTORY: Bernard Creek is named for **Captain Reuben F. Bernard**, who had command of the army in the **Sheepeater War of 1879**. After unsuccessfully chasing the Indians from May 31, 1879 till August 26, 1879, Captain Bernard and 60 of his men had covered 1168 miles, lost 63 head of stock, and had completely depleted their supplies. After losing the Indian's trail here, they began their retreat back to Boise by way of Loon Creek.

They had found the river below this point to run through an **"Impassable Canyon"** with no trails and 2000 foot vertical walls. Even today, the lower 18 miles can only be reached by water.

A.D. "Asa" Clark built a cabin here during the Thunder Mountain gold rush in the early 1900s. He ingeniously put pack saddles on a herd of milk cows and used them for pack animals carrying supplies from Meyers Cove to Thunder Mountain. During the summer, he would sell the milk to the miners and on his last trip in the fall would slaughter the cows and sell the meat.

The Forest Service built a guard station on the foundation of the Clark cabin.

HUNTING & FISHING: This is a great stretch of river to fish. In between stretches of whitewater, the water slows down into a series of deep holes. Large cutthroat trout lurk in the holes and will move into the shallower water to feed.

The **"Flying B Ranch"** located one mile upstream provides guided hunting trips for elk, deer, moose, goat, sheep, bear, cougar, predators, and forest grouse. They also offer fishing, trailrides, and backpacking. Units 20A, 26, and 27. For more information, contact: Flying Resort Ranches, Inc., Box 770, Salmon, Idaho 83467 (208)756-6295.

MAPS, LOCAL CONDITIONS, AND INFORMATION:

Salmon National Forest, Box 729, Salmon, Idaho 83467 (208)756-2215.

BIG BAR

HIGHLIGHT ✈ *On the banks of the Snake River, in the bottom of Hells Canyon, Big Bar offers great fishing and canyon scenery.*

- - - - -

AIRPORT DESCRIPTION: Big Bar is currently the only Hells Canyon airstrip on the Idaho side of the river. The airstrip is in a field without the aid of runway markings, windsocks, or tiedowns.

CAMPING: There are no developed camp sites at Big Bar but there are some very nice undeveloped sites along the river. When camping along the river, be aware of widely fluctuating water levels, or you may get a free float trip.

HISTORY: There are two Big Bars in Hells Canyon; both have had airstrips on them. The Big Bar upstream from Hells Canyon Dam, near Bar Creek, is now under several feet of water and is less desirable to land on. This Big Bar is near Meyers Creek and is the site of a murder.

Sheep sheds and corrals on Big Bar in 1952, looking north down river. Courtesy: Backeddy Press.

Mac Meyers, once described as having a disposition as sweet as sour milk, had a rock cabin just over the hill from Big Bar on what is now known as Meyers Creek. Meyers raised a garden near his cabin for his own personal consumption.

However, the cattle from nearby Big Bar considered the garden existed for their own personal consumption. Meyers exchanged heated words with the local cowboys responsible for the cattle, and threatened that they would be grabbing the wrong end of a branding iron if their cattle entered his garden again.

On May 18, 1904, Mac returned to his cabin to find that cattle had once again been allowed to graze in his garden. Madder than a bull in bumble bees, he grabbed his 30-30 and set off to find those responsible. He set up an ambush in what is now known as "Brownlee Saddle" and waited for the cattle drive to pass through. As George Brownlee rode unsuspectingly through the saddle, Meyers shot him in the back, killing him instantly. He then turned his rifle on Wallace Jarrett, and wounded him in the arm. Jarrett hightailed it out of the area to report the crime.

Big Bar in the foreground. Hay was slid down a chute to a barn on the lower flat.
Courtesy Backeddy Press.

Meyers was soon apprehended and taken to White Bird for a preliminary hearing. It was determined that there was enough evidence that he should be tried by the District Judge in Grangeville. That night, as Meyers was being held prisoner in the Newman Hotel, an angry lynch mob was forming outside.

Two ladies, spending the night in the hotel, were feeling a little peaked. The lynch mob (gentlemen as they were) deferred their activities until the following morning so as not to further distress the ladies.

Early the following morning, the two men escorting Meyers out of the hotel were overtaken by 30 armed men. The prisoner was taken a short distance to the George Bentz ranch on White Bird Creek and hanged from a cottonwood tree.

After Bentz returned home and learned the story from his wife, he rode into town and demanded that the men return and cut the body down. Out of disgust, Bentz later cut the tree down. The body was taken back to White Bird, ending the story of the disgruntled gardener from Big Bar.

MAPS, LOCAL CONDITIONS, AND INFORMATION:

Hells Canyon National Recreation Area, Box 699, 2355 Riverside Drive, Clarkston, Washington 99403 (509)758-0616.

For more information, refer to Hells Canyon overview on page I-3.

BIG CREEK

HIGHLIGHT → *Two rustic lodges offer food, trailrides, and lodging. Airplane camping at its best. High mountain valley.*

- - - - -

AIRPORT DESCRIPTION: For sheer beauty, this strip might receive top honors. It is situated immediately outside the western edge of the Frank Church River of No Return Wilderness, high in the upper basin of Big Creek, a major tributary of the Middle Fork.

There are several private and public strips in the area but this one sits at the headwaters. Mountains reaching above 9,000 ft. to the south sit in a semicircle separating the Big Creek drainage from the South Fork of the Salmon and the famous historic mining towns of Yellowpine, Stibnite, Thunder Mountain, and Roosevelt. The high, lush misty mountain meadow attracts moose in the willows at the north end and deer in the pasture by the Guard Station.

If you arrive early, it seems as if you have caught the little valley before waking to the morning sun. The sweet mountain dew is still on the grass and misty puffs are still hugging the valley floor. A dirt road runs by the airstrip back toward civilization, 80 grueling, rough and dusty miles away. Tiedowns are located at the south end of the airstrip.

TRANSPORTATION: Cars would definitely be out of place here. Horses are available to rent from the Big Creek Lodge or bring your own mountain bike.

SERVICES & LODGING: Civilization has finally encroached on this Idaho gem. A small hydroelectric generator has been installed to provide electricity to the Big Creek Lodge. I regret such civility but am certain the operators of the lodge greatly appreciate its convenience. Still no telephone, but limited radio communication is available at the Forest Service, Big Creek Lodge, and Gillihan's Lodge.

The **US Forest Service** has a guard station located on the field and it's a good source of information and maps.

Big Creek Lodge sits at the south end of the field and offers breakfasts and lunches for $7.50 and dinners for $10 to $15. Reservations are requested for

dinner. Lodging is available for $85 person per day, which includes three meals. Guided pack trips for fishing are available for $45 per person including lunch.

Guided hunting trips for elk, deer, bear, and moose are available in unit 20A. For reservations and information, call Howard Manly (208)375-4921.

Gillihan's Lodge is located one mile south of the airstrip. Contact them on 122.9 for transportation. Reservations for meals are not required in June, September, and October. During July and August, make advance reservations through Arnold Aviation at (208)382-4336. Breakfast and lunch run $4 to $6, and dinners run $10 to $20.

The lodge is a small bed and breakfast accommodating approximately twelve guests. The five private bedrooms share bath facilities. Family style meals, by reservation, are served at indoor and outdoor dining areas.

Room and board at the lodge is available at $80 per person, couples - $70 per person. Horse trail rides - $45 per person. Overnight all-expense pack trips, $150 per person per day. For more information, call (208)365-5384.

The Big Creek Lodge features great food and overnight accommodations.

CAMPING: The ****Big Creek Campground** has eight nice campsites with tables, stoves, and a new pit toilet. Drinking water is now available. The grassy campground is set back in the trees and is protected by rocks at the entry to discourage vehicle traffic. It is maintained by the State of Idaho and the Treasure Valley Aviation Association.

EXPLORING BIG CREEK: This tranquil mountain setting may be explored by horseback, foot or mountain bike. I found great mountain bike adventures.

MOUNTAIN BIKE RIDES:

BIG CREEK TO WERDENHOFF MINE General Description: This is a 14 mile round trip ride from the Big Creek Airstrip up Smith Creek to the **Werdenhoff Mine**. Numerous old mining cabins and buildings exist along the road. The road is primarily decomposed granite with quite a few chunks not quite so decomposed.

Trees line the roadway to provide a canopy of shade for a pleasant ride. From the airstrip, the road descends 320 feet in 2.4 miles and then climbs another 820 feet in 4.6 miles.

Finding the Trailhead: From the tiedown area at the airstrip, intercept the road paralleling the west side of the runway. The Forest Service Guard Station has maps and information. Follow the road downstream (northeast).

The Ride: The road descends gradually to the mouth of Smith Creek at 2.4 miles as Big Creek drops quickly away from the road to begin its tumultuous trip to the Middle Fork. The Big Creek/Smith Creek Trailhead, at this confluence, has a livestock loading ramp, a clean pit toilet, and a tribute to Frank Church who was instrumental in setting aside much of the Idaho Wilderness. A gate across the road continuing down Big Creek marks the boundary of the Frank Church River of No Return Wilderness - no bikes this way!

Remnants of the Werdenhoff Mill. The weathered siding was removed to decorate someone's home.

The main road turns up Smith Creek. Near this location was the old camp of the Smith Creek Hydraulic Mining Company.

At 2.9 miles is the huge Werdenhoff Mill and remnants of three associated buildings. It appears as if someone has removed all the exterior boards from the mill to remodel their living room. Inside is what's left of a seven foot wood cook stove - also vandalized. I'm sure the mining cook flipped a lot of flapjacks over this stove in its lifetime.

At 4.3 miles, three buildings and an ore dump cling to the side of the road. At 6.2 miles, a small sign points to the Smith Creek Cutoff Trail. A steep trail switchbacks up the hill past several decomposing cabins, presumably bypassing the switchback on the main road. You're on your own exploring this trail. It didn't appear to be mountain bike material to me.

Continuing on the main road, ford the North Fork of Smith Creek (a cold foot soaker), until reaching the fork in the road at 6.7 miles. Take the switchback uphill to the right. Numerous mining buildings still exist. Please leave them intact.

Return along the same route, or for the more adventurous, return to the fork in the road at 6.7 miles and continue up to the head of the South Fork of Smith Creek approximately 3.5 miles to the **Independence Mine**, which was located in 1898.

BIG CREEK TO PROFILE GAP SUMMIT: General Description: This is a 21.2 mile round trip climb and return descent, with an elevation gain of 1862'.

The Trailhead: From the Big Creek airstrip, follow the main road south past the Big Creek Lodge.

The Ride: Follow rolling hills along lower Big Creek Drainage with various unimproved campsites along the road. Lick Creek Trail branches off to the east and climbs up to Cougar Basin. At about 4.3 miles, just past Jacobs Ladder Creek, the ride begins its steady climb to the summit, 7.7 miles further. The ride is gradual and of a consistent pitch to the top. This is beautiful country, especially the basin below Big Creek Point and Profile Peak.

Profile Sam's Camp at the head of Profile Creek. Circa 1908. Courtesy: Idaho Historical Society.

OPTIONAL RIDE - PROFILE GAP SUMMIT TO RED METALS MINE: General Description: From Profile Gap Summit, this trip adds 3.6 miles to the round trip from Big Creek Airstrip.

The Ride: Drop over Profile Summit Gap and head south down Profile Creek Drainage for 1.5 miles, where a two track dirt road branches off the right side. Follow the double track for another 0.4 miles until you reach the mine. If you explore the area, use extreme caution; many of the

Red Metals Mine on Profile Gap Summit.

structures are old and unstable. Also, open mine shafts still exist. To the west of the prominent structures runs the Crater Lake outlet, which cascades over the steep, rocky terrain.

OPTIONAL HIKE:

Red Metals Mine to Crater Lake: This is an additional 1 mile round trip hike from the Red Metals Mine.

Finding the Trailhead: From Red Metals Mine, there is a rock cairn.

The Hike: The trail follows the right (north) side of the Crater Lake Drainage. It is somewhat primitive, but distinguishable. The lake itself is nestled between jagged granite peaks, and provides a nice overnight destination. In late June, the water had a layer of broken ice on its surface. Several other lakes lie to the southeast, but to my knowledge, are not accessible by trail. This doesn't mean you can't get there; easy scrambling up any of the outlets will lead you to them. Middle Lake and Fish Lake lie respectively to the south. The Wilson and Lotspiech Mine also lie in this basin.

The ice is just leaving Crater Lake in early July.

HISTORY: The Big Creek Airport was obtained by the Forest Service in 1926, for the purpose of feeding stock and the first travel there was recorded in 1929. Many times it was a one-way trip, with the plane being grounded in the pasture because of high density altitude.

The Division of Aeronautics finished grading and sodding under a special use permit in 1960. The Big Creek Airstrip plays an important role as an emergency strip for flyers and provides access to the upper Big Creek area when roads are impassable.

It was this rough country that delayed development of mining on Big Creek. An 1100 ft. by 60 ft. outcrop of parallel veined silver ore was discovered in 1884. Within a year, 150 miners had located 100 mining claims, but development required an 85 mile wagon road to haul the ore out. Although individual ore samples were quite rich, the average only ran $1 to $2 a ton.

It wasn't until the early 1900s that improved mining techniques and better transportation allowed for profitable mining in the area. In 1904, the W.A. Edwards claim between Logan and Government Creeks, justified importing a stamp mill.

That created Logan City (later known as Edwardsburg). That same summer, up went a saloon, store, butcher shop, a house on Big Creek flat, and later in 1906, the four stamp mill arrived. The mill met with limited success, but Mrs. Edwards continued to run the post office and Edwardsburg served this remote country for many years. Between 1906 and 1942, most of Big Creek's production was realized, a yield of about $400,000.

MAPS, LOCAL CONDITIONS, AND INFORMATION:

Current local conditions: Division of Aeronautics (208)334-8775.

Topographical Maps: Distribution Section, U.S. Geological Survey, Federal Center, Denver, CO 80225.

USFS Nez Perce & Bitterroot Nat'l Forest: U.S. Dept. of Agriculture Forest Service, Northern Region Information, Receptionist, Box 7669, Missoula, MT 59807.

USFS Payette & Salmon Nat'l Forest: U.S. Dept. of Agriculture, Forest Service, Intermountain Region, Room 1407 Federal Bldg., 324 25th St., Ogden, UT 84401.

Charley Myers riding up Big Creek towards Profile Gap.
Due to a hip injury, he rode his horse off-center. Circa 1920.
Courtesy: Idaho County Free Press.

BIG SOUTHERN BUTTE

HIGHLIGHT → *A desert strip located at the base of pioneer Idaho's most recognized landmark, Big Butte, site of the Big Butte Stage Stop, where a late 1800s stage robbery resulted in a lost fortune of gold.*

- - - - -

AIRPORT DESCRIPTION: The runway is basically dirt with clumps of grass and an occasional sagebrush growing on it. It slopes uphill to the south. Strong afternoon winds out of the southwest are prevalent. There are tiedowns at the south end but they are overgrown with weeds and hard to find. The tiedowns also slope downhill from the runway which encourages pulling rocks through your propellor when leaving.

A log cabin, log barn with sod roof, and corrals are located at the south end of the runway. Apparently, it is used in the summer for running cattle in the desert. There are no telephones or electricity. A small holding pond behind the cabin is filled from a spring on the Butte.

EXPLORING BIG SOUTHERN BUTTE: A few cow skulls decorate the sage covered desert. Miles of uninhabited desert lie in all directions. For the desert explorer, this nothingness is everything.

HIKES: BIG BUTTE HIKE OR MOUNTAIN BIKE RIDE - From the south end of the airstrip, follow the road through the ranch to a sign designating the road

Big Butte cow camp; notice the barn with sod roof and wagon with singletrees. Photo 1993.

to Big Butte. It climbs 2500 feet in 5 miles to an incredible 360 degree view of the Snake River Plains. This famous landmark shows up on the maps of nearly all the early explorers as it can be seen from hundred of miles in all directions.

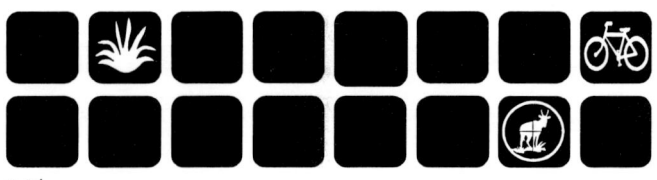

HISTORY: In the late 1800s, a stage route ran near Big Butte with a stage station located here. A lone gunman purportedly held up the Custer Mine stagecoach on Root Hog Divide, a few miles east of the Butte. He made off with gold coins and two 150 pound gold bars. The two heavy gold bars were buried in a desert cave as the bandit made his way to Salmon City.

In the late 1800s the stagecoach which ran between Blackfoot, Big Butte, Antelope, and Mackay was held up near Root Hog Divide, resulting in a fortune in gold lost in the desert.

A posse later apprehended him near the site of the robbery, along with some of the loot. He agreed to lead them to the hiding place of the two gold bars in the cave. However, as darkness arrived, the bandit escaped, never to return.

Thirty years later, a New Mexico man arrived in the area with a map drawn by the bandit but his search was fruitless. Locals believe

Big Butte juts 2500' above the desert floor, providing an historic landmark on the Oregon Trail.

that the cave may be within the confines of the INEL; waiting to be discovered.

MAPS, LOCAL CONDITIONS, AND INFORMATION:

Maps and area recreational information:

Bureau of Land Management, U.S. Dept. of the Interior, 400 West F Street, Shoshone, Idaho 83352 (208)886-2206.

Airport information:

Division of Aeronautics, 3483 Rickenbacker, Boise, Idaho 83705 (208)334-8775.

For more informaiton, refer to Arco-Kimama overview on page I-1.

BRUCE MEADOWS

HIGHLIGHT ✈ *Hike to hot springs or watch springtime elk herds graze along the runway. Float and fish Bear Valley Creek where huge salmon populations once attracted herds of bears.*

- - - - -

AIRPORT DESCRIPTION: Bruce Meadows lies a mile south of the Frank Church River of No Return Wilderness, 20 miles northwest of Stanley in Bear Valley next to the junction of Bear Valley Rd. and Boundary Creek Rd. The large grassy meadow is a haven for elk in the springtime. Later in the season, cattle graze in the valley, and by hunting season, the elk have found more secluded hiding areas.

Because Boundary Creek Campground is a loading area for white water float trips on the upper Middle Fork, the dirt road draws considerable traffic until the water level drops and outfitters put in farther downstream.

CAMPING: ****Bruce Meadows Airport Campsite**. The State of Idaho has installed one campsite with a picnic table, fire pit, and pit toilet in the trees at the northeast end of the airstrip near the tiedown area.

The ****USFS Bruce Meadows Campground** is located about a mile west of the tiedown area. Follow the dirt road.

*Fir Creek Campground is a good place to set up camp if you intend to partake in the Bear Valley Hot Springs.

EXPLORING BRUCE MEADOWS: The **Bear Valley Hot Springs Hike** is a rewarding and easy nine-mile round trip with a wonderful series of warm water pools. Hiking into this secluded valley is very special and privacy is almost guaranteed, except for the occasional airplane. The hot springs are located just upstream from the confluence of Bear Valley Creek and Marsh Creek which join to form the headwaters of the famous Middle Fork of the Salmon.

Finding the trailhead: From the Bruce Creek Airport, head east along the dirt road approximately one mile and follow the turnoff to Marsh Creek Trail and Fir Creek Campground. There are really two trails that lead to the springs.

The USFS trail starts at the **Fir Creek Packbridge** and requires a stream fording about 1.5 downstream. This can be a little treacherous until late August, depending on weather conditions.

A primitive trail following the south bank of Bear Valley Creek can be picked up at the Fir Creek Campground and followed until the junction of the USFS trail at the ford. This trail does erode away and is quite steep in places.

The Hike: For the USFS trail, cross the Fir Creek Packbridge and proceed downstream 1.5 miles. In a large meadow, look for orange flagging on both sides of the creek to indicate the ford. At 3.5 miles, look for a tree with HS carved on it. Faint paths lead down to the first murky spring. Continue downstream to the series of pools stepping down to the creek. Enjoy.

Early day salmon fishing trip in Bear Valley.
Notice the "fly rod" the fellow on the right is using. Circa 1930.

HISTORY: Bear Valley was once the site of two active dredges. After standing like statues in the open meadow for many years, they were dismantled in 1970 and hauled away. They were powered by electricity generated from a plant on the east side of the valley. Unlike other dredges, they sought the rare metals of columbium, tantalum, and monazite not gold.

Two beautiful salmon caught in Bear Valley Creek circa 1930.
Courtesy: Idaho Historical Society.

Mt. McGowan overlooks the beautiful Stanley Basin.
Courtesy: Idaho Historical Society.

MAPS, LOCAL CONDITIONS, AND INFORMATION:

Airport conditions: Division of Aeronautics, 3483 Rickenbacker St., Boise, Idaho 83705 (208)334-8775.

Maps and forest information: Lowman Ranger District, Boise National Forest, Lowman, Idaho 83637 (208)259-3361.

CABIN CREEK

HIGHLIGHT ✈ *Wilderness airstrip at the historic battleground of the Sheepeater War. Great fishing.*

- - - - -

AIRPORT DESCRIPTION: Do not attempt landing here without first being shown the approach by one of the experienced local pilots. It is not difficult if done correctly. A couple of hours with one of the pilots listed in the appendix will save you the embarrassment of adding your name to the list that didn't make it.

When the approach is flown properly, not to be confused with a "standard approach pattern", the outcroppings of rock and selected pine trees work as a VASI to provide a gentle descent to what could otherwise be a harsh learning experience. There is no go-around. You must do it right the first time and every time.

The runway has a pretty good upslope in addition to a dogleg. The approach end crosses over Cabin Creek and the cool air provides quite a sink just before touchdown. Rubber waterbars traverse the runway to divert water from running down the strip. They are quite flexible and appear more ominous than they really are.

The airstrip lies about twelve miles upstream from the confluence of Big Creek and the Middle Fork of the Salmon on Cabin Creek. This was an early ranch site with two barns and numerous other buildings. The Forest Service has removed most of the buildings and buried the bulldozer that built the airstrip.

CAMPING: The only facility here for camping is a pit toilet. This is wilderness camping at its best. Reports of rattlesnakes suggest leaving your pooch at home.

EXPLORING CABIN CREEK: Cabin Creek should be high on the history buff's list. This is the site of **Catley's Retreat** in the Sheepeater War of 1879, and the steep ridge west of the airstrip is known as Vinegar Hill. One report claims that Catley's troops sought shelter in the caves on the hillside after the Indians set fire to the base of the hill. (See history, below).

As far as hiking goes, the more civilized, loop-trail day hikes are not found here, but there are several trails accessible from Cabin Creek. Trail busters had

one thing in mind...to get somewhere else. The incentive was either the gold rush du'jour or the shortest route to packing supplies. Consequently, we are treated to a different kind of adventure: the trail-less hike. It is a special treat to explore areas of trackless wilderness, a treasure worth preserving for future generations.

HISTORY: Lieutenant Catley and Vinegar Hill: Lieutenant Catley led 50 men from Camp Howard, at Grangeville, in the spring of 1879, into the Middle Fork country searching for the Sheepeater Indians. They proceeded through Florence, Burgdorf Hot Springs, Warren, Rains Ranch on the South Fork of the Salmon, and then into Chamberlain Basin. From Chamberlain, they proceeded southwards toward Big Creek.

The first cabin built on the Caswell Ranch was later used by Rex Lanham as a hunting lodge. Courtesy: Idaho County Free Press.

On the afternoon of July 28, 1879, one of the Catley's packers reported having seen two Indian horses and moccasin tracks about eight miles below their camp on Big Creek. Lieutenant Catley, who was busy fishing when the report came, is reported to have admonished the messenger for having caused him to lose two fish. Two hours later, Catley returned to camp and asked for details of the reported Indian sighting. After the story was retold, Catley responded "if I had more time I would have gone down that evening, but it was too late to start".

The following morning, July 29th, without placing advance guards in front or flankers on both sides of Big Creek, Catley and his men proceeded directly through the bottom of the narrow canyon where Indians had been only two hours previously. After about two miles, the Indians who were well hidden up the canyon walls, opened fire about 100 yards off on Catley's men below.

Catley immediately dismounted and hid behind a large tree. In his exuberance to seek shelter, Catley failed to give any orders to his men. Confusion arose, and the men eventually followed suit; dismounting and seeking shelter. Two soldiers were seriously wounded in the skirmish. Catley ordered a retreat and spent the night at the base of what later became known Vinegar Hill.

The following morning, the wounded men were put on litters and carried up a ridge on Vinegar Hill. Thinking, incorrectly, that this ridge would eventually lead to the route which he had followed into Big Creek, he observed Indians in fortified positions above him and below him. He ordered his command to unload all of their supplies and hold this position if the Indians attempted to approach.

The Indians, seeing this determination, set the base of the mountain on fire. The wind was high, and the terrible roaring of smoke and flame seemed to approach from every direction. In an attempt to save themselves from the impending conflagration, one of the men set a backfire . This effort, and the fact that the wind seemed to shift just as they were in greatest danger, alone saved the command. After being trapped on the hillside for 14 hours and exhausting their water supply, the troops drank from a keg of vinegar - thus the name Vinegar Hill.

During the night, the men moved back down from their precarious position on Vinegar Hill and ascended a parallel ridge to begin their retreat to Camp Howard. Within 30 hours they had reached Cold Meadows. From there they proceeded on to the Rains Ranch and Burgdorf.

When hearing of Catley's retreat, Colonel Wheaton, commander of the District of the Clearwater, dispatched Captain Forse, First Cavalry, with 25 men of his company to turn Catley back toward the South Fork.

By August 11, the retreating Lieutenant Catley met up with Colonel Bernard and his 60 men at confluence of Elk Creek and the South Fork of the Salmon. The following day Troop D 1st Cavalry joined forces with an additional 24 men. Bernard relieved Lieutenant Catley of his command and ordered him to stay with the pack train. The combined forces returned down Big Creek to the site of Catley's retreat and on to Soldiers Bar for another confrontation with the Indians.

One source said there may have been as few as 15 warriors surrounding Catley's troops. Catley was court-martialed in July, 1880, for his retreat and earlier conduct, but President Hayes later set aside the court martial verdict.

Early Homesteaders: The four **Caswell brothers** built a ranch on Cabin Creek in the 1890s. They raised sheep and hay, had an orchard and trapped, hunted and prospected. After striking gold on Thunder Mountain, they sold it.

The ranch changed hands several times and in 1925, **Merle Wallace**, a former Forest Service Ranger, bought the ranch and constructed the airstrip. He ran an outfitting business from the ranch which he called the Flying W.

In 1953, **Rex Lanham** bought part of the Cabin Creek Ranch for an outfitting headquarters. In 1956, Lanham drove a caterpillar bulldozer from Chamberlain to Cabin Creek to lengthen the landing strip. He built guest cabins,

The Caswell brothers, discoverers of Thunder Mountain gold, appear to be expecting company. Circa 1900. Courtesy: Idaho State Historical Society.

a dam, and a Pelton Wheel for electricity. Lanham did the flying for a National Geographic film, "Last of the Big Cats", filmed at Cabin Creek. In 1973. the Forest Service purchased the ranch for $1.6 million.

HUNTING & FISHING: I have had good reports of the trout fishing in Big Creek but have not yet been able to confirm them. I have also been cautioned to watch for rattlesnakes.

MAPS, LOCAL CONDITIONS, AND INFORMATION:

Payette Forest Air Officer, Box 1026, McCall, Idaho 83638 (208)634-8151.

CAVANAUGH BAY

HIGHLIGHT → *Airplane camping with hot showers on shore of beautiful Priest Lake. 20 pound lake trout are still common and catchable.*

- - - - -

AIRPORT DESCRIPTION: This beautiful grass airstrip has its approach directly over Priest Lake. Dense timber surrounds the lake. If Idaho has a rain forest, this is probably it. Slate gray clouds reflect their mood in the deep waters of lake. Early morning fog and low level strata add to the mysterious beauty of this Idaho gem.

TRANSPORTATION: A State courtesy car is available while the State employed caretaker is here - generally from the end of May to the middle of September. Call the Division of Aeronautics (208)334-8775 if necessary to confirm its availability.

SERVICES & LODGING:

Elkins on Priest Lake - HCO 1, Box 40, Nordman, ID, 83848, (208)443-2432. Two miles east of Nordman, halfway up the west side of Priest Lake. 28 cabins, $70-180, LH, R, P, CU, CC, AB.

Grandview Lodge & Resort - HCO 1, Box 48, Nordman, ID, 83848, (208)443-2433, 36 units, $69-145, LH, R, CU, TV, SP, CC, AB, MR(25).

Hill's Resort - HCR 5, Box 168A, (208)443-2551. On Luby Bay. 52 units, $80-225, P, TV, AB, R, CU, CC, MR(125), PH.

Kaniksu Resort - HCO 1, Box 152, Nordman, ID, (208)443-2609. On the west shore of Priest Lake. 77 camp sites, 14 units, $10.50 - 100, LH, R, P, CU, TV, CC, AB, L/R, L, HU, DS, SH, MM.

Outlet Bay Resort - HC 5, Box 138, Priest Lake, ID, 83586, (208)443-2444. 7 units, $45-150, LH, R, CU, CC, AB.

Showboat Lodge - Box 11, Coolin, ID, 83821 (208)443-2191. On southeast shore of Priest Lake at Coolin. 5 campsites, 9 units, $14-45, HA, R, P, CU, TV, CC, AB, MR, HU, DS.

CAMPING: Another Ritz Carlton campground. Ranking a Level 6 by the State Division of Aeronuautics, *****Cavanaugh Bay Airport** resembles Johnson Creek and Smiley Creek in creature comforts. There are three campsites with tables, stoves, toilets, and hot showers. Drinking water is available and you'll find lodging, boating and swimming nearby. The summer caretaker irrigates, keeps the campground clean and rents out the courtesy car.

Priest Lake RV Resort and Marina - HCR 5, Box 172, Priest Lake, ID, 83856, (208)443-2405. On the water, Kalispell Bay, Priest Lake. 16 camp sites. $6-10, HA, R, P, CC, AB, L, HU, DS, SH, LP.

EXPLORING CAVANAUGH BAY: Northern Idaho's Priest Lake is paradise. Seventy miles of shoreline is dressed in dense ferns, spruce, and hemlock. Rising 7,000 feet above the lake are peaks on the eastern shore reflecting their glacial spires on the glassy surface.

The lake plays host to several year-round resorts, serving fine cuisine, to the surprise of many guests. The **Roosevelt Grove of Ancient Cedars** holds court on the west side of Priest Lake, reaching 150 feet high with girths 12 feet wide. A walk through this virgin forest of shaggy giants makes dwarfs out of most of us.

A trail to **Granite Falls** will take you to a cool cascade of whitewater spraying over the moss-covered rocks, giving you your first clue as to why the "big tree country" is so lush. Heavy annual rain and snowfall, water the healthy growth of lichen and moss covering the huge western cedars, Douglas fir and spruce. This lichen provides the major source of food for the only band of mountain caribou existing in the United States. Only old-growth forest will do for this majestic animal's habitat. Another occasional visitor is the grizzly bear who wanders down from Canada in an attempt to re-establish itself in a former range.

HISTORY: Claude & Catherine Simpson describe the early settlement of Priest Lake in their book, *North of the Narrows* as follows:

"Jesuit missionaries called Kaniksus, the Indian word meaning priests in black robes, arrived in 1846. Father Peter Jean De Smet in 1846 was the first man of the order to arrive in the Priest Lake country. He was a gifted writer with a special interest in giving names to various landmarks.

He named Priest Lake, Lake Roothaan, for one of his teachers, Father J.P. Roothaan, of the Society of Jesus in Rome. Mt. Roothaan is one of the few names given to landmarks by Father De Smet that remains today.

Many of the names were too difficult for the Indians and the early pioneers to pronounce. Examples are: Riviere des Robes for Priest River; Hollandoise and Lyonnaise for Reeder and Granite Creeks; Triandoise for Kalispel Creek. As would be expected, the majority of the permanent identifying names in the Kaniksus are of Indian or pioneer origin. A few examples would include: Squawman, Tepee Creek, Kaniksu, Phoebe Tip, Eddy Peak, Goblin Knob, Trapper and Gold Creeks."

HUNTING & FISHING: Fish for trophy cutthroat and rainbow trout. Priest Lake is also famous for its big Mackinaw. In summer, fishing charters are available to help you land the big one, and you can also rent any craft that takes to the water, from sailboats to powerboats to wind surfers to jet skis.

MAPS, LOCAL CONDITIONS, AND INFORMATION: Visitor Information:

Priest Lake Chamber of Commerce, Steamboat Bay Road #121, Coolin, Idaho 83821 (208)443-3191.

Priest Lake, Idaho.
Courtesy: Idaho State Historical Society, Ross Hall Studio.

CAYUSE CREEK

HIGHLIGHT ✈ *Undeveloped airstrip with great potential for airplane camping. Set on a tributary of the Clearwater River in mountains and lots of trees. Excellent trout fishing.*

- - - - -

AIRPORT DESCRIPTION: Cayuse Creek is a U.S. Forest Service Guard Station on the Powell District of the Clearwater National Forest. East of the Bitterroot Mountains, separating Montana and Idaho, the area has roads but is extremely remote.

The airstrip is not currently maintained by the Forest Service and is therefore listed as an Emergency airfield. However, it holds great potential for development as a wilderness reliever strip. The Idaho Aviation Association is working with the Forest Service in an attempt to maintain this beautiful strip.

Apparently, 10 to 15 years ago, some teeth were broken on the mower used to mow the landing strip. Because it takes three hours to drive in and out of Cayuse, the Forest Service felt it was too costly to repair the mower and continue maintenance of the strip. Therefore, the classification of the airstrip is that of Emergency Only.

This is a sleeper of an airstrip. Follow the developments in reopening this strip as a recreational wilderness reliever and volunteer to support the maintenance of it if you can.

CAMPING: There are presently no camping facilities at the airstrip, but wilderness camping along the beautiful Cayuse Creek is hard to beat - not to mention the fishing.

HISTORY: Cayuse Creek flows northeast from the airstrip about five miles to its confluence with Kelly Creek. Kelly Creek then flows 15 miles westward to its confluence with the North Fork of the Clearwater River. This area is rich in history, much of it yet to be recorded and interpreted.

Archaeological diggings indicate that the area was widely used by **Aboriginals** as early as 6000 years ago. The camps were used in the summer and fall as hunting, fishing, and probably berry picking camps.

Ocean run salmon and steelhead were harvested from the crystal clear waters. Pit ovens, along the river banks, were then used to process the fish and possibly berries, using a technique similar to the Hawaiian Luau. Holes were dug and lined with burning coals. The coals were layered with wet leaves and fish. The pit was then covered with dirt and allowed to bake.

There is some evidence that the aboriginals "improved" the habitat in this already food-rich environment by setting fire to native stands of timber. Berry bushes and grasses replaced the burned timber. Not only did the aboriginals crave the sugar from the huckleberries, serviceberries and elderberries, so did bears and other wild game. Bighorn sheep and deer benefitted from the lush grasses. Even today, while flying over the area, it is common to see vast hillside areas covered with shrubs and grasses while similar hillsides remain heavily forested.

In more recent times, the Nez Perce, Flathead, and Salish Indians used the area for much the same purposes as their ancestors. A trade route across the Bitterroot Mountains made trade possible with the Plains Indians of Montana, Wyoming, Nebraska and the Dakotas. This was their closest access to anadromous fish. The Indians probably processed the salmon, game, and berries into pemmican, a jerky-like food rich in sugar and fat.

As late as the 1920s and 1930s, long after the camas and bison had disappeared from the Plains, bands of Plains Indians continued to travel across the Bitterroots into the Clearwater country to gather foods as they had done for centuries.

It is unknown if the trappers of Hudson Bay Company explored the area. It is also unlikely that Lewis and Clark strayed off their route to the Pacific into Cayuse Creek. The hardships caused by the Rocky Mountains were largely unexpected and they just weren't in the mood to take adventurous side trips.

In 1858, **Captain Elias Davidson Pierce** was lured from the gold fields of California to the North Fork of the Clearwater by a story told by an Indian - a story of seeing a great shining ball on a canyon wall as he lay in his camp and watched the moon come over the Bitterroots. However, the area described by the Indian was within an exclusive Nez Perce territory guaranteed in 1805 by a treaty with the U.S. Government.

Pierce befriended the Nez Perce chieftain Timothy and eventually Chief Timothy's daughter guided Pierce to the North Fork of the Clearwater River and the junction of Canal Gulch and Oro Fino Creek. There, in the fall of 1859, Pierce was the first white man to discover gold in what is today Idaho.

During 1861 and 1862 the town of Pierce boomed. Miners poured in from the played out gold fields of California. As the Confederacy implemented a compulsory draft for men to serve in the War Between the States, many dissenters sought their fortune in the gold fields of Idaho.

The overflow of Pierce miners quickly scattered throughout the region. It was during this period that mining came to Cayuse Creek. **Moose City**, about six miles north of Cayuse Creek, popped into existence to support the area miners. Today, little of Moose City is left but some piles of rubble and remnants of foundations.

The techniques of utilizing hydraulics in the placer mining operations was characteristic of those used in the California gold fields. Hard rock or lode mining soon followed.

While the hustle and bustle of the 1860s gold rush left Cayuse Creek, there are still active mining claims in the area. The miner's dream of striking it rich is still alive, and could very well still occur in Cayuse Creek.

Origin of Name - Cayuse Creek

When two miners, Crane and Altmiller, left the Blacklead country in the spring of 1887 to work their way to Pierce, they dropped down into what is now known as Cayuse Creek. There they found a pony or cayuse that had spent the winter there. They called the stream Cayuse.

Gravesite of Shoecraft and Gorman

In 1907, George Gorman and Clayton Shoecraft, were accused of killing a man in Deerlodge, Montana. They were acquitted of the charge, but public opinion was so strong against them they thought it would be better to seek refuge in the Idaho Wilderness.

In Lolo Hot Springs, they found a packer who agreed to pack them into the Cayuse Creek country. They had little money left to purchase supplies and decided they would subsist from the land.

Arriving in Cayuse Creek in the fall of 1907, they either built a cabin or moved into one already existing. According to their diary, they killed two elk and salted them down. They ran a trap line up Cayuse Creek.

In mid-winter they began to suffer with an ailment they believed to be rheumatism. Their joints swelled, they had pains in their limbs and their teeth loosened; almost sure signs of scurvy. In their last diary entry, one man reported that his partner was dead and that he was no longer able to get out of bed.

When their bodies were found, they were buried with a cedar slab marking their grave. In 1922, the Forest Service remarked the grave with a permanent marker near the airstrip.

Their misfortune left the following geographical names: Scurvy Mountain, Scurvy Creek, Scurvy Lake, Never Creek, Never Again Ridge, Never Again Flats, Shoecraft Creek, Gorman Creek, Clayton Creek, and Gorman Mountain.

The author recommends taking a lime along as garnish for your gin and tonics purely as a medicinal precautionary measure.

The Cayuse Airstrip was used by Johnson Flying Service, out of Missoula, Montana, as early as 1932. Harvey Grasser, Orofino, recalls helping with a lot of the improvements to the airstrip in 1936.

The area was used for sheep and cattle grazing during the 1950s and 1960s with a sheep drive trail leading through Cayuse into Montana.

HUNTING & FISHING: The Cayuse Outfitters are licensed outfitters in this area and set up a base camp near the Cayuse Airstrip. They offer guided trailrides/ fishing trips and guided hunting trips for bear and cougar, with good success. For more information contact: Rich & Patti Armiger, HCR 11, Box 74, Kamiah, Idaho 83536. (208)935-0859.

MAPS, LOCAL CONDITIONS, AND INFORMATION:

Local conditions and airport information: Powell Ranger District, Lolo, Montana 59847 (208)942-3113.

Maps: Clearwater National Forest, 12730 Highway 12, Orofino, Idaho 83544 (208)476-4541.

HIGHLIGHT ➔ *The second longest wilderness airstrip. Every fall, Chamberlain Basin fills with elk hunters while moose graze on the runway.*

- - - - -

AIRPORT DESCRIPTION: Chamberlain Basin Country is big country...about 600 square miles of rolling forest in the Frank Church River of No Return Wilderness. The airstrip is 4100' long and 200' wide, but don't let that lull you into complacency as the airstrip is surrounded by deceptively rising terrain. RWY 25 is generally favored for landing and RWY 07 favored for departure.

The surface is dirt/thin turf and rough. Use of a soft field landing technique will prolong the life of your undercarriage, not to mention your airplane's. Ground squirrels, gophers, deer, elk, and moose have done a good job of making the surface rough. RWY 15/33 is not in good condition and has nose wheel size badger holes.

Chamberlain is used as a transfer camp for packing hunters and fishermen further into the wilderness. Packstrings of horses and mules are loaded at both ends of RWY 07/25. Take a good look for critters on the runway before landing.

CAMPING: *Chamberlain Campsites are located on the south side of RWY 07/25 and next to the trees east of RWY 15/33. Drinking water is available at the Guard Station. Picnic tables have existed, but the Forest Service, in a very controversial move, has burned them. The fire pits are in need of repair. Pack out your own garbage.

EXPLORING CHAMBERLAIN: After a recent landing at Chamberlain, I had just finished tying down my airplane when a bull moose casually strolled down the runway, crossed over and ambled by my airplane, then through our camp.

Oblivious to landing traffic, and big enough not to care, this moose has earned a reputation for being a little sweet on airplanes. Actually, I can relate. I think airplanes are better looking than cow moose too.

Nevertheless, he can cause damage to your one and only. Shouting, arm

W.A. (Al) Stonebraker was one of the first settlers in Chamberlain Basin. Courtesy: Idaho County Free Press.

waving, and swearing may divert his attentions away from your airplane....to you. Moose don't climb trees, but they can sure shake them!

If Chamberlain rumors are to be believed, this particular moose prefers taildraggers. Be forewarned. Those not intimidated by the moose may want to take advantage of the wonderful hiking opportunities. My favorite is No Name Creek.

HIKES: No Name Creek - General description: There are several well documented hikes leading from Chamberlain but this hike is my favorite. It is an easy hike following the beautiful No Name Creek as it runs up against vertical sheer rock and forms crystal clear wading pools warmed by the sun peeking through the towering firs. There is no trail, so those of you who enjoy the security of a nose and tail hike would be better off trying the **Flossie Lake Trail** hike.

Finding the trailhead: From the southwest corner of the airstrip, pick up the trail (003) leading to Red Top Meadows. Follow the trail westward for about a mile and look to the south for the secluded No Name Creek drainage. (There are no signs or trail.) Walk across two meadows until you find the confluence of No Name Creek and Chamberlain Creek.

The hike: Follow No Name Creek upstream. There are numerous game trails. If you are quiet, you can almost bet on seeing elk and moose grazing in the meadows. Drink in a quiet and serene moment while in this truly idyllic setting. It is why we're here isn't it?

Either return the way you came or climb up the ridge to the east of the stream and intercept the Chamberlain Trail (001) and follow it north back to the airstrip.

HISTORY: Hudson Bay Company trappers trapped beaver on Chamberlain Creek during the winter of 1821-1822. Placer deposits of gold on Chamberlain Creek were worked during the gold rushes of the 1850s and 1870s. But the first full time settler was John Chamberlain, a mule packer who settled here in 1895.

In 1900, the historic **Three Blaze Trail**, was built to provide a northern route for eager miners headed to Thunder Mountain. The trail lead from Dixie, across the Salmon River at Campbell's Ferry, through Chamberlain Basin, and on to Thunder Mountain. To mark the trail, trees were blazed with three squares in a column. A winter shelter cabin called the Smokehouse, was built at the junction of Three Blaze Trail and the Chamberlain. The remains of this cabin are about 2.5 miles west of the airstrip on the **Red Top Meadows Trail**.

In preparation for the great Thunder Mountain rush, the cities of Weiser, Emmett, Grangeville, Dixie, Salmon, Mackay, and Ketchum began to advertise their routes to Thunder Mountain. But the 28,000 hopeful miners were stopped in their tracks by deep snow. They piled up in surrounding towns, ready to seek their fortune as soon as an opportunity should offer.

The Old Smoke House (named because the fireplace smoked so badly) was a prominent landmark on the Three Blaze Trail. Courtesy: Idaho County Free Press.

Stage lines from Union Pacific Railroad Stations in Ketchum, Mackay, and Red Rock, Montana, prepared to offer service over nonexistent roads through country where roads still don't exist 90 years later.

Ultimately, impatient men were killed in avalanches trying to get to Thunder Mountain before conditions permitted. For those men who had spent the winter at Roosevelt, food was extremely scarce. Dog sleds, with up to a ton of supplies, were brought in from Boise, Grangeville, and Bear Valley (see Bruce Meadows).

Homesteaders in the Chamberlain Basin raised cattle to supply the Thunder Mountain miners. But when the miners left, so did the cattle business.

The first log cabin for the ranger station was built in 1907. The airstrip was constructed in 1928, and was first used by firefighting crews in 1931. The modern log buildings were constructed at the Chamberlain Ranger Station in 1937 and the present landing field in 1940.

HUNTING & FISHING: Mackay Bar Outfitters provide guided hunting and fishing trips out of Chamberlain. They can be contacted at (800)854-9904, Box 7968, Boise, Idaho 83707.

Trout fishing in Chamberlain Creek behind the airstrip can be very rewarding. Salmon can occasionally be seen in the stream, but don't molest them. They are struggling for a comeback. Besides, the season is closed.

MAPS, LOCAL CONDITIONS, AND INFORMATION:

Krassel Ranger District, Payette National Forest, Lake Street, P.O. Box 1026 McCall, Idaho 83638 (208)634-0700.

Chamberlain Guard Station, 1993.

COLD MEADOWS

HIGHLIGHT ✈ *Wilderness airstrip popular with elk hunters. Used little during summer months.*

. . . . .

AIRPORT DESCRIPTION: The terrain surrounding Cold Meadows shares physical similarities with the nearby Root Ranch and Chamberlain Basin. The elevation is high, 6000', but the terrain is not as rugged as that of the Middle Fork country or Sawtooth or Bitterroot Mountains.

The mountains are gentle rolling giants covered with coniferous trees. Rock outcroppings and jutting rocks, so typical of much of the Idaho back country, are scarce here. Large open basins and meadows covered with grasses and willows make this the ideal habitat for elk and moose.

A fire burned much of the timber surrounding Cold Meadows. The wildlife, however, seems to have fared well, as beautiful green grasses flourish under the standing dead trees.

CAMPING: Wilderness camping is the modus operandi at Cold Meadows as there are no formal camping amenities here, toilets, picnic tables, fire rings, etc. Plan on bringing in your own water or water filter system. I haven't checked for availability of water at the Forest Service Guard Station here, but suspect they have spring water that could be used to fill your canteens in an emergency.

On a visit in 1991, the Forest Service employees were at the airstrip picking up their supplies from a charter plane. They used a large cart type wheel barrow to transfer their supplies from the plane to the Guard Station, while a couple of llamas were grazing in the pasture. When asked why they didn't use the llamas to pack the supplies, the Forest Service employees let it be known in no uncertain terms, the questionable value of these llamas as pack animals, accompanied by comments as to the llamas' ancestry.

As I understand the wilderness rules, all wheeled conveyances are illegal to use in the wilderness. I can only assume these same rules apply to the Forest Service. In which case, I hope the fences between the Forest Service and its llamas have been mended, or at least a pack mule has been brought in.

EXPLORING COLD MEADOWS: Margaret Fuller has described a strenuous 21.4 mile round trip hike from Cold Meadows to Black Lake, in her excellent book, *Trails of the Frank Church-River of No Return Wilderness*. This author has not taken this hike and can only defer to Margaret's description. This hike is on the author's list of Things To Do - Soon.

HISTORY: After Lieutenant Calley's brush with the Sheepeater Indians at Vinegar Hill in 1879, Calley led his men in a prompt retreat through Cold Meadows on the way to the South Fork of the Salmon.

The origin of the geographical names in the Cold Meadows area can not directly be tied to the soldiers retreat, but someone, at some time must not have had too great of a time here with names like: Disappointment Creek, Hungry Creek, Starvation Creek, Dismal Creek, Cold Mountain, and Cold Meadows.

Oh well, what's in a name anyway? For a real getaway, Cold Meadows has a lot of appeal to perverted isolationists.

HUNTING & FISHING: Several outfitters provide guided hunting trips for whitetail and mule deer, elk, goat, sheep, moose, bear, cougar, and predators in this area. Three outfitters picked at random are:

Chamberlain Basin Outfitters, Inc., Route 1, Box 240 AD, Salmon, Idaho 83467 (208)756-3715.

Mackay Bar Corp., Box 7968, Boise, Idaho 83707 (208)344-1881.

Stanley Potts, HC 64, Box 61, Shoup, Idaho 83469 (208)394-2135.

For a complete listing of outfitters request a free directory from:

Idaho Outfitters and Guides Assoc., Box 95, Boise, ID 83701 (208)342-1919.

MAPS, LOCAL CONDITIONS, AND INFORMATION:

Payette Forest Air Officer, 106 W. Park Street, McCall, ID 83638 (208)634-0746.

COPPER BASIN

HIGHLIGHT ✈ *High elevation airstrip in large basin with many small lakes in the surrounding mountains. Antelope outnumber people 10 to 1.*

▪ ▪ ▪ ▪ ▪

AIRPORT DESCRIPTION: Copper Basin sits in the southern part of the Challis National Forest. It is a remote, yet beautiful sage-covered valley with the Pioneer Mountains skirting the western edge of the basin and the White Knob Mountains to the east. The headwaters of the East Fork of the Big Lost River originate in the area referred to as "The Swamps" just one mile southeast of the airstrip. Directly east of the airstrip sits the Copper Basin Mine.

CAMPING: The airstrip currently (1993) is up for adoption by the Division of Aeronautics. No camping facilities exist but this shouldn't prevent visitors from camping here to fish or to hunt for sage hens. Five miles away, southwest of the airstrip on the Copper Basin Loop Road, you will locate the Lake Creek Trailhead, a good airplane/mountain bike/camping destination. From the airstrip, follow the road northwest toward the Copper Basin Guard Station. The road intersects with Forest Route 138. Take 138 to the southwest about four miles to the Lake Creek Trailhead. The elevation is 8,100 feet, a 200 ft. climb from the airstrip. No amenities whatsoever, but you will find shade trees, a rare and welcome site for much of the stark yet unforgettable basin.

EXPLORING COPPER BASIN: While most tourists visiting the world famous Ketchum/Sun Valley area will drive due north toward the Sawtooth National Recreation Area, locals and those in the know like to hop over Trail Creek Summit, east of the resort, into Copper Basin. Admittedly, a hairy dirt road must be navigated; the reward however, a day in Copper Basin, is well worth the nail biting. This guide could not possibly list all the hiking and exploring opportunities, but here is a suggestion.

View of the Copper Basin mine sites from the airstrip.

HIKES:
Round, Long, Rough, Big and Golden Lake hike or mountain bike ride:

General Description: This is a 12.7 mile round trip hike or bike ride from the Lake Creek Trail Head. Add an additional 2.2 mile loop hike to visit all five lakes. This is a strenuous hike, so count on an overnight trip. The trail is also open to motorcycles, all-terrain vehicles, and mountain bikes.

Finding the Trailhead: See Lake Creek Trailhead under "Camping" above.

The Hike: From the **Lake Creek Trailhead**, an old jeep road leads through a gate. The trail leaves the old road occasionally as it proceeds up the valley. At 3 miles are the ruins of an old log cabin. At 3.5 miles the Big Lake Trail and the Round Lake trails meet to form a loop.

The trail to **Round Lake** first is an easier climb - 640 ft. in 2 miles as opposed to 960 ft. in 1.2 miles to Big Lake. The route to Round Lake crosses a boulder field and two streams at 5 miles, and climbs a wooded ridge to the Round Lake turnoff at 5.5 miles.

Camping at Round Lake one evening, we were treated to nature's light show as huge black clouds came roaring over the nearby mountain peaks. Deafening cracks of thunder reverberated in the surrounding confines and blinding flashes of lightning illuminated the ceiling of our tent. In a short time, it was over as quickly as it had started. Nature has a way of humbling one's perspectives.

To continue on to **Long Lake**, follow the main trail .2 mile and take the left branch of the trail at an unsigned junction. Follow this trail .3 mile to the lake.

From Long Lake, the main trail crosses the outlet and then climbs to the west over the ridge to a junction at 6.5 miles. Take the left trail and climb 200 yards to **Rough Lake**.

To reach **Big Lake** from the Rough Lake junction, follow the trail signed **Golden Lake**. The trail crosses the outlet of Rough Lake and climbs to Big Lake at 8 miles.

For a side trip to Golden Lake, follow the path around the upper end of Big Lake and climb .5 miles to the lake.

To continue the loop to its origin, return to Big Lake and proceed north at the junction where the Rough Lake trail reaches Big Lake. Follow the trail on the ridge not along the shore line and cross the outlet of Big Lake. The loop junction is at 9.2 miles and the trailhead continues down Lake Creek another 3.5 miles.

HISTORY: Not surprisingly, it was copper ore discovered in 1888 that put Copper Basin on the map. Assays of 35 to 55 per cent were found and silver values raised the ores to $145 a ton in a 35 foot vein. After several years, preparations were made to haul the ore down the steep Trail Creek Summit to Ketchum for shipment to a Salt Lake City smelter.

Horace Lewis, of Ketchum, had 25 freight wagons constructed to haul ore from the surrounding mining camps to the Philadelphia Smelter in Ketchum, carrying freight on the return trip. The Lewis Lead was the largest freight wagon in the world. Built entirely in Ketchum, the wagon box was 16 feet long, 6 1/2 feet high and weighed 4900 pounds empty. It had a carrying capacity of 18,000 pounds, with the wheels on the wagon standing over 7 feet high.

Several wagons were hooked in tandem and pulled over the treacherous Trail Creek Road by 10 pairs of mules. Each animal was trained individually to stop, start, steer and pull, but their actions were highly synchronized. The teams worked by voice command and jerk line. The driver did not sit on the lead wagon but rather on the "wheel mule", and gave voice commands along with tugs on the jerk line. A chain running between the mules had to be stepped over to turn the wagons. Mules were trained to cross the haul chain on command. They always took the same place in the lineup. A mule trained to the left side, for instance, was never moved to the right.

The ore wagons were the mode of transportation which made and maintained Ketchum as a commercial mining center for the 30 years between 1890 and 1910. When the jerkline operator wasn't bringing ore downhill from the mountains, he was driving mules back up the steep passes with supplies for the miners.

HUNTING & FISHING: The wide open high arid desert covered with sagebrush and cheat grass with willows in the creek bottoms present excellent habitat for sage hens and antelope. Higher in the surrounding mountains live elk, deer, bear, and cougar.

Fishing in the small streams was sensational during the early 1960s. But fishing has continued to decline. The guides and outfitters place the blame on "flatland meat fishermen" accused of spending the summer filling their freezers; the locals blame the guides for making a profit while selling out the "secret" of Copper Basin fishing.

The Fish and Game Department attributes the decline to low waters caused by seven years of drought. The unusually low water levels resulted in a high mortality rate during the winter months as ice forms from the bottom up covering the stream bottoms and source of food.

While all or none of the reasons may be valid, it's a sad fact that the quality fishing we once experienced in this area is gone. It is still legal to keep fish caught here but please release them until this fishery is back on track and we will all benefit.

MAPS, LOCAL CONDITIONS, AND INFORMATION:

Maps and Forest Information: Lost River Ranger District, Highway 93 North, Box 507, Mackay, ID 83251 (208)588-2224.

Airport Conditions: Division of Aeronautics, 3483 Rickenbacker, Boise, Idaho 83705 (208)334-8775.

COX'S WELL

HIGHLIGHT ✈ *Desert airstrip with good turf. Good place to practice your short/soft field techniques. Occasional coyote, jackrabbit, and rattlesnake but no people in 50 miles any direction.*

- - - - -

AIRPORT DESCRIPTION: Cox's Well is probably in as good of a condition as any in the Arco Desert. It doesn't seem to have the damage caused by livestock that the other strips have. The grass is in good condition, especially considering that there is no irrigation water for it. The runway shows signs of being mowed and generally well taken care of. The tiedowns are visible and in good repair.

For a flying club looking for an offbeat place to have a fly-in barbeque, this may be exactly what they are looking for. There certainly wouldn't be any noise complaints or party crashers and it is a forgiving place to practice your soft/short field techniques.

MAPS, LOCAL CONDITIONS, AND INFORMATION:

Maps and area recreational information:
Bureau of Land Management
U.S. Department of the Interior
Shoshone District Office
400 West F Street
Shoshone, Idaho 83352
(208)886-2206

Airport information:
Division of Aeronautics
3483 Rickenbacker St.
Boise, Idaho 83705
(208)334-8775

For more information, refer to Arco-Kimama overview on page I-1.

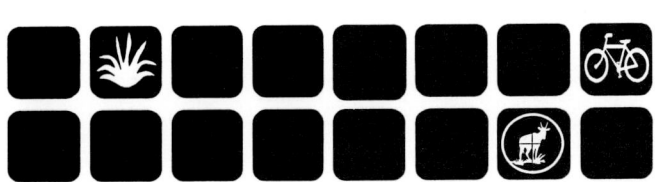

DEADWOOD

HIGHLIGHT ✈ *Spectacular lake setting surrounded by timber covered mountains. Plan your visit for other than a holiday and enjoy the utmost in privacy and fishing.*

- - - - -

AIRPORT DESCRIPTION: Deadwood Reservoir is located 23 nm southeast of Cascade. The dam creates a picturesque clear mountain lake in a setting of lodgepole and ponderosa pine. It is in the Lowman Ranger District of the Boise National Forest. The runway itself is at the southeast end of the reservoir near the dam. Several Forest Service and Bureau of Reclamation buildings sit at the approach end of the runway. The approach is over the lake and the runway makes a remarkably steep climb up the hill. At the top of the hill (i.e. runway), a road intersects. Use caution while crossing the road and park in the flat area atop the hill.

There are no tie downs or runway markings visible, however there is a windsock at the upper end. Ruts run along both sides of the runway with some signs of erosion going right down the middle. Tall trees surround the runway and a few three footers are growing on the low end. The runway surface is decomposed granite mixed with a few grasses and wildflowers.

The landing roll is significantly reduced due to the uphill climb. In fact, power is required to get to the end of the strip. Conversely, the downhill roll on takeoff is a big help.

CAMPING: There are four campgrounds to choose from, and one Forest Service "Vacation Cabin".

**Cozy Cove Campground - From the upper end of the runway, follow the road to the south. The road quickly descends the hill and switchbacks below the dam. A bridge crosses the Deadwood River and the road climbs back up to the level of the lake. The road follows the shore line. At 2.1 miles from the airstrip, a Forest Service Sign designates the Cozy Cove Campground. It has nine campsites with picnic tables, fire pits, and pit toilets set in the shady lodgepole pines along the shore line.

Both airplane and passengers require skis for this 1931 winter landing on Deadwood Reservoir. Courtesy: Idaho Historical Society.

Three more campgrounds are on the east shore line, listed in sequence: ****Howers Campground** about 4 miles north of the airstrip - five campsites with picnic tables, fire rings, and pit toilets. ****Barneys Campground** is located just past Howers - six campsites with picnic tables, fire rings, and pit toilets. ****Riverside Campground** is about 7 miles north of the airstrip on the inlet to the lake. It has nine campsites with picnic tables, fire rings, and pit toilets.

A Forest Service **Vacation Cabin** is located at the approach end of the Deadwood airstrip. It requires advance reservations. Accommodations are described as "basic". Summer rates are $30 per night (unlimited occupants) and winter rates are $20 per night (access by snow machine in winter). Contact the Lowman Ranger District (208)259-3361.

EXPLORING DEADWOOD RESERVOIR: Fishing and whitewater kayaking take the lead here in the recreation department. The reservoir provides excellent fishing while the Deadwood River Canyon rates as a Class IV river. The upper run is 14 miles with a 60 fpm gradient. Considered a "secluded wilderness run," it takes about three hours in a kayak. Rumors of a box canyon and some unrunnable falls kept people out of the river until 1976 when Tulio Celano and Roger Hazelwood made the first descent. The rumors were squelched when all they found was a beautiful wilderness river close to Boise with a number of dangerous log jams. For details refer to *Idaho - The Whitewater State: a guidebook.*

HISTORY: Construction on the Deadwood Dam was begun in 1929 and completed in 1931. It was designed to provide water storage for irrigation and flood control.

When full, it contains 191,600 acre-feet of water. The surface of the reservoir is 3000 acres with wooded shoreline surrounding it. The dam is built from concrete and is 165 feet high, 9 feet wide at the top, and 749 feet long. It contains 55,463 cubic yards of concrete.

The Bureau of Reclamation keeps a caretaker at the facility during the summer months. A small hydroelectric generator provides electricity for the Bureau's local use. A radio/telephone at the facility can be used in the event of an emergency but is not available for general public use.

HUNTING & FISHING: The reservoir provides fishing for rainbows, cutthroats, hybrid rainbow/cutthroats, kokanee, Atlantic salmon, and whitefish. During the spring, try fishing the inlet to the reservoir as the fish tend to migrate upstream out of the reservoir.

The fishing in the river below the dam is also good. Use caution due to fluctuating water levels. The Bureau of Reclamation schedules water releases from the dam at nighttime but be alert for unscheduled releases.

Harry Nock's 12 dog team on the way to Deadwood Dam.
Courtesy: Idaho Historical Society.

MAPS, LOCAL CONDITIONS, AND INFORMATION:

Information on Camping/Vacation Cabins and Forest Maps, Lowman Ranger District, Highway 21, HC-77, Box 3020, Lowman, Idaho 83627 (208)259-3361.

Supervisor, Boise Natl. Forest, 1750 Front St., Boise, ID 83702 (208)364-4100.

Airport conditions: U.S. Bur. of Rec., Box 9, Cascade, ID 83611 (208)382-4258.

HIGHLIGHT ✈ *Extremely difficult wilderness airstrip on Big Creek. If you must go, have a local pro go with you. Blue ribbon fishing for native trout.*

- - - - -

AIRPORT DESCRIPTION: Dewey Moore is located at the confluence of Big Creek and Acorn Creek, about 5 miles upstream from Vines. This is a particularly difficult strip as the approach is blind and the runway is short (700 ft.). On takeoff, a hard left and then right (low and slow) turn downstream is necessary to avoid terrain. If the departure stall/spin doesn't ruin your day, the terrain probably will. Do not attempt this without first being checked out by one of the local charter pilots familiar with the strip.

HISTORY: Shorty Yardley started ranching here around 1900. He sold the ranch to John Routson who supported his wife and six children by raising cattle, packing, and working for the mines. The children made most of their own toys but didn't have much time for play as their lives were kept busy gardening, chopping wood, cutting hay, doing laundry, and running a trapline.

Routson sold the ranch to Phil Beal in the late 1930s. Beal referred to the ranch as the "Rhubarb Ranch" because of the rhubarb he grew. Fruit was a real scarcity in Big Creek and neighbors would come from miles around to gather a little rhubarb for pies and jam.

Laurence Johnson displays a salmon he caught at Dewey Moore. Circa 1950. Courtesy: Pete Johnson.

Laurence Johnson, center, with his Beech Staggerwing and a couple fishing partners at Dewey Moore. Circa 1950. Courtesy: Pete Johnson.

In 1945, Beal sold the ranch to Dewey Moore. Moore, an apparent visionary, once elucidated the 1920 Christmas celebration in Yellow Pine (see Johnson Creek) as the "wildest gathering of drunken prospectors and dogfights a man ever saw." His insight is still accurate 75 years later.

Moore developed a spring, and built a log cabin, barn, and landing strip on the ranch. Dewey had an aversion to shoes and usually went barefoot. One winter while shoeing horses, barefoot in the snow, he stepped on a piece of red hot metal he had cut off a horseshoe. It wasn't until he smelled burning meat that he realized his foot was on fire...tough country - tough men (tough feet anyway).

MAPS, LOCAL CONDITIONS, AND INFORMATION:

Payette Forest
Air Officer
Box 1026
McCall, Idaho 83638
(208)634-0746

Laurence Johnson, center, demonstrating his fishing techniques. Circa 1950. Courtesy: Pete Johnson.

DIXIE TOWN

HIGHLIGHT ✈ *Land one block from main street and have breakfast in an historic mining community that refuses to die.*

- - - - -

AIRPORT DESCRIPTION: This is a private strip where the owner allows landing at your own risk. Contact John Wenzel (208)842-2467 for current runway conditions. It is located three miles northeast of USFS Dixie airstrip. There is a downhill slope to the approach end of the runway with erosion cutting across it. The spring visitors will find themselves tying their plane down in a field of wild strawberries.

TRANSPORTATION: Transportation isn't really necessary since the airstrip immediately parallels main street. A mountain bike would be ideal; lacking a bike, you might make an offer on a local horse.

SERVICES & LODGING: Everything you need can be found in the heart of Dixie. The **Dixie Store** provides basics including supplies, post office, gas, and seven motel units ranging from $35 to $45 per night. The store is owned by a friendly couple, LaVern and Lee Miller, who are more than happy to share good information about the area. If you are lucky enough to meet Lee, you will become mesmerized with his historical knowledge of the region.

Directly across the street is the **Lodgepole Pine Inn**, a combination restaurant and good sized bar.

The **Dixie Lodge** is a hunting lodge that seasonally offers beds to its guests.

CAMPING: Limited camping is allowed in the trees adjacent to the runway across from the homes. No facilities are provided.

EXPLORING DIXIE TOWN: And a sweetheart of a town it is. It wasn't until 1980 that electricity found its way to Dixie Town, to give you an idea of how far away you have come from civilization. After you've seen the Dixie Store, the Lodgepole Pine Inn, and the impressive log cabin owned by the Dixie Outfitters, you've just about seen Dixie Town, and you are ready to begin exploring. But before you go,

make note of several historical buildings...the tiny log school house, the stage barn, and the Rory Burk cabin (rumored to have housed two women of ill repute).

Far away from any other town or permanent habitation, there are 15 miles of wilderness road which separates Dixie from the Red River Ranger Station to the north. To the south, Dixie Town is still considered the "jumping off place" to the Salmon River (literally - it's 3000 ft. down!). Roads are primitive and impassable in winter.

To the south, over 100 miles of mountain wilderness separate you from a major highway and nearly 80 miles of the rugged Bitterroot Mountains lie between Dixie and Gibbonsville. The historic mining towns of Lucile and Slate Creek are 40 miles West.

(Above) The Dixie Outfitter's log barn at the end of Main Street, Dixie. (Below) Local sentiment runs strongly against radical environmentalists infiltrating the area.

The fun here is found on foot. Old mines surrounding the town become the destination for fascinating day hikes, and the charming pioneer cemetery, a short walk from town, is not to be missed.

THIS PUBLIC TELEPHONE IS ON **PRIVATE** PROPERTY. EARTH FIRST!ERS USING THE TELEPHONE WILL BE LIMITED TO **ONLY ONE** PERSON ON THIS PORCH AT ANY ONE TIME!

HISTORY: In August of 1862, two prospectors who also happened to be Confederate sympathizers, discovered ore in a gulch 26 miles due south of Elk City. They named the place Dixie Gulch.

In search of supplies, one of the men set off for Elk City, and unfortunately failed to return. His partner formed a search party in Elk City and discovered his partner had been killed by Indians. Through the ordeal, word got out about the gold in Dixie Gulch and the rush was on.

The Dixie mines suggest that all the mining methods of the day were used: panning, sluicing, rocking, hydraulic-ing, dredging, pick and shovel, steel and single jack. There were both placer and quartz operations.

Booms and busts were repeated through the years, as innovative mining methods, more sophisticated recovery procedures, improved transportation, wars, and the price of gold fluctuated.

ANNUAL EVENTS AND ACTIVITIES: As in many of Idaho's towns of all sizes, Dixie Town celebrates the Fourth of July.

HUNTING & FISHING: Dixie Outfitters, Inc., Box 33-0, Dixie, Idaho 83525, (208)842-2417, offers guided hunting trips in Units 19 and 20 for deer, elk, moose, goat, sheep, bear, and cougar. Also available are fishing pack trips and trail rides.

MAPS, LOCAL CONDITIONS, AND INFORMATION:

For local information, supplies, and lodging, contact Lee Graves at the Dixie Store. For airstrip conditions, contact John Wenzel (208)842-2467. Remember, however, that Mr. Wenzel is not a paid airport employee. He owns this strip and allows visitors to land at their own risk. Do not make a nuisance of yourself. He doesn't have to permit anyone to land.

Downtown Dixie. Five hundred pounds of freight could be pulled by wrapping it in rawhide and dragging it behind a horse. Courtesy: Idaho State Historical Society.

DIXIE USFS

HIGHLIGHT ✈ *On the outskirts of the wilderness, this is a beautiful turf strip with a challenging approach and an historic mining district with much to explore.*

AIRPORT DESCRIPTION This airstrip lies three miles southwest of town and serves the Forest Service station located adjacent to the field. The strip is good sized for the Idaho Backcountry, being 4500 feet long and 100 feet wide, and covered with grass. Do not confuse this with the Dixie Town airstrip located adjacent to town. It lies in a wooded valley above the Salmon River Canyon. The approaches can be blind, so be sure and stay on the radio, announcing your position and intentions. During the fire season, summer and fall, the strip can get heavy use from Forest Service fire fighters.

CAMPING Pit toilets are available at the Dixie USFS airstrip but no camping facilities are available on the strip.

The ****Halfway House Campground** is one half mile down Crooked Creek. From the south end of the airstrip follow the road to the campground. It features designated campsites and pit toilets.

HUNTING/FISHING Excellent trout fishing can be found in the tumbling Crooked Creek. Steelhead and trout fishing can also be found in the Salmon River, 20 some miles down Crooked Creek.

MAPS, LOCAL CONDITIONS, AND INFORMATION
Nezperce National Forest
Red River Ranger District
Elk City, Idaho 83525
(208)842-2255

Dixie pioneer cemetery.

DUG BAR

HIGHLIGHT ✈ *Hells Canyon airstrip along the Snake River. Land in a field and fish for 12 foot sturgeon, smallmouth bass, trout, and steelhead.*

- - - - -

AIRPORT DESCRIPTION: Use extreme caution for the power transmission lines crossing the canyon three miles downstream from Dug Bar (three miles upstream from Salmon Bar). The top wires are marked with orange balls but many less visible lines lie below these. These insidious lines cross the canyon mid-level and have been the nemesis of more than one pilot. Scud running below the canyon rim is asking for trouble.

The airstrip is located on the Oregon side of the river and is really more of a field than an airstrip, lacking a windsock, runway markings, tiedowns, tire tracks, or any indications of where the runway actually is. The runway markings on the color aerial shots have been added to help in identification but do not exist in real life. This is the longest strip in the bottom of the canyon and would be an excellent one for future development.

CAMPING: There is an administrative building at the site with water and toilets. There are no formal camp sites, but it is possible that future development may

Chief Joseph's home, Nespelem, Washington, 1902.
Courtesy: Idaho State Historical Society.

result in primitive camp sites with potable water. An NRA map indicates toilets and camp sites 1/4 upstream from the airstrip at the mouth of Robinson Gulch. This camping area is unconfirmed but worth future investigation.

On his historic flight for freedom, Chief Joseph led his band of Nez Perce across the Snake River at Dug Bar.

HISTORY: In the spring of 1877, **General Howard** and Indian Agent Montieth, gave **Chief Joseph** and his Wallowa Band of Nez Perce Indians 30 days to gather their herds of cattle and horses along with their personal belongings and relocate to the Lapwai Indian Reservation. The General also made it clear that any abandoned livestock would become property of the white settlers.

Chief Joseph felt it was better to lead the Indians to freedom in Canada than to suffer confinement on a reservation run by religious zealots. His flight led to the swollen flood waters of the Snake River near this location.

The Indians had no boats, but wrapped their belongings in the watertight hides of the teepees and pulled them across the river with ropes, while women and children hung on tightly in the raging flood waters. Incredibly, there was no loss of life. However, there were heavy losses of livestock as these animals were unable to swim the river.

Renegade whites quickly gathered up the straggling livestock which became the foundation stock of some of the local ranchers.

The following year, 1878, saw the first white settler in the area, **Thomas Douglas.** He built a cabin here and left his name on Dug Bar, Dug Creek, and Dug Basin. A map maker with a perverted sense of humor lists Dug Creek, Doug Creek, and Dog Creek all within the immediate vicinity of Dug Bar.

By 1887, the ownership of the ranch changed to George Craig. After Craig relocated his cattle to winter range, a band of outlaws moved into Craig's abandoned cabin. It is believed that these outlaws were involved in the nearby

Chinese Massacre of 1887. The outlaws had a well organized horse thief ring going on by transporting stolen horses back and forth across the Oregon-Idaho border.

MAPS, LOCAL CONDITIONS, AND INFORMATION:

Hells Canyon National Recreation Area
Clarkston, Washington
(509)758-0616

Fishing licenses and information:
Oregon Fish and Wildlife
2501 SW 1st.
Box 59
Portland, OR 97207
(503)229-5403

For more information, refer to the Hells Canyon overview on page I-3.

A view of the incredibly rugged Hells Canyon.
Courtesy: Idaho State Historical Society.

ELK CITY

HIGHLIGHT ✈ *This is your chance to land on a semi-circular runway and visit a small mountain community that offers some of the best elk hunting in Idaho.*

· · · · ·

AIRPORT DESCRIPTION: The airstrip provides access for the community of Elk City. Because of the curved runway, the alignment is also listed elsewhere as RWY 14/35 and 15/33. It may be advisable to report "landing to the south" or "departing to the north" to avoid confusion. The surface is turf with a 40' wide dirt-gravel strip down the runway centerline.

TRANSPORTATION: No courtesy car, however, and "town" is just a gentle five-minute downhill walk away.

SERVICES & LODGING

BB - **Canterbury House Inn Bed and Breakfast**, 501 Elk Creek Road, Box 276 , Elk City, Idaho 83525, (208)842-2366, 3/4 mile from Elk City. 2 rooms, $40-50, P, CU, CC, MR (10)

M - **Elk City Hotel**, Box 327, Elk City, Idaho 83858, (208)842-2452, 15 units, $14-36, R, CU, TV, CC

M - **Elk City Lodge**, Box 143, Elk City, Idaho 83858, (208)842-2250, 21 units, $20-30, P, CU, TV, C/M, CC

M - **Junction Lodge**, HC #67, Box 98, Grangeville, Idaho 83530, (208)842-2459, 5 1/2 miles west of Elk City on Highway 14, 1 space, 6 units, $32.10-36.38, P, TV, C/M, AB, R, CB, HU

CAMPING: No camping facilities are located on the field. However, several motels are in the area. Since no car rentals are available, one is limited to staying in town or bringing a mountain bike.

*Crooked River Campground - This campground has 5 campsites for tents and trailers. It has pit toilets, picnic tables, but no drinking water. It is located about 7 miles from the airport. Take Forest Route #283 southwest out of

town about 2 miles to its junction with State Highway 14. Turn right and follow the South Fork of the Clearwater River downstream about 3 miles to its junction with Crooked River. Turn up Crooked River about 2 miles to the campground.

EXPLORING ELK CITY: Situated in the heart of the Nez Perce National Forest, Elk City is surrounded by literally millions of acres of backcountry. You probably would find it difficult, if not impossible to identify another spot in the lower 48 states that mixes just the right amount of civilization with everything that the outdoor recreationist could ask for.

The population is sparse, about 400 "locals" live in this town, located about 60 miles east of Grangeville, Idaho. Elk City offers a grocery store, several restaurants and taverns, overnight lodging, gas stations, and a small laundromat.

1901 view of Elk City Main Street. Courtesy: Idaho State Historical Society.

Most Elk City residents are employed by the timber industry but current mining activity can be seen in the area, in keeping with Elk City's history. Another major employer is the U.S. Forest Service.

A busy little community, where the kids still ride their horses to town, Elk City's main attraction is its surrounding backcountry. Fellow visitors will most probably be campers and fishing enthusiasts during summer, but in the fall visitors will see Elk City come to life. This backwoods community attracts thousands of sportsmen for some of this country's best elk hunting. In fact, many will boast it is indeed the best elk hunting in the United States.

HISTORY: It all began in May of 1861, when 22 prospectors from Pierce, Idaho had the good fortune to discover the Elk City mines. A gold rush followed, and that summer the number of miners in town mushroomed to 1,000. In August, 40 stores, saloons, and cabins, taking only one month to build, were ready for winter use.

It should be noted here that 52 prospectors were in the original party. Since there was a treaty with the Nez Perce Indians discouraging this sort of thing, Chief Looking Glass caught 30 of the prospectors and they turned back.

That same year all but 75 of the miners moved on to nearby Florence for yet another bonanza. Those that remained achieved the incredible feat of building ditches anywhere from three to 17 miles long to provide water to their hillside claims. This sluicing operation was eventually taken over by hydraulic giants.

From 1872 to 1884, Chinese miners leased the ditches to work the claims. During the peak of this 12-year venture, nearly 1500 Chinese and only 12 white men lived in Elk City. By 1887, a judge ruled that aliens could not hold mining claims and a subsequent Chinese exodus began in 1889.

An estimated $5 million quartz lode operation began in 1902. Elk City became the "mountain metropolis" for most people settling on the north side of the Salmon River.

Hydraulic mining in the Buffalo Pit - Elk City, Idaho. Courtesy: Idaho State Historical Society.

Fire threatened Elk City in 1910, during the Great Idaho Fire. In 1930 most of Main Street went up in flames; and again in 1939, when the last hotel was reduced to ashes. Not as vulnerable, old mining equipment exists in abundance and can be seen scattered throughout the forest.

As would be expected, stories of Wild West characters and folklore are abundant. Idaho's most famous outlaw, **Henry Plummer**, made Elk City his headquarters after he and his gang survived a shootout in Lewiston in 1863. Plummer's gang made their living by ambushing pack trains taking the gold out of the remote camps.

Plummer became sheriff to avoid the nasty business of dealing with the law.

Vigilantes and a hangman's noose finally brought an end to his reign of terror.

Another colorful character was Bill Mayfield, one of Plummer's gang and an escaped convict from Carson City, Nevada. Another outlaw, Cherokee Bob and Cynthia, the fallen wife of a very worthy man, all got together for a trip from Lewiston to Florence. Not above "bestowing her favors where they would command the most money," Cynthia soon became flirtatious with Cherokee Bob, he being the richer of the two gentlemen. Foolishly Mayfield was confident of Cynthia's affections and resolved to bring the matter to an end. Not surprisingly, Cynthia chose Cherokee because he, "was settled in business," referring to his gun-point acquisition of a saloon the previous day.

Later on, the socialites of Florence refused Cynthia's attendance at a New Year's dance. Subsequently, Cherokee Bob was killed in a gun fight attempting to restore Cynthia's reputation. A gentleman to the end, Cherokee's dying request was that Cynthia return to her previous lover, Bill Mayfield. The reunion was short-lived. Mayfield was shot and killed during a Placerville card game that spring.

It is written of Cynthia, "she has been the cause of more personal collisions and estrangements than any other woman in the Rocky Mountains."

HUNTING & FISHING: As previously mentioned, many believe that the best trophy elk hunting in the continental United States is right here in the Nez Perce National Forest. And, if big game is your bag, you can hunt trophy whitetail and mule deer, elk, bighorn sheep, moose, mountain goat, black bear, and mountain lion on your own or with a licensed outfitter.

The fishing is also exceptional. Hooking a 20 pound steelhead promises a thrill of a lifetime on the Clearwater or Salmon River. The largest steelhead in the world regularly thrill anglers. Also, alpine lakes and bubbling mountain streams offer resident cutthroat and rainbow trout.

ANNUAL EVENTS/ACTIVITIES: **Elk City Days** is held the second weekend in August and is considered a major Idaho County event. A parade, logging events, gymkana, cow pasture golf, dancing, and a big beef barbecue are all part of the fun.

Not to be overlooked for another trip to Central Idaho, is the historic **Elk City Wagon Road**. Either by car or by mountain bike, this 53-mile tour starts at Harpster, 12 miles from Grangeville, on Highway 13. Most of the road is unpaved and continues to Elk City, taking four to six hours driving time. Much of the road parallels the **Old Nez Perce Trail**. An informative brochure about this "trip through time" is available through the Nez Perce Forest Service headquarters.

MAPS, LOCAL CONDITIONS, AND INFORMATION:

Maps & local information: Nez Perce National Forest, Elk City Ranger District, Elk City, Idaho (208)842-2245.

Airport information: Trent Wood, Airport Manager (208)842-2275.

FAIRFIELD

HIGHLIGHT ✈ *A prairie town that offers pilot breakfasts and lots of hangar talk. Walk one block from your airplane to the restaurant.*

- - - - -

AIRPORT DESCRIPTION: The runway parallels Highway 20 and provides easy access to the town across the street. For the purposes of this book, Fairfield may not fit in the mold of a "backcountry airstrip", but it gets heavily used by Idaho pilots looking for a "hundred dollar" breakfast and lots of hangar talk.

It is a nice strip, approachable from both directions. Decomposed granite covers the runway and taxiway. Invariably, I pick up more prop erosion on this strip than any other in the backcountry. I really can't explain it because the strip is in excellent condition.

SERVICES & LODGING: Sullivan's Restaurant, 200 yards from the airport, is the scene for early morning hangar talk as pilots from Sun Valley, Buhl, and Twin Falls regularly fly in for breakfast. The menu is standard Idaho fare, where coffee, toast and tip will get you in and out for $2.00. All the usual breakfast items like eggs, pancakes, and biscuits and gravy are also available.

Unlike "true" backcountry airports, the morning paper is available in vending machines outside the restaurant (also a good place to tie your dog, horse, or unruly relative) and a telephone inside.

The **Country Inn**, is a comfortable motel next to Sullivan's Restaurant. 16 units. $30-38, TV, C/M, HT, WO, AB, CC, MR(50). For information and reservations: Box 393, Fairfield, Idaho 83327, (208)764-2247.

EXPLORING FAIRFIELD: With any luck, you may run into octogenarian **Captain Ben Hurtig** with his Super Cub and sidekick **Pete Johnson** (age undisclosed) in his J-3 Cub. Only the weather keeps them from flying every day, after first calling the "Friendlies" to check the winds...at uncivilized early morning hours.

Only their love of life surpasses their love of flying. And if you overhear one of their breakfast stories, your life will forever be enriched. If you do run into them, a little prodding may get them to relive their tale of discovering a UFO. But just in case you miss them...

FAIRLY RELIABLE PILOTS DISCOVER UFOs: After departing Hailey on one of their early morning reconnaissance missions (i.e., looking for elk or chasing coyotes in Ben's Super Cub) they saw a very bright metallic object with red flames shooting out of the back it, traveling through the side canyons west of Hailey.

I had just departed Hailey in my 182 headed north and keyed up 122.9 to give a position report. Super Cub 39 Zulu immediately replied with his usual good morning but added that he and Pete had seen a UFO and were going to investigate. Assuming they were suffering from the effects of high altitude flying (i.e., higher than their usual tree top level) I promptly dismissed the comment and headed the opposite direction.

Early log home on Soldier Creek. Occupants display rattlesnakes hanging from stick.
Courtesy: Idaho State Historical Society.

Ben, who flies a Super Cub as well as anyone, decided he would make a close pass at the UFO as it was slowly crossing sage covered ridges. It appeared totally unintimidated by their presence until they flew within a few feet of it and then it would rapidly accelerate in a drastic evasive maneuver and then return to its slow cruise mode.

Ben figured that no UFO could outmaneuver his Super Cub and considered it a challenge of his aviation skills to demand a little respect from the aliens. In one of the tight tactical turns, Pete, who was riding as copilot in the rear, claims to have seen the nose of their Super Cub head south while he was heading north.

With all due respect to Ben's flying skills, the UFO continued to outmaneuver the Super Cub using its advanced evasive maneuvers. After a prolonged dogfight, the UFO decided to concede victory and land in a sagebrush ravine. No one got out...

Figuring no one would believe their story, let alone their tenuous victory, Ben and Pete flew back to Hailey to get the station wagon for a ground confrontation.

After Pete told his wife, Kate, what they were up to, she suggested they better take a gun in case there were little green men... not a bad idea. So they loaded up two shotguns and plenty of bullets in their armored personnel carrier (Ben's Country Squire station wagon with vinyl wood grain camouflage on the sides) and tore out of town in a cloud of dust.

As they turned up the dirt road to the landing area, they could see the brilliant metallic UFO pulsing and throbbing as red flames continuing to shoot out in different directions. It may have been defeated but it was definitely not out of commission.

The details of the land assault on the UFO are sketchy but it wasn't much of a skirmish. As it turned out, the little green men didn't even get out of the UFO.

Close inspection of the "spacecraft" revealed that it was a cluster of three metallic helium filled birthday balloons tied together. One of the balloons was

Soldier, Idaho parade celebrating the coming of the settlers. Circa 1900.
Courtesy: Idaho State Historical Society.

a metallic red. As the wind would turn the balloons the sun would reflect off of them and the red reflection appeared to be a burst of flames. The evasive maneuvers were caused by the Super Cub's propwash blowing the balloons helter skelter as they tried their best to catch it.

It's reported that the "UFO" is being held captive by one of the wives for such a time when a Super Cub fighter pilot needs an appropriate serving of humble-pie.

For the more serious minded, Fairfield has three museums: Union Pacific Train Depot (listed in the National Register of Historic Buildings); Manni Shaw's Music Museum (noted Idaho fiddler); Camas County Historical Museum.

HISTORY: Donald Mackenzie's party of trappers discovered this Camas Prairie in 1820, (not to be confused with the Camas Prairie near Grangeville). This Camas Prairie later contained a shortcut toll road for the Oregon Trail known as **Goodale's Cutoff**.

For years, the camas, an edible blue flower of the lily family, was a staple of the Native American's diet. Thus, the Camas Prairie attracted annual migrations of Bannock Indians who came to harvest the bulb. The Bannock Treaty of 1869 guaranteed the continued use of this centuries old practice. However, a "typographical error" listed Camas Prairie as Kansas Prairie, which gave the whites reason not to recognize the treaty.

Assuming that if no camas existed the Indians would disappear, the white settlers started raising pigs which would root out the bulbs and destroy the camas. This was the principle cause of the Bannock War of 1878.

The town of **Soldier** was built in 1880, about two miles north of present day Fairfield, and named for the soldiers in the Bannock War. When the railroad came through Camas Prairie in 1911, it passed two miles north of Soldier so a new town was built along the tracks and called New Soldier and later Fairfield.

HUNTING & FISHING: Seven years of drought severely affected the area's fishing. With the hope that the drought ended with the winter of 1992/1993, Mormon Reservoir is again filled with water. This reservoir is located about 5 miles directly south of the airport.

Some incredible rainbow trout have been taken out of here in the past. The fresh water shrimp contribute to the rapid growth and the salmon colored meat of these fine eating fish.

Camas Prairie is also known for its excellent goose hunting. Ducks Unlimited has taken over management of the Centennial Marsh, south of Hill City, which should greatly enhance the goose habitat.

MAPS, LOCAL CONDITIONS, AND INFORMATION:

Airport Information: Camas County Sheriff, Box 216, Fairfield, Idaho 83327

Visitor Information: Camas County Civic Organization, Box 337, Fairfield, Idaho 83324.

FISH LAKE

HIGHLIGHT ✈ *Moose alert! They love the lake as much as the native cutthroat. Beautiful Wilderness camping.*

- - - - -

AIRPORT DESCRIPTION Fish Lake is set in the Selway-Bitterroot Wilderness. The approach to the runway is directly over the lake itself. The runway surface is grass and a little soft from sub water. Be sure to stay in the middle of the runway as boggy areas with standing water are hidden in the grass along the edges of the runway. While taxiing, it is a good idea to have someone walking ahead of you - looking for gopher holes and mud bogs.

A sign near the ranger station cautions pilots about density altitude and downdrafts over the lake. Heed the advice. The runway is relatively long at 2800', but the combination of soft runway surface, prevalent tail winds, high density altitude, and downdrafts over the lake have resulted in six airplane crashes - five in the lake - and eight fatalities.

CAMPING Wilderness camp sites are located in the trees near the lake at the east end of the runway. Bring plenty of insect repellent, give the moose a wide berth, and don't feed the deer in your camp and you will have a wonderful wilderness experience.

EXPLORING FISH LAKE MOOSE ALERT - I had heard for years the axiom that there were moose at Fish Lake and fish at Moose Creek. I had sampled the fishing at Moose Creek and could verify that half of the axiom was true, and was eager to confirm the second half.

In August of 1993, while photographer

Roger DeWeese samples the cutthroat fishing while keeping an eye on nearby moose.

John Plummer and I were doing the aerial photography for this book, we spotted three moose swimming off the north shore of the lake and a bull moose wading on the east bank. I knew then that I would have to return for a closer look.

Two weeks later, Roger DeWeese, a 205 pilot out of San Diego and I decided to return for a closer look. As we overflew the airstrip for a runway examination, we spotted a Forest Service employee mowing the airstrip with a small lawn

The author pretends he is a stump while photographing a passing moose. The ploy worked - too bad he forgot to load film in the camera. Courtesy: Rich Hall.

tractor - just like rolling out the red carpet! On short final, however, we noticed a deer frolicking on the runway threshold. We managed to avoid both the mower and deer and made an uneventful landing.

Apparently Fish Lake campers started feeding the deer, and now it has become quite a pest begging for food, following campers, and hanging around the campsites. I hope it becomes educated before the opening of hunting season.

Roger's assignment was to sample the fishing potential while I photographed the moose. Roger caught two cutthroats in the 10-11" class with his first two casts.

A cow and calf moose were wading in the shallows off the north shore. I was able to walk through the trees along the shore line and get within 50 yards of them. It was a special treat to quietly watch these large animals feeding in their natural environment, unafraid of something as inconsequential as a human.

Roger, satisfied with his fishing success, shares my fascination with these behemoths in this very special wilderness setting.

HISTORY Bert Zimmerly used the airstrip at Fish Lake as early as 1937 to transport elk hunters in his Zenith airplane. The hunt was described as a "mercy" elk hunt on the Selway game preserve. There were no accommodations for hunters and they were required to take their own equipment. Packer John Hazelbaker of Kooskia used a string of horses to pack game to the field where it was loaded into the plane.

In 1939, beavers were trapped and transported out of the Fish Lake area. The beavers had plugged the drainage ditches and flooded the airstrip. It appears to be an ongoing problem.

MAPS, LOCAL CONDITIONS, AND INFORMATION:

Clearwater National Forest
12730 Highway 12
Orofino, Idaho 83544
(208)476-4541

Fish Lake Ranger Station. 1993.

FLYING "B"

HIGHLIGHT ✈ *Private guest ranch with all the amenities in the heart of the wilderness along the Middle Fork of the Salmon.*

- - - - -

AIRPORT DESCRIPTION: The Flying B's lush green hay fields stand out in stark contrast to the dry arid canyon walls along this section of the Middle Fork. It is an oasis surrounded by very unforgiving country. It has been used as a refuge for adventurers for the last 6000 years. Fifty miles from civilization by air and a hundred by foot, the "B" offers pampered accommodations and sustenance to modern day adventurers and hunters.

Don't let the road that leads between the airstrip and the lodge fool you. That's as far as it goes. You can only get here by air, boat, or foot.

The beautiful turf strip is short and becomes even shorter in the heat of the day. Plan your arrival and departure early or late to minimize the effects of high density altitude.

SERVICES & LODGING: The Flying B is a private resort that offers breakfast and lunch to non-members for $10 and dinners for $14. Lodging is available for $66/person/night. A $25 landing fee and prior permission is currently required for landing.

EXPLORING THE FLYING B RANCH: The **Bernard Creek Bridge** was constructed from cables flown in by Bob Johnson from McCall. They weighed 1800 pounds and were wrapped around the outside of the airplane. The first load was delivered when the air was cool and arrived with no real problems. However, by the time the second load was delivered, the air had warmed and increased the density altitude to the extent that full power was required just to land. He delivered the cable alright but damaged the undercarriage of his airplane and had his license suspended for some time.

HISTORY: When **Captain Bernard** arrived at this location in 1879, he discovered six large lodges that had been occupied by the Sheepeater Indians. Some time after this discovery, miners erected a log cabin here.

After hearing about the area from **Cougar Dave Lewis, Albert Kurry** and his wife moved in 1912. Albert's brother, Henry, put a herd of cattle across the river on the Mormon Ranch. A cable and basket arrangement was used to cross back and forth across the river.

George Crandall and his wife pack a bear on the Middle Fork.
Courtesy: Idaho County Free Press.

The year of 1919 was tough on Albert. The winter destroyed 270 of his 300 cattle and early that same summer his wife died. Her last request had been to be buried in Boise. Her body was packed 20 miles up Camas Creek to Meyers Cove and then 60 miles by horse and wagon to Salmon, then 800 miles by train packed in ice for the final leg of the journey. Albert returned to the Middle Fork and filed a patented claim to 160 acres and acquired title in 1920.

In the late '20s, the ranch was sold to **George Crandall** and his wife. It was a lonely life for Mrs. Crandall. She seldom saw more than two or three women a year. However, in 16 years she never left the ranch until it was sold in the early 1940s to **A.A. Bennett.**

Bennett was a World War I fighter pilot. He flew a Ford Trimotor in and out of the Idaho back country for many years. He is credited with laying out many of the back country airstrips. Despite his adventures as a mountain bush pilot, Bennett lived nearly to the century mark.

Bennett converted the marginal cattle ranch into the fly-in resort you see today. The Flying B and the Root Ranch have consolidated into a time share arrangement known as the Flying Resort Ranches, Inc. Membership totals around 150, enjoying the good life, vacationing, hunting, and fishing on the ranch.

HUNTING & FISHING: The Flying Resort Ranches, Inc. offer guided hunting trips for elk, deer, moose, goat, sheep, bear, cougar, predators, and forest grouse. They also offer fishing trips, trailrides, and backpacking in Units 20A, 26, and 27.

MAPS, LOCAL CONDITIONS, AND INFORMATION:

Flying Resort Ranches, Inc., Box 770, Salmon, Idaho 83467 (208)756-6295.

The Flying B is a beautiful oasis in the heart of the wilderness.

GARDEN VALLEY

HIGHLIGHT ✈ *Natural hot springs, manicured airplane campsites overlooking the river, and access to a small mountain community make Garden Valley a must-do.*

- - - - -

AIRPORT DESCRIPTION: The airport is located two miles southeast of the town of Garden Valley. The runway surface is gravel and turf. The area surrounding the airport is mountainous but the width of the valley permits relatively safe approaches. Tiedowns are located the south side of the airstrip.

The first observation you will make here is how aptly this area has been named. Lush green in innumerable shades is this valley floor. The grassy meadows sit at a low elevation, looking much like golf courses and are protected by surrounding mountains.

TRANSPORTATION: A mountain bike is your best bet. Bring your own.

SERVICES & LODGING: The **Longhorn Saloon** located in Crouch is the gathering place in these parts. Its about six miles west of the airport on a highway that makes a 360 degree loop around the saloon - handy for finding your way home if you get looped. The Saloon has a long bar running the full length of the building, and it's busy. The restaurant is open for breakfast, lunch, and dinner.

Craig Creek Cottages, HC 76 Box 2976, Garden Valley, Idaho 83622, (208)462-3033. 5 units $60-$150

Terrace Lakes Resort is located 4 miles north of Crouch. The 18 hole golf course is nestled in the mountains with trees and streams. It has a natural hot water swimming pool, clubhouse with restaurant and bar, and tennis courts. Overnight accommodations are limited to 8 rental units for guests of members or anyone interested in buying a membership. For more information contact: Terrace Lakes, Garden Valley, Idaho 83622 (208)462-3250.

CAMPING: The ****Garden Valley Airport Campground** has three camp sites with covered picnic tables, stoves, garbage cans, and flush toilets. Wooden stairs conveniently lead from the airstrip down to the campground. The beautiful grass

covered camping area is regularly mowed and irrigated. Due to the underground sprinkling system, check the irrigation schedule to avoid a late night drenching. The campsites overlook the beautiful South Fork of the Payette River.

The **U.S.F.S. Hot Springs Campground** is located about 1.5 miles east of the airstrip past the Garden Valley Forest Service Office. This campground has 5 individual campsites and two group picnic areas. It has picnic tables, stoves, and pit toilets. Ponderosa Pines tower over the grass covered area. The hot springs are located across the highway. Concrete steps lead down a steep embankment to a lovely warm water pool overlooking the river. This is a fee charge campground.

EXPLORING GARDEN VALLEY: Garden Valley served as the area's bread basket during the mining boom of the 1860s and 1870s. Vegetables were grown here to supply local mining camps. Today Garden Valley is still home to the largest wholesale greenhouses in the state, located here for the natural hot water.

Crouch sits at the western end of the valley near the confluence of the South Fork and Middle Fork of the Payette River. Both streams offer excellent fishing, and the South Fork is one of the best whitewater rafting streams in the state.

For an exhilarating mountain bike ride, try the **Anderson Creek/Granite Basin Road.** From the airstrip, go west two miles to the mouth of Anderson Creek, located just past the convenience store on the right. The road climbs 12 miles to a dead end. The creek has cut a deep canyon through the granite. Ponderosa pines cling to towering mountains. Elk are thick as house flies.

MAPS, LOCAL CONDITIONS, AND INFORMATION:

U.S. Forest Service, Garden Valley Ranger Station, HC77, Box 2900, Garden Valley, ID 83622 (208)462-3241.
West Boise Chamber of Commerce, Box 105, Garden Valley, Idaho 83622.

Garden Valley baseball team prior to a game with Placerville.
Early day Idaho - I hope! Courtesy: Idaho State Historical Society.

GRAHAM

HIGHLIGHT ✈ *Site of an 1880s boom town, today it is as remote and isolated as it was 100 years ago. Not much left but great hunting and fishing.*

· · · · ·

AIRPORT DESCRIPTION: Fairly remote and seldom used, this scenic strip on the North Fork of the Boise River is the perfect spot for those searching for a place to get away from everything.

In the Boise National Forest, just two miles outside the Sawtooth Wilderness Area, a Forest Service Guard Station sits adjacent to the airstrip. The airstrip has runway end markers and a windsock. Bring your own tiedowns.

TRANSPORTATION: You are on your own. A mountain bike would be ideal for exploring the historic mining operations.

CAMPING: All three campsites existing in the area are located on the river and offer picnic tables, firepits, and pit toilets. You may choose to camp under your wing or, upstream one-half miles is the ****Graham Bridge Campground**, with four campsites. ****Johnson Creek Campground** (not to be confused with Johnson Creek Campground near Yellowpine) is located one mile downstream from the airstrip and has three campsites. Bring your own water and take out your trash. This is a remote mountain area and only practically accessible by airplane. A gravel road ending at Johnson Creek Campground travels about 27 miles to reach the paved Lowman Road, and then another 15 miles to reach the only civilization around - Idaho City. Last minute supplies could be picked up in Atlanta, 15 miles southeast by air and 60 miles by car on a dirt road.

EXPLORING GRAHAM: The mines are up on Silver Mountain behind the old mill site. A long tramway was built to haul the ore from the mines down to the mill. Some of the wooden tram towers are still standing, well supported by trees that have grown much taller. The rotting remains of many old cabins are scattered throughout the trees on either side of the mill.

HISTORY: In 1885, **Matthew Graham** created quite an interest in the dull red outcrops on Silver Mountain, just west of the present airstrip. He maintained the area offered great possibilities of large scale quartz mining. Assays of some good gold ore samples (of questionable origin) confirmed his expectations.

During the 1860s, Mr. Graham had been successful in promoting the Atlanta mines, 16 miles southeast, by obtaining large investments from New York and London. There wasn't enough high quality ore to keep the mills open and in a few short years the investors went bankrupt.

But this time was different. Graham reported veins on Silver Mountain four to six feet wide with surface assays of $50 to $2000 of free-milling gold and largely metallic silver for which no complicated reduction would be required. More New York and London investors returned with more money and by 1888, the new town

Ruins of a cabin at Graham taken on an Historical Society field trip, 1962.
Courtesy: Idaho State Historical Society.

A fishing party from nearby Atlanta pose for a photograph. Notice the salmon spears. Courtesy: Idaho State Historical Society.

of Graham boasted of having six saloons, a store, two blacksmith shops, a jail, a Justice of the Peace and Deputy Sheriff, a butcher shop, two faro games, three livery stables, a fine hall, 300 men, 41 ladies, and the controlling vote of Boise County.

What they didn't have, however, was ore. Upon completion of the $350,000 mill, it ran only eight hours before it became obvious that all it could produce was crushed rocks. Matt Graham spent the winter of 1888 in New York City trying to obtain more British capital to develop the necessary ore bodies...unsuccessfully. The $350,000 mill was sold at a Sheriff's sale for $9,500 and the tramway, buildings, and the thirteen mines sold for $500.

It's estimated that over $1 million was spent to prove that gold and silver was lacking at Graham. In 1980, efforts were resumed to find the large ore body.

HUNTING & FISHING: Good fishing can be found in the North Fork of the Boise River. **Sawtooth Wilderness Outfitters** provides guided pack trips for elk, deer, cougar, bear, and fish in Units 35 & 39. For more information, call or write Darl Allred, Box 81, Garden Valley, Idaho 83622. Phone (208)462-3416 winter and (208)259-3408 summer.

MAPS, LOCAL CONDITIONS, AND INFORMATION:

US Forest Service, Boise National Forest, Idaho City Ranger District, Box 129 Idaho City, Idaho 83631 (208)392-6681.

GRASMERE

HIGHLIGHT ✈ *A wide spot on one side of the road in the middle of the Bruneau Desert. As far as the eye can see, desert in all directions. These small desert oases are pure Americana and are quickly vanishing. Catch this one while you can.*

- - - - -

AIRPORT DESCRIPTION: The airstrip is a nice long strip that ends in a gravel pit. It is turf and alkali covered with lots of livestock imprints. As nice as it looks it is deceivingly rough. Located in the Bruneau Desert, this is probably the least populated corner of the state.

Going to town means driving 36 miles north on highway 51 to the town of Bruneau (pop. 100) or south 20 miles to Riddle (pop. 25) and the Duck Valley Indian Reservation.

SERVICES & LODGING: When you reach the **Grasmere Station**, just a half-mile north of the airstrip, you have just been to Grasmere...all of it. A desert gas station/restaurant/bar is reminiscent of old Highway 30 during the '40's and '50's. A porte cochere shelters the gas pumps and a neon Oly sign in the window beckons thirsty travelers off the highway. A diesel generator out back provides the electricity.

As you walk through the front door, you'll see a pay phone to your right, a beer bar on the left (complete with a couple of desert folk wetting their whistles with cold Buds), another bar on the right offering standard Idaho fare, and a pool table straight ahead. The juke box in back will probably be playing Conway Twitty.

Even the harsh Bruneau Desert has its moments of beauty.

Bruneau Canyon. Courtesy: Idaho Historical Society.

With the exception of a few mobile homes and an auto graveyard, this is Grasmere. Saving the best news for last, you can buy the whole town for around $150,000 because it has been for sale for a couple of years.

EXPLORING GRASMERE: This is a remote desert experience. The current proprietors, Ralph and Thelma Crane, have leased the operation to get away from it all. She serves cold beer and hot hamburgers while Ralph takes care of the rest. They hope to offer lodging in the future. Grasmere...the perfect destination for pilots in search of a hot spot and a cold sarsaparilla.

HUNTING & FISHING: The **Grasmere Reservoir** is located about 3 miles west of the town

(Above) The first OPEN sign I've ever noticed on a town. (Below) Grasmere, Idaho, 1993.

and is stocked annually with Lahonton Cutthroat fingerlings. The water level fluctuates according to irrigation needs - and so does the fishing. Native Red Band Rainbows are

also believed to inhabit the reservoir migrating in from feeder streams.

Sage hen hunting can be very good, depending on the spring weather. A wet spring kills the baby chicks. The plains are ideal antelope range with the canyons providing homes to chukars and mule deer.

MAPS, LOCAL CONDITIONS, AND INFORMATION:

Airport information: Division of Aeronautics, 3483 Rickenbacker Street, Boise, Idaho 83705 (208)334-8775.

Local information: Grasmere Station, CH 58, Box 24, Bruneau, Idaho 83604 (208)759-9930.

HENRY'S LAKE

HIGHLIGHT → *Fish! Some of the best trout fishing in the world in a very scenic area appropriately named "Vacationlands". Several local resorts cater to your every whim.*

- - - - -

AIRPORT DESCRIPTION: Henry's Lake lies tucked into eastern corner of Idaho and borders Montana and Wyoming. The unique geologic setting is at the center of three mountain passes and surrounded on three sides by the Continental Divide.

Next door is the great Yellowstone Park, western entrance. Appropriately named "Vacationlands", this area is within the Targhee National Forest, and offers semi-desert, sagebrush dotted arid land, timbered highlands, peaks over 10,000 feet high, streams, lakes, waterfalls, and wilderness. Summer highs will get up to 80 degrees and evenings will drop 20 to 30 degrees. It may even snow during the summer.

TRANSPORTATION: The State does not have a courtesy car available at the airport but Mack's Inn will provide airport pickup for guests using their facilities. Call ahead of time (208)558-7272 to arrange a pickup since there is no telephone at the airport.

SERVICES & LODGING: Mack's Inn Resort, located 15 miles south of the airport on the Henry's Fork, offers 65 rooms, a 6000 square foot convention center, float trips, boat rentals, bicycle rentals, and limited shuttle service. For information and reservations contact: Mack's Inn Resort, Box 10, Island Park, Idaho 83429 (208)558-7272.

Elk Lake Camp offers a first class dining experience.

Staley Springs Lodge is located on the west side of Henry's Lake about five miles from the airstrip. They offer rustic log cabins with 1,2,3, and 4 bedrooms. The restaurant is open for breakfast and dinner serving family style home cooking. The lodge also has a lounge with TV and fireplace. A store provides sundries and your favorite fly or lure.

The dining room is decorated with lodgepole pine furniture complementing a red and white checkerboard linoleum floor. Age has taken its toll on the gently rolling floor, but an hour in the lounge seems to smooth it out. For information and reservations, contact: Staley Springs Lodge, HC66, Box 102, Island Park, Idaho 83429 (208)558-7471.

Wild Rose Ranch is on the north shore of Henry's Lake about three miles north of the airstrip on Highway 87. They offer 18 cabins and condominiums for rent along with boat rentals and a small restaurant. For information and reservations, contact: Wild Rose Ranch, HC 66, Box 140, Island Park, Idaho 83429, (208)558-7201.

Elk Lake Camp.

Elk Lake Camp offers a place for you to relax, renew, and explore in first-class, rustic comfort. The lovely lodge and cabins sit on the edge of Montana's unspoiled and beautiful Centennial Valley approximately 25 miles west of Henry's Lake over Red Rock Pass.

Private cabins are grouped around the lodge. They vary in size and sleep from one to six. Each has its own woodstove and bath, and comfortable queen size and twin beds are covered with goose down comforters.

The dining is first class! What a relief to see linen napkins, proper wine glasses, and candles on your table. Elegance in a very remote setting, but the setting is only exceeded by the quality and presentation of the food. Guests may choose from an array of entrees each night, including tender steaks, barbecued ribs or succulent fish cooked over a mesquite grill. All the desserts are homemade. The wine list is limited but intelligent, obviously created by someone who understands, appreciates, and enjoys wine.

Our dinner of mesquite grilled rack of lamb, cooked to perfection, and served sprinkled with freshly picked sage leaves was memorable. The burning embers of sage leaves created ruby like reflections in our polished glasses of Cabernet. The very chocolate dessert brought to mind the saying "Living well is the best revenge".

Dusty contemplates the beauty of Big Springs...or maybe the huge trout swimming in the crystal clear water.

For information and reservations, contact: Elk Lake Camp, Box 916, West Yellowstone, MT 59758. (406)276-3282.

CAMPING: The ****Henry's Lake Airport Campground** has recently been improved and contains two camp sites, picnic tables, stoves, potable water, and pit toilets.

**Upper Coffee Pot Campground -An interesting canoe/camping trip would be to arrange for Mack's Inn to pick you up at the airport, rent a canoe, and shuttle you to Big Springs. Load your camping gear in the canoe and do a 6 mile float trip downstream to the Upper Coffee Pot Campground. The campground offers 14 campsites with picnic tables and pit toilets. What a great opportunity to try your fly fishing skills. Pre-arrange a pickup for you and your canoe from Mack's Inn.

Henry's Lake State Park is located on the south shore of the lake about three miles from the airstrip. The campsites are grass covered with picnic tables, flush toilets, drinking water, and showers. The fee is $8.00 per night with an additional $3.00 fee for an electrical hookup.

EXPLORING HENRY'S LAKE: It takes several visits to feel like you know the territory. Here are a few suggestions to get you started.

Big Spring - Big Spring is one of the 40 largest springs in the country; it produces about 120,000,000 gallons of water each day, enough to supply a city of nearly 1,000,000 people. It is the main source of the Henry's Fork River. Fishing is strictly against the rules at the bridge over the spring run, where schools of oversized, overfed and perpetually ravenous trout beg tirelessly for handouts. From Henry's Lake Airport, take Highway 20 south 10 miles to Mack's Inn and turn left on the road to Big Springs - five miles.

Upper and Lower Mesa Falls - From Henry's Lake Airport, take HWY 20 south 22 miles to the turnoff to HWY 47, "Mesa Falls Scenic Byway" for approximately 16 miles.

These falls have been described as two of the last undisturbed waterfalls of consequence in the West. **Lower Mesa Falls** is easily seen at the Grandview campground, where you can actually touch the edge of the waters plunging into roaring, white foam. The cataract is a feature of the Henry's Fork of the Snake River where the river is squeezed into a gorge that drops 65 feet. This secluded spot along the Henry's Fork offers excellent trout fishing and camping.

Upriver you can hear the waters of **Upper Mesa Falls** pounding on the rocks. To get there, follow the highway north of the campgrounds a little over 1/2 mile to a gravel road on the west side. These glassy waters froth to mist in a 114 foot plunge.

HIKES: The Targhee National Forest created the first **National Recreation Water Trail**, a five mile float on calm water where bald eagles, osprey, moose, deer, and elk can be observed in their natural settings. The float can be made in almost any small shallow draft boat with oars, such as a McKenzie boat, small aluminum fishing boats, and canoes.

Boat and canoe rentals can be made at Mack's Inn, 10 miles south of the airport on Highway 20. From Mack's Inn, turn east on the Big Springs road. At about 4.5 miles, look for the boat ramp and parking area. The takeout area is Mack's Inn. It is also possible to continue the float past Mack's Inn another 1.5 to 2 miles and take out at Upper Coffee Pot Campground.

HISTORY: The lake was first discovered by **Major Andrew Henry** in 1810. **Jim Bridger** camped on its shores with trappers and Flathead Indians in 1835 and 1838. After the battle of Big Hole, in 1877, Nez Perce bands of **Chiefs Joseph**, **White Bird** and **Looking Glass** built their fires along this scenic mountain lake.

Mysterious floating and disappearing islands in the lake once served as the Nez Perce Indians burial grounds. They erected scaffolds on the islands on which they placed their dead. The islands would vanish and then reappear with their cargo. Legend has it that this ensured a happy future for the soul of the Indian.

5.2 miles north of Henry's Lake is the Targhee Pass leading into Montana. The pass honors Targhee, the head chief of all the Bannocks, and in an effort to maintain peace between the whites and his tribe, he met the Governors of Utah and Idaho in the 1860s. Years later, in an epic flight of the Nez Perce across this pass, Chief Joseph eluded General Howard's pursuit.

HUNTING & FISHING: Hunting and fishing are very popular activities in the area and require state licenses. Game species are moose, elk, antelope, mule deer, mountain goat, whitetail deer, bighorn sheep, black bear, small animals, and game birds. The area is world-renowned for its excellent stream and lake fly fishing opportunities. Game fish are rainbow, eastern brook, brown, and cutthroat, kokanee salmon, and whitefish.

The Eastern Idaho geology contains limestone which is conducive to the production of microbiologically rich waters. These microorganisms start the food chain that gives phenomenal growth to the fish. Henry's Lake has been described as a "fish grocery store".

Contact the following outfitters for a guided fishing and/or hunting trip: Teton Valley Lodge, (208)354-2386; Three Rivers Ranch, (208)652-3750; Last Chance Lodge, (208)558-7068; Henry's Fork Anglers (208)558-7525; B.S. Flies, (208)558-7879.

MAPS, LOCAL CONDITIONS, AND INFORMATION:

For information on the National Recreation Water Trail and Forest Service maps, stop by or call: Island Park Ranger District (located 15 miles south of the airport on highway 20), Box 20, Island Park, Idaho 83429 (208)558-7301.

For boat, canoe, and bicycle rentals, contact: Mack's Inn Resort, Box 10, Mack's Inn, Idaho 83433 (208)558-7272.

HOLLOW TOP

HIGHLIGHT ✈ *Springtime brings great turf to this Arco Desert airstrip. Good place to practice your soft/short field technique. No noise abatement procedures here!*

- - - - -

AIRPORT DESCRIPTION: Hollow Top gets its name from the large hollow top volcanic butte directly east of the airstrip. Springtime brings lush green grass to the runway, much to the delight of the open range cattle.

HUNTING & FISHING: Not a chance on catching a fish here - they are so fussy about demanding water. However, avid varmint hunters might glass Hollow Top Butte over carefully for the elusive Yellow-Bellied Marmot from early spring through the end of July. The lava rock and green grass, not to mention lots of privacy, are rock chuck prerequisites.

Dispatching a few of the furry critters inhabiting the airstrip would be doing us all a favor - especially those of us still using training wheels on our airplanes (i.e. nose wheels).

MAPS, LOCAL CONDITIONS, AND INFORMATION:

Maps and area recreational information:
Bureau of Land Management
U.S. Department of the Interior
Shoshone District Office
400 West F Street
Shoshone, Idaho 83352
(208)886-2206

Airport information:
Division of Aeronautics
3483 Rickenbacker Street
Boise, Idaho 83705
(208)334-8775

For more information, refer to Arco-Kimama overview on page I-1.

IDAHO CITY

HIGHLIGHT ✈ *Historic living ghost town. At one time the largest city in the Northwest. Proud of its old west heritage, Idaho City offers restaurants and hotels to today's "prospectors."*

- - - - -

AIRPORT DESCRIPTION: The airstrip sits on the west edge of town, amidst piles of mining tailings and white pine. The runway surface is primarily gravel and is in good shape. There is a paved turn around at the approach end of RWY 21. A large open ended hangar is located at the northeast end, presumably used by the Forest Service. A sign identifies a telephone that is now gone. There are lots of good tiedown areas but we didn't find any tiedowns per se. From the pavement, head toward the windsock to pick up the 1/2 mile trail into town.

SERVICES & LODGING:

The **Idaho City Hotel**, Box 70, Idaho City, 83631, (208)392-4290. 5 units, $29.50-46.50, P, TV, C/M, CC, PH, MR(6).

The **Prospector Motel**, Box 70, Idaho City, 83631, (208)392-4290. 7 units, $29.50-46.50, LH, P, CU, TV, C/M, CC, PH.

Calamity Jane's is a small restaurant on the corner of Main Street and Highway 21. They serve a great breakfast and have tables inside and out in an apropos historic setting. (Easy walking distance from the airstrip).

CAMPING: No camping facilities exist on the airport, but the ****Grayback Gulch Campground** is located 2.4 miles southwest of Idaho City on Highway 21. It has 14 designated campsites with drinking water, picnic tables, fire pits, and pit toilets. Be forewarned, the campsite is accessible to RV's exiting from the highway. Reservations are available through MISTIX (800)283-CAMP.

EXPLORING IDAHO CITY: A quaint old western mining town with a population of 300, Idaho City once was the largest city in the Northwest, and briefly the capital of Idaho Territory. Rich with history, with a few remaining buildings from the 1800s, the "Merc" has been operating in its current location since 1865. However, you will notice immediately that the little town is up to date.

Services and restaurants are more than adequate and the folks are eager to share, not only their town, but other points of interest as well. A visit to the Idaho City Cemetery brings to life the rugged and sometimes tragic lives endured by the former residents. The experience brings to heart the fact that not even 10 per cent of the men died of natural causes in the Idaho Territory mining camps.

HISTORY: It only took one year for the population of Idaho City to jump from one to 6,267...gold again. It was the winter of 1862 and a disgruntled miner from Pioneerville was digging a well. At 18 feet he discovered gold and Bannock City (called West Bannock to differentiate it from Bannock, Montana), and later known as Idaho City.

Even the early day miners found time for a little recreation.
Courtesy: Idaho State Historical Society.

In two years the town had two main streets, each a half-mile long. A printing office, eight bakeries, nine restaurants, 25 saloons (at least), about 50 variety stores, 20 doctors, 25 or so attorneys, seven blacksmith shops, four sawmills, two dentists, three express offices, five auctioneers, three drug stores, four butchers, three billiard tables, two bowling alleys, three painters, three livery stables, four breweries, one harness shop, one mattress factory, two jewelers and four theaters, (attracting traveling troupes from New York to San Francisco), caused Idaho City to surpass Portland, Oregon in becoming the largest city in the Northwest.

Montgomery Street was said to be literally panning up to $16 a pan. Miners were mining under the houses and in the street. Buildings were raised up on pilings so the ground beneath could be mined...as so humorously portrayed in "Paint Your Wagon".

A fire swept through town in 1865 and what wasn't destroyed then was taken by another fire in 1867, destroying most of the early day landmarks.

Ya-hoo! Let 'er buck! Main Street, Idaho, City. Circa 1920. Courtesy: Idaho State Historical Society.

ANNUAL EVENTS AND ACTIVITIES:

Arts & Crafts Fair - Idaho Arts Council - Check for June date.

July 4th Fireworks & Games - Idaho City Chamber of Commerce. July 4th.

Basin of Gold Days & Pioneer Picnic - Sponsored by the Idaho City Historical Society to celebrate the anniversary of the discovery of gold in the Boise Basin. Picnic and potluck held in Brogan park. Check for August date.

Black Powder Rendezvous - A muzzleloaders shooting event. October date.

MAPS, LOCAL CONDITIONS, AND INFORMATION:

Visitor information: Idaho City Chamber of Commerce, Box 70, Idaho City, Idaho 83631 (208)392-4290.

Museums: Boise Basin Historical Museum, Main Street & Highway 21, Idaho City, Idaho 83631.

Airport and camping information: Idaho City Ranger District, Boise National Forest, Box 129, Idaho City, Idaho 83631 (208)392-6681.

Chamber of Commerce, Box 70, Idaho City, Idaho 83631 (208)392-4290.

INDIAN CREEK

HIGHLIGHT → *Popular whitewater boat launch on the Middle Fork of the Salmon. The longest airstrip in the FC-RONR Wilderness. Wilderness camping on America's most beautiful river.*

- - - - -

AIRPORT DESCRIPTION: Indian Creek is the best airstrip on the Middle Fork and a very busy place. More than 4,400 aircraft land within the Wilderness Area each year and most of this traffic is shared between Chamberlain Basin and Indian Creek.

Indian Creek's popularity is due to float-boating on the Middle Fork. Charter operations ferry passengers and gear several times a day during mid summer. All traffic is confined to the narrow canyon with Little Soldier Mountain at 8,813 ft. to the southeast and Big Baldy at 9,705 ft. to the northwest. Stay on the radio announcing your position and intentions.

CAMPING: The ****Indian Creek Airstrip Campground** lies adjacent the airstrip overlooking the river. Except for the picnic tables within the Forest Service fenced

National Geographic Society Expedition, 1935. Courtesy: Idaho State Historical Society.

area, signed "authorized personnel only", and for a pit toilet near the boat launch area, all camping amenities have been removed from Indian Creek. Potable water is seasonally available outside the Forest Service guard station, but tastes like it ran off someone's boot.

For a little tranquility, the best time to camp here is early June through the end of July. In late summer, there is a lot of float-boat activity. Watching the launching of the rafts, the preparation and the excitement of the rafters will probably entice you to take a trip someday.

Two *Indian Creek Camps** are located 1 mile downstream from the end of RWY 22. Follow the **Middle Fork Trail** (007) downstream to the Indian Creek Pack Bridge. The camp sites are located on each side of the mouth of Indian Creek as it dumps into the Middle Fork. No facilities are located here but the beauty of the site makes the wilderness camping experience worthwhile. Fishing is also very good here (catch and release) for rainbow, cutthroat, dolly varden, and brook trout.

EXPLORING INDIAN CREEK: The Middle Fork of the Salmon River was one of the eight original rivers to be designated Wild and Scenic on October 2, 1968. It originates 20 miles northwest of Stanley, with the merging of Bear Valley and Marsh Creeks. Flowing 106 miles northeast through one of the deepest gorges in North America, the Middle Fork is indeed a national treasure.

July boat frenzie at Indian Creek.

In July, 1980, the President of the United States established the "River of No Return Wilderness" encompassing the wild and scenic river in its entirety. Senator James McClure (R-Idaho) introduced a bill adding the name of Frank Church to the title. In March, 1984, President Ronald Reagan signed the bill creating the Frank Church River of No Return Wilderness protecting this 2.2 million acres.

National Geographic Society Expedition, 1935.

This includes parts of the Bitterroot, Boise, Challis, Nez Perce, Payette and Salmon National Forests. It is now set aside to preserve and protect its natural state forever. To maintain this environment, motorized equipment or transportation is not allowed, except by airplane, and then only to established landing strips.

HISTORY: Indian Creek Bar was first settled, in 1914, by a Mr. Watson who built several small cabins there. Lured by stories from a passing prospector, he left the area in 1919 looking for greener pastures. Fred Paulsen worked a mining prospect up behind Indian Creek Bar. Eventually the site was withdrawn by the Forest Service for administrative purposes and the old cabins were burned.

Pungo Creek is located 2.3 miles downstream from the airstrip. In 1933, John Minshew (aka Harry Jones) built two cabins and had a good sized garden at Pungo. He trapped marten for their furs, and supplemented his existence by hunting and fishing. In 1936, Minshew took on a partner to help with his trap lines - Eddie Budell.

When W.W.II came around, the men felt they should do something for their country. Minshew, at the age of 60, found a job in Pocatello with the railroad. Figuring he would never get back to the Middle Fork, Minshew gave Budell the homestead at Pungo.

Budell failed the army physical for having "multiple sclerosis." Since he couldn't produce a birth certificate, he couldn't do any other defense work so headed back to the Middle Fork. He decided to work a quartz prospect which turned out to be high grade flurospar - much in demand for the war time effort.

Budell, with a sound knowledge of drilling, blasting and blacksmithing, hauled 75 tons of ore in a wheelbarrow to his stockpile below the mine. Bob Johnson, of Johnson Flying Service, figured he could fly out of Indian Creek in a Ford Trimotor, carrying 3000 pounds of ore at a time. Budell proceeded to build some wooden mule-loading docks (which can still be seen on the flat) to haul the ore to Indian Creek airstrip; but after some careful calculations, figured at best he could only break even on the project. At that point, Budell decided to sell his claim for $5000, and run a long pack string from 1951 to 1965 for the Forest Service ...quite a life for a man rejected from the Army for having multiple sclerosis.

The claims were allowed to lapse, and the Forest Service withdrew the area from mineral entry for administrative site purposes and burned the cabins at Pungo Creek.

HUNTING & FISHING: Hunting and fishing regulations can be picked up at license vendors or by calling or writing: Idaho Department of Fish and Game, 600 S. Walnut, Box 25, Boise, Idaho 83707, (208)334-3700.

MAPS, LOCAL CONDITIONS, AND INFORMATION:

Middle Fork Ranger District, Box 337, Challis, Idaho 83226 (208)879-4321.

JOHNSON CREEK

HIGHLIGHT → *Idaho's premier airplane campsite - all amenities including hot showers. Nearby historic mining community. Lodging and restaurant in town. Johnson Creek has it all.*

- - - - -

AIRPORT DESCRIPTION: The gem of the Gem State, and possibly all of the West is the Johnson Creek airstrip. The Division of Aeronautics and Idaho volunteer pilots have all joined together to make this a superb fly-in picnicking and camping destination.

The well irrigated runway is groomed to perfection by the full-time caretaker. If this is your first visit, don't panic when you see sprinkler pipe on the runway. It is plenty wide so you can land to either side.

TRANSPORTATION: Two marvelous coaches are provided by the State of Idaho. The early 1960s vintage pumpkin orange Dodge Panel Wagons are affectionately named "Great Pumpkin I and II" and cost $5 to drive, plus $.30 per mile. Don't worry about the charge, you can only go to Yellow Pine.

If your thirst takes you by the Yellow Pine Bar, it's best to designate a driver before you go in. Even stone sober the Great Pumpkins drive like they are in a forward slip. The adventure is truly part of the over-all Johnson Creek experience...not to be missed.

SERVICES & LODGING: Since **Yellow Pine** is the sole destination allowed of the Great Pumpkins, and since no other town exists within 60 miles, on dust choking roads, I would highly suggest visiting Yellow Pine.

In all truthfulness, you wouldn't want to miss Yellow Pine anyway. There is limited lodging available and a restaurant/bar, and small store.

No need to worry about having to choose the right long distance phone company while in Yellow Pine - phone service has not yet arrived. It was almost a disappointment to see the arrival of a satellite dish outside the bar!

Yellow Pine Lodge has 6 rooms from $5-20, LH, P, R. For information and reservations write: Yellow Pine Lodge, Box 77, Yellow Pine, ID 83677 no phone.

The **Wapiti Meadow Ranch** is located just upstream a few miles from Johnson Creek Airstrip. Shortly after requesting a brochure on the ranch from owner, Diana Haynes, I received a beautifully organized packet of information...it knocked my socks off!

Diana, a graduate of Northwestern University and East Coast horsewoman, divided her time between homes in Virginia and Washington, D.C. where her gourmet catering business launched a career into the world of professional entertaining. For 25 years she challenged her abilities with classic fox hunting, dressage competition, and trailriding the foothills of the Alleghenies.

Repeated visits to the River of No Return Wilderness fueled her dream to relocate here and build a home and business, helping to open the doors of the wilderness to others.

Wapiti Meadow Ranch.

Managing Agent, Barry Bryant, a graduate of Washington State University draws on his business background and life in the Idaho backcountry, hunting and fishing this area for over four decades. Barry knows the country like the back of his hand and understands the ways of the animals who live there. He is also a licensed backcountry pilot and loves to share his enthusiasm and knowledge of flying with guests.

Together, they have created a wilderness retreat guaranteed to make you forget telephones, televisions and traffic. Four private guest cabins are scrupulously clean, light and airy with new carpet. When you open your door, you'll be greeted with fresh flowers, snacking goodies, a refrigerator filled with soft drinks, your own coffee maker, and a fruit basket brimming with seasonal selections.

The lodge dining room seats 18 comfortably. Service is on fine china with silver appointments, and the glow of warm candlelight sets the mood. Three memorable meals a day include such entrees as:

* Marinated Grilled Flank Steak * Roast Cornish Game Hens with Cranberry

Glaze * Grilled Fresh Salmon on a bed of Belgian Endive with Lemon Dressing * Savory Prime Rib.

If you tire of being pampered in luxury, you may opt for a trailride, trout fishing, a packtrip, river rafting, huckleberry picking, hot tub soaking, a historic mining tour, or a 9 day guided hunting trip for elk, deer, bear, sheep, goat, and cougar.

Don't miss this one...For reservations and information, contact: Wapiti Meadow Ranch and Outfitters, HC 72, Cascade, Idaho 83611, Radio-Phone (208)382-4336. Reservations always required.

CAMPING: Numerous and varied are the campsites along the banks of Johnson Creek bordering the airstrip. Tall ponderosa and lodgepole pines and Douglas firs provide the privacy between campsites which come with axes to split your own firewood - which is usually stacked up right at your feet. And it keeps getting better.

Firepits, charcoal grills, picnic tables, drinking water and best of all...hot showers, electricity, and new toilets. For those who lack a tent, two bunk houses with fold down plywood beds are available with a horseshoe pit out back.

It comes as no surprise that the word is out on Johnson Creek. The Cessna 185 Club's annual fly-in has attracted 85 planes at one time. You should be able to enjoy the solitude of just a few other planes with mid-week plans.

On a four day trip in mid May, only two lonely elk grazing on the runway were there to greet us.

EXPLORING JOHNSON CREEK: Yellow Pine is what Idaho was 100 years ago and America was 200 years ago. A mining town that didn't die, Yellow Pine is remote and isolated and still without telephones. It has let the 20th Century go its way while it continued on its own...probably for the best. The residents are hard working, hard playing, beer drinking, God fearing individuals.

The Yellow Pine Bar jumps on Saturday night accompanied by the tunes of local "musicians". Known as the Yellow Pine Stomp...it is. A "stranger in town" easily stands out and is advised to keep a low profile. I wouldn't advise "ladies" to attend unescorted.

Fist fights are a common form of entertainment with usually no permanent damage. These are tough, working men...if you find yourself in a pinch, generally an offer to buy the "gentleman" a drink will smooth things over.

Visiting Yellow Pine is like participating in a game of Virtual Reality. It is a unique opportunity to look at America's roots. Not in a history book, not a western made for television, but in real life with self participation. These are the same people who led the gold rush to Thunder Mountain, Roosevelt, Dixie, and Warren a hundred years ago. Here the individualistic attitude, the strength and the perseverance that made America great is alive and well. It may be a little selfish, but I hope the phone never rings in Yellow Pine...we have so much to lose.

HIKES: DAY/OVERNIGHT HIKE TO RIORDAN LAKE FROM JOHNSON CREEK AIRSTRIP: General Description: This is a 12 mile round trip hike with the first two miles difficult hiking on the two track road.

Finding the Trailhead: From the airstrip, head south on the road that parallels the airstrip and campgrounds. Pass through a gate and cross the bridge. Turn left after the bridge and head north for 1/4 mile. Look for the first road that

Riordan Lake.

Yellow Pine, Idaho. Courtesy: Idaho Historical Society.

branches to the right and follow it as it climbs up the steep and rocky hillside. After about 2 miles, the pitch slackens, and a meadow can be seen on the right. Look for a post, with the sign missing, which marks the trailhead to the right.

The Hike: Continue on foot on the trail, keeping the stream on your right. At about 2 miles the trail crosses the North Fork of Riordan Creek, and shortly after branches. Stay left, and continue for about another mile to the lake. A pleasant hike, and the lake offers some nice campsites. When near Hennessey Meadow, look for game down in the beaver ponds - especially moose.

The hike from Hennessey Meadow to Riordan Lake is easy, about 3 miles and about a 100 foot climb in elevation. The difficult part of the hike is the beginning on the old road - about 500 foot gain in 2 miles. A four wheel drive vehicle or ATV would be ideal to take to Hennessey Meadow and start the hike from there.

Note: The Forest Service is altering sections of the trail for revegetation. If the trail becomes highly cluttered with debris, look around for the new alternate route which is marked by two large tic marks in a nearby tree's bark. Please follow the new route. It helps to aid the environment and the Forest Service's efforts.

HUNTING & FISHING: The fishing in Johnson Creek, adjacent to the camp sites, is excellent. Rainbow and brook trout are the predominant fish. The area directly below the campground gets a lot of pressure. You can catch fish there but would probably be more successful farther up or down the stream, away from the campgrounds. While it is legal to keep fish caught in this section of water, limit your catch rather than catch your limit. Let's preserve this resource. Besides, around the campfire, it's easier to add a couple of inches to a fish that was released than one in the frying pan.

HISTORY: The following anecdotes are taken from *"Yellow Pine, Idaho"* a book of stories compiled by Nancy G. Sumner, aka "The Flatlander".

A.C. BEHNE, FOUNDER OF YELLOW PINE

Mr. Behne is given credit for founding Yellow Pine after the gold rush to Thunder Mountain in about 1906. He became the first Postmaster of the town (which at that time had three cabins). He was a well respected old boy, and prior to his passing away at the age of 91 in 1945, he wrote down very specific instructions for his burial. Unfortunately, the people he gave his burial instructions to were out of town when he died.

Miners came from all over the area to pay their last respects, and after a proper service, planted him on a hillside instead of his chosen spot.

"His close friends were perturbed for several reasons. Behne was a Mason and he wasn't buried facing the east, so they knew he wasn't resting well. Too, his grave was covered with rocks and debris from road machinery and heavy snow.

Some years later, his old friends thought it best to move his remains to the cemetery where it could be properly marked. Money was solicited from the community, but somehow the moving never materialized. You know how it is when friends get together over a bottle of whiskey. It took days to arrive at a solution to their problems and the 'reburial' funds had literally gone down the drain! In another three years, some good friends of Behne had him put down where he wanted to be."

AL HENNESSEY   In the mid-50s, Al Hennessey had a tent house set on some mining claims on Buck Creek. The planes flying between Boise and Stibnite would keep track of his activities from tracks in the snow and smoke from his shack. They reported no tracks and no smoke seen for several days. A good sized pack of food, including whiskey, was dropped in the snow near the shack. The next day a pilot reported tracks from the shack to the package, but no smoke.

Hennessey had made it out to the food drop, drank the whiskey, fell into bed, pulled the covers over himself and apparently passed out. When rescuers found him, one foot had frozen. This resulted in his foot being amputated.

PICCOLO PETE STROMBERG - In the early days, the only bathtub in Yellow Pine country was located at the Bryant Ranch. An assortment of people came from all around bringing fish, steak or other foods, towels and soap, and also sociability.

Piccolo was one of the men who visited at the house, but he shunned the bathtub. When asked if he wanted a bath, his answer was, "No, I just roll in the sand," and so far as anyone knows, that is just what he did.

Piccolo was a hardy bowlegged Swede who was a so-so miner but an expert on skis. At one time he was hired to teach Claudette Colbert, the movie star, to ski at Sun Valley - hopefully after a good roll in the sand.

ANNUAL EVENTS AND ACTIVITIES: Annual Harmonica Contest...a playoff to salute the importance of the harmonica in the musical history of the Old West. A foot-stompin' musical celebration with cash prizes for participants. A three day event, generally held in early August featuring barbeques, a pancake feed, street jam sessions, street booths, and tours of gold mines. For information and registration write to: Dave Imel, Box 23, Yellow Pine, Idaho 83677 (no phones).

MAPS, LOCAL CONDITIONS, AND INFORMATION:

Division of Aeronautics, 3483 Rickenbacker St., Boise, ID 83705 (208)334-8775.

Boise National Forest, 1750 Front Street, Boise, ID 83702 (208)334-1516.

Payette National Forest, Box 1026, McCall, Idaho 83638 (208)634-0600.

KRASSEL

HIGHLIGHT ✈ *Access to upper section of historic South Fork of Salmon. Whitewater rafting, fishing, and hunting.*

- - - - -

AIRPORT DESCRIPTION: Krassel, surrounded by stately ponderosa pines, sits high on a bluff overlooking the South Fork of the Salmon. The ends of the runway drop off sharply to the swirling waters below. A helipad and guard station are located on the east side of the field.

During summer months, the Forest Service maintains a helitack crew here for fire suppression. When they aren't fighting fire, their attention is focused on maintenance and the turf reflects their efforts. The runway is short and unforgiving. Trees obstruct the departure end.

CAMPING: There are no camping facilities at Krassel, and even if there were, the helicopters and work crews coming and going probably wouldn't be conducive to ones tranquility.

The ****Buckhorn Bar Campground** is located about 3.5 miles upstream from Krassel. It has 10 designated campsites with picnic tables, fire rings, potable water, and pit toilets.

EXPLORING KRASSEL: The surrounding timber covered mountains are lovely, but the big attraction here is the river. Whitewater rafting and kayaking rule supreme. The South Fork of the Salmon is becoming a popular whitewater run. It has a perfect mix of whitewater, scenery, and seclusion.

The stretch of river in the immediate vicinity of Krassel, is rated as Class II water but as the river progresses downstream toward the mouths of the East Fork of the South Fork of the Salmon and the Secesh Rivers, the water becomes increasingly more challenging.

HISTORY: Gunfight at the Reed Ranch - In 1914, **William Reed**, aka "**Deadshot**" **Reed**, homesteaded on the south end of a bar, six miles upstream from Krassel Airstrip, on what was to become known as Reed Ranch. Deadshot was reputed to be an ex-Texas Ranger who moved to Idaho in hopes of leaving his past behind.

Meanwhile, **George Krassel,** a local placer miner and occasional Forest Service employee, decided to settle on an abandoned homestead on the north end of the same bar. Krassel also erected the first cabin on Dutchman's Bar across Indian Creek from the Guard Station.

In the fall of 1918, Krassel returned to the South Fork with his winter supplies only to discover Reed's cattle had gotten out and were contentedly grazing on his hay. Enraged, Krassel decided to pay Deadshot a visit - with his rifle.

As was common with gunfights in the Old West, there were no witnesses and we are left with only one side of the story. Krassel, purportedly, rode up to the Reed Ranch house, concealing his rifle behind the withers of his horse. Deadshot was out in the field cutting hay as Krassel approached the house. When Mrs. Reed noticed Krassel's hidden rifle, she wrapped Deadshot's pistol in a dishtowel and sent her daughter scurrying to deliver it.

Krassel approached Reed on horseback and there were unfriendly words. As Krassel began to raise his rifle, Deadshot drew his pistol and opened fire. The past that Deadshot was hoping to escape, reared its ugly head as Krassel fell dead from his horse. Krassel was buried below the first bend in the road downstream from the airfield.

With Krassel gone, Deadshot Reed filed on the Krassel land and was granted a patent. Deadshot proceeded to farm the bar and supported his wife and 14 children. Reed sold his holdings in 1929, but the ranch still carries the name of this ex-Texas Ranger looking for a new beginning in the Idaho Backcountry.

HUNTING & FISHING: The South Fork of the Salmon continues to have dwindling runs of Pacific Chinook Salmon. The numbers no longer justify a season. An interpretive sign at Krassel describes the life cycle and plight of the salmon.

MAPS, LOCAL CONDITIONS, AND INFORMATION:

Krassel Ranger District
Payette National Forest
Box 1026
McCall, Idaho 83638
(208)634-0600

LAIDLAW CORRALS

HIGHLIGHT ✈ *Arco Desert airstrip with a nearby ice cave. Very private. Home of the Sage Grouse, antelope, and desert mulie.*

- - - - -

AIRPORT DESCRIPTION: The Laidlaw Corrals Airstrip is named after the Laidlaw family - long-time ranchers in the area. An old corral and cabin are located on the east end of the airport. There is also nearby a large ice cave, reported to house a healthy population of rattlesnakes.

    Laidlaw Park is the name given to the large surrounding area of native grassland - ideal country for plant ecologists, but to the untrained eye (the author's included), it's hard to see past the lava rocks, sagebrush, tumbleweeds, and rattlesnakes to really appreciate the area.

MAPS, LOCAL CONDITIONS, AND INFORMATION:

Maps and area recreational information: Bureau of Land Management, U.S. Department of the Interior, Shoshone District Office, 400 West F Street, Shoshone, Idaho 83352 (208)886-2206.

Airport information: Division of Aeronautics, 3483 Rickenbacker Street, Boise, Idaho 83705 (208)334-8775.

For more information, refer to Arco-Kimama overview on page I-1.

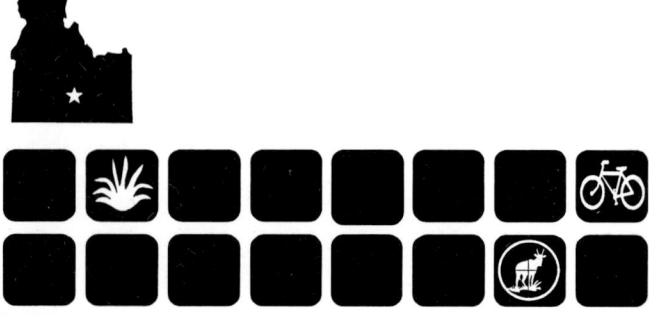

LANDMARK

HIGHLIGHT ✈ *A timbered setting along the headwaters of Johnson Creek. Landmark has good potential as a wilderness reliever airstrip. Two resorts on Warm Lake will transport you.*

- - - - -

AIRPORT DESCRIPTION: This airstrip appears deceptively easy, however, the surrounding terrain is not as flat as it appears from the air. Erratic winds and downdrafts combined with high density altitude and tall trees on the approach will keep even an experienced pilot on his toes.

The airstrip is in the Salmon River Mountains - Boise National Forest, 2 miles southeast of the Landmark Ranger Station. Picturesque Johnson Creek slowly winds its way through this high mountain meadow surrounded with lodgepole pines.

SERVICES & LODGING: Located about 11 miles west of the airstrip, the **Warm Lake Lodge & Resort** has a restaurant, cocktail lounge, and 12 rooms available at $45-80 per night. They also have boat rentals and a grocery store. The Lodge will provide round trip transportation from the Landmark airstrip for guests. Fishing in Warm Lake is excellent. The manager, Mike Rowland, may also be encouraged to reveal the location of remote mountain lakes for day hikes and fishing. For reservations and information contact: Warm Lake Lodge & Resort, Box 450, Cascade, Idaho 83611. (208)257-2221 (summer) or (208)382-4274 (winter). HA, R, CU, CC, AB, MR(50), L, no pets.

Warm Lake's North Shore Lodge is also located on Warm Lake, about 12 miles west of the airstrip. They have 8 cabins to rent for $50-80. They have a cafe, bar, store, and boat and canoe rentals. They will also provide roundtrip transportation from the Landmark airstrip for guests. For reservations and information contact: Warm Lake's North Shore Lodge, 175 N. Shoreline Drive, Cascade, Idaho 83611. (208)257-2219. P, AB, R, CU, CC, MR(10).

CAMPING: Landmark has a great airplane camping...potential. At present there is a pit toilet and nothing else. A campground set in the shady lodgepoles on the

banks of Johnson Creek would be a great reliever field for some of the wilderness strips.

**Pen Basin Campground has six campsites with picnic tables, fire rings, and pit toilets about 3.5 miles from the airstrip. From the tiedown area at the airstrip, follow the access road north to its junction with the Warm Lake Road. Turn left and cross the bridge at Johnson Creek. The Forest Service buildings are on the right (couldn't find anyone around July 1). Turn left at the road to Deadwood Reservoir (FS Highway 570) and follow it another 2.5 miles. If a bridge were constructed at the south end of the airstrip, it would make this campground accessible within 1/2 mile from the airport as opposed to 3.5 miles.

HUNTING & FISHING: Warm Lake provides an excellent fishery for rainbow trout, kamloops, brook trout, cutthroat, kokanee, and Mackinaws. The lake is 684 acres in size, and over 200 feet deep. Boat rentals are available from the Warm Lake Lodge and Warm Lake's North Shore Lodge.

MAPS, LOCAL CONDITIONS, AND INFORMATION:

Maps and airport information: Forest Supervisor, Boise National Forest 1750 Front Street, Boise, Idaho 83702 (208)334-1516.

Cascade Ranger District, Box 696, Cascade, Idaho 83611 (208)382-4271.

LORD FLAT

HIGHLIGHT → *Oregon airstrip high on the rim of Hells Canyon. Unlimited views and lots of privacy. Elk hunting.*

- - - - -

AIRPORT DESCRIPTION: Lord Flat sits high on a ridge overlooking Hells Canyon from the Oregon side of the river. The green grass and patches of trees provide stark contrast to the tan cheat grass covered slopes of the canyon. A windsock is located on the east side of the runway, midfield.

CAMPING: Lord Flat has no improved camp sites but elk season finds hunters camped along the runway. There is a USFS administrative facility with potable water one mile south of the airstrip at the Dorrance Cow Camp.

HISTORY: The name Lord Flat, has its origin from an early day settler, **James Lord**, who ranged his cattle and hunted this area between 1878 and the late 1800s. The area was also referred to as Buckaroo Flat.

Apparently, the prehistoric peoples inhabiting the Hells Canyon area preferred to live along the Snake River as opposed to the canyon rim areas such as Lord Flat and Memaloose. In contrast to extensive evidence of prehistoric inhabitation along the river, very little has been discovered on Lord Flat.

However, single prehistoric Indian graves have been uncovered in both Memaloose and the Lord Flat areas. It is conceivable that these areas were reserved as sacred burial grounds for very special people, while the common Indians were buried closer to home. It would have taken a determined burial party to carry a body up and out of the deepest gorge in North America. Only two motives, come to mind, would lead to such a determined action - fear or respect; but more likely, a combination of both.

MAPS, LOCAL CONDITIONS, AND INFORMATION:

Hells Canyon Natl. Rec. Area, Clarkston, WA (509)758-0616.
Hunting licenses and information: Oregon Fish and Wildlife, 2501 SW 1st, Box 59, Portland, OR 97207 (503)229-5403.

For more information, refer to Hell's Canyon overview on page I-3.

LOWER LOON

HIGHLIGHT → *Incredible hot springs on lower Middle Fork of the Salmon. Very difficult airstrip - take a local professional pilot with you the first time.*

- - - - -

AIRPORT DESCRIPTION: The approach must be done precisely, as the runway is only 860 feet long with a ditch across the upper end and a go around is generally not feasible. Regardless of your experience, have a local professional pilot go with you the first time. The airstrip is open to the general public.

Previously known as "Simplot", after the Idaho businessman J.R. Simplot who owns some of the surrounding land and cabins, Loon Creek is located at the confluence of Loon Creek and the Middle Fork of the Salmon River. Other surrounding land is owned by Idaho Fish and Game, who lease some of it to an outfitter. So, if you plan a fall trip - expect company.

The runway surface is a combination of thin turf and gravel. A windsock is located on the northeast edge of the runway. There are no runway markings. The parking area is opposite the windsock along the northwest edge of the runway.

CAMPING: Camping is not allowed in the fenced runway environment. However, ***Big Loon Camp** is a wilderness campground located nearby on the bar at the mouth of Loon Creek. Because of the well known hot springs further up Loon Creek, this camp is popular during the summer months with boaters.

EXPLORING LOWER LOON:

LOWER LOON CREEK HOT SPRINGS: From the airstrip, walk south toward the Simplot cabins and cross the Lower Loon Creek Bridge. Follow the trail upstream about 1 mile to the hot springs. It is a large pool created by hand hewn longs, approximately 10 X 20 feet and 3-4 feet deep. A long hose feeds 120 degree water from several springs into the crystal clear pool. Overhanging pine boughs provide shade on one side of the pool while a few boards on the other side of the pool provide a sunning deck.

HISTORY: **Bob Ramey**, a descendent of **John S. Ramey**, a guide in the Sheepeater War, was the first settler on the flat at the mouth of Loon Creek. Ramey built an irrigation system to divert water from nearby Cache Creek to the ranch. With an ideal exposure to sun, he was able to raise fruit, vegetables, hay, beef, and horses.

The property changed hands several times and eventually ended up in the hands of Idaho businessman **J.R. Simplot.** He retained the acreage with cabins, and sold the rest to the Idaho Fish and Game.

HUNTING & FISHING: The trout fishing in both the Middle Fork and Loon Creek is excellent. The 1993 regulations allow catch and release fishing with single barbless hooks on artificial lures on both the Middle Fork and Loon Creek. A possession limit of 2 fish is allowed on the tributaries of Loon Creek. Be sure to check current regulations.

To book a guided hunting trip out of Lower Loon Creek, call the Idaho Fish & Game (208)756-2271 to determine which outfitter currently has the lease. Then refer to the free Idaho Hunting and Land Based Recreation Directory to contact the outfitter.

MAPS, LOCAL CONDITIONS, AND INFORMATION:

Maps: Challis National Forest, Box 404, Challis, Idaho 83226, (208)879-2285. Middle Fork Ranger District, Box 337, Challis, Idaho 83226 (208)879-4321.

Airport conditions: Bob's Aviation, Box 525, Challis, Idaho 83226 (208)879-2364.

Outfitter Information: Idaho Outfitters and Guides Association, Box 95, Boise, Idaho 83701 (208)342-1919.

MACKAY BAR

HIGHLIGHT ✈ *Private guest ranch. Lodging, trailrides, fishing, hunting, jet boat trips, and long soaks in a hot tub. Pilot breakfasts by prior arrangements.*

- - - - -

AIRPORT DESCRIPTION: At the confluence of the South Fork of the Salmon and the Main Salmon River sits the beautiful **Mackay Bar Salmon River Ranch**- a private guest ranch, accessible by jet boat, airplane, or horse.

LANDING FEE: A $25 landing fee is universally charged on all private aircraft, whether stopping in for breakfast or staying overnight.

SERVICES & LODGING: Whether it's trailrides or packtrips to fish the high mountain lakes in the Frank Church Wilderness, backpacking and nature hikes into the historic Southfork area, jet boating the River of No Return, or just plain relaxing in a hot tub, the professional staff and guides at Mackay Bar are devoted to one thing: Making your wilderness adventure the most exciting comfortable, safe and memorable one of your life.

Lodging for 26 guests is provided in three individual cabins and two lodges. Rates for lodging are $115/person/day including three hearty meals. Trailrides and jet boat rides are also offered at an additional cost.

Pilots are welcome to stop in for meals as long as prior reservations are made. For reservations and information call: (800)854-9904

HISTORY: Archaeological discoveries indicate that there were prehistoric concentrations of native people in the Mackay Bar vicinity. Its relatively mild climate and abundance of fish and wildlife made it as attractive 10,000 years ago as it is to modern recreation seekers.

The more recent (18th and 19th century) Mountain Sheepeater Indians also used the area for winter camps.

Mackay Bar got its name from its first white settler, William B. Mackay, who build a cabin around 1900. He died in 1916 and is buried on the bar.

In 1937, Mackay Bar was purchased by **John Oberllig** of the Salmon River Placer Company. Plans to mine gold at the confluence of the South Fork of the Salmon and the Main Salmon required extending the road down the canyon wall from Dixie, building a tunnel to divert waters from the South Fork to operate a hydroelectric generator, and flying in 400 tons of machinery from McCall.

The outbreak of World War II prevented the mine from successfully starting production. The site of the mining operation is still visible on the scree slope downstream from the ranch.

HUNTING & FISHING: Mackay Bar is a permittee of the Payette, Nez Perce, Salmon and Boise National Forests. The staff at Mackay Bar provides guided hunts in Units 19, 19A, 20, and 20A. Mackay Bar is reputed to have the best and most productive hunt area in North America for elk, deer, moose, goat, sheep, bear, cougar, predators, chukar, and forest grouse. They also offer guided trips for steelhead and trout, trailrides, backpacking, and jet boat rides.

MAPS, LOCAL CONDITIONS, AND INFORMATION:

Maps: Payette National Forest, Box 1026, McCall, Idaho 83638 (208)634-2255. Frank Church-River of No Return Wilderness, Big Creek District Ranger, McCall, Idaho 83638 (208)634-2255.

Reservations and information for lodging/meals: Mackay Bar Corporation, Box 7968, Boise, Idaho 83707 (800)854-9904.

Hunting & Fishing information and booking: (208)365-3753.

Cables for the Mackay Bar bridge looped from mule to mule. The packers are about to leave Warren for the river. Courtesy: Idaho State Historical Society.

MAGEE

HIGHLIGHT ✈ *Panhandle get-away. Historic interpretive site. Airplane camping.*

- - - - -

AIRPORT DESCRIPTION: Situated in the heart of Idaho's Panhandle National Forest, at the junction of Tepee and Trail Creek, Magee Airport is located 23 miles northeast of Coeur d'Alene. It is a beauty, ranking right along with Johnson Creek, Cavanaugh Bay, and Big Creek.

The runway surface is covered with lush grass which can extend the takeoff roll considerably, especially if it hasn't been mowed for a while or is wet. Beavers occasionally dam the streams and flood the area. A Forest Service Guard Station and work camp is located adjacent to the airstrip.

CAMPING: The ****Magee Airstrip Campground** has two campsites with tables, stoves, fire pits and a pit toilet. Magee is not in wilderness area and as such, permits non-wilderness activities (bicycles, motorized vehicles, and generators). This is not to say that these modern conveniences are necessary but rather, they are allowed. Choose your comfort level but don't disrupt your neighbor's tranquility.

EXPLORING MAGEE: The **Magee Historic Site** was the site of a local Forest Service Administrative Headquarters from 1908 until 1973. The first recorded settlement in the Trail Creek-Tepee Creek drainage was a 160 acre homestead claim made by **Charles Magee** in the early 1900s.

In June 1908, the site, including part of Charley Magee's original homestead was reserved as a Forest Service administration site. Most of the existing buildings at the Magee site were constructed between 1922 and 1935. In its most active period, about 50 people were seasonally employed here. The site was placed on the National Register of Historic Places in 1981. Remnants of 14 historic buildings are left to explore and enjoy.

HISTORY: In 1943, the Army Corps of Engineers filled in a swamp with thousands of tons of fill dirt and rerouted Tepee and Trail Creek. This was to become an

emergency airport for combat fighter aircraft. It is questionable whether an F-51 could land on a 2200' strip at the bottom of this timbered canyon, so it is fortunate it never had to be used in such an emergency.

It also was fortunate that in its spare time, the Corps built a substantial log barracks building for the adjacent Magee Ranger Station. Following the war, the Forest Service became landlord of the strip for use in fire control and administrative flights.

Historic Magee Ranger Station.

In 1974, the northern third of the airstrip was destroyed by flood and the Forest Service abandoned the facility. In 1980, reconstruction began after the Division of Aeronautics applied for a Special Use Permit.

Those who enjoy this beautiful Northern Idaho airstrip may give thanks to an on-going volunteer and cooperative effort by the Idaho Aviation Association and the Division of Aeronautics.

HUNTING & FISHING: Excellent trout fishing in Trail Creek.

MAPS, LOCAL CONDITIONS, AND INFORMATION:

Maps and area camping information: Fernan Ranger District, 2502 East Sherman Avenue, Coeur d'Alene, Idaho 83814 (208)765-7381.

Airport Conditions:, Division of Aeronautics, 3483 Rickenbacker St., Boise, Idaho 83705, (208)334-8775 (800)346-9134 in state.

MAGIC RESERVOIR

HIGHLIGHT → *Idaho's own Baja beach community. Fishing and windsurfing. Nearby restaurants, lodging, golf, and hunting preserve.*

- - - - -

AIRPORT DESCRIPTION: Magic Reservoir is located 15 miles southwest of Hailey in the sage and lava rock covered desert. The airport boasts intersecting turf covered runways. The surface of RWY 3-21 is a little rough with more gravel than turf. The shorter RWY 6-27 has better turf but requires consideration of density altitude and increased roll during takeoff due to the tall grass.

The area is characterized by rolling, rugged hills, rocky basalt outcroppings and desert rangeland. Sagebrush dominates the landscape but chokecherry, aspen, and willows may be found in shaded canyons or wetter areas.

SERVICES & LODGING: The **Magic Lake Resort** can be found at the east end of the airport overlooking the lake. It has a full liquor bar, dance floor, and seasonal restaurant. (208)487-2022

The **West Shore Lodge**, located at the west end of the airport offers a restaurant, motel, golf course, and private shooting preserve. The rates for the motel are $30/night for two people. The golf course is a 3 par 1300 yard, chip and putt course. The rates are $8 for 18 holes. The shooting preserve is open from September 15 to March 1 for pheasant hunting. Shuttle service from the airport to the lodge is available. Call Don Farnes, (208)487-3636 for reservations and information.

Magic City, also known as **Baja Magic** is located on the east side of the reservoir. It has some similarities to the fishing villages found in the desert peninsula of Baja California. Windsurfing was the popular sport here in the years before the reservoir dried up. Now that there is water it is likely that windsurfing will again flourish.

CAMPING: Camping is permitted on the air strip. Tiedowns, picnic tables, stoves,

and pit toilets are located here. Check at nearby West Magic Resort for potable water. The lack of any trees taller than a sagebrush limit the scenic value of the area, but for a weekend of prime fishing, this is the spot.

The Magic Reservoir Area has nine semi-developed sites which include boat ramps, docks, water access, restrooms, signs, cattleguards, and cattle enclosures.

EXPLORING MAGIC: Fishing is the big attraction here, and Idahoans are optimistic that the seven year drought is finally over (winter of 1992-93). This is especially good news for anglers because the refilled reservoir had its bottom aerated during the drought. Rainbow trout feed on the fresh water shrimp here, giving them rapid growth and delicious salmon-colored meat. Most fishing methods are successful...lures, trolling, float tubing with flies, or bank fishing with worms and marshmallows.

HIKES: Following the springtime snowmelt, the desert comes to life. Wildflowers abound, the sagebrush blooms, and dirt roads lead for miles through the desert.

There are no formal hiking trails because of the openness of the country. A variety of upland game birds and animals

Site of the local sportsman's club at West Magic.

can be seen including antelope, mule deer, elk, coyotes, badgers, rock chucks, ground squirrels, sage hens, Hungarian partridge, chukar partridge, doves and a variety of song birds. Early morning risers could be fortunate enough to find sage hens performing their ritualistic mating dance.

HISTORY: At a cost of 3 million dollars, Magic Dam was built in 1910 to supply irrigation water to the farms around Richfield, Dietrich, and Shoshone. Although electrical generators were added to the dam in 1988, irrigation storage and controlled water delivery remain the primary functions of the reservoir. The Big Wood River, Camas Creek, and Rock Creek all flow into the reservoir. When full, the reservoir is approximately 3,740 acres and 135 feet deep at the dam.

HUNTING & FISHING: Both good. As previously stated, the main attraction through the years has been the excellent fishing opportunities here. Numerous deer also inhabit the desert and a resident elk herd lives in the vicinity. Coyotes, jackrabbits, and rattlesnakes complete the desert scene.

The West Shore Lodge has established a shooting preserve for pheasants. For more information, contact the West Shore Lodge at (208)479-3636.

ANNUAL EVENTS/ACTIVITIES: The West Magic Sportsman Club has activities throughout the year...barbecues, fishing contests, Mother's Day brunch, dances, weddings, and wakes. For more information, contact the West Lake Resort (208)487-2022.

MAPS, LOCAL CONDITIONS, AND INFORMATION:

Maps and area recreational information: Bureau of Land Management, U.S. Department of the Interior, Shoshone District Office, 400 West F Street, Shoshone, Idaho 83352 (208)886-2206.

Airport Information: Division of Aeronautics, 3483 Rickenbacker St., Boise, Idaho 83705 (208)334-8775.

Local Conditions: West Shore Lodge (208)479-3636.

Jim Herbert is greeted at the West Shore Lodge.

MAHONEY CREEK

HIGHLIGHT ✈ *Wilderness airstrip overlooking the Middle Fork of the Salmon. Dropoff point for hunters.*

- - - - -

AIRPORT DESCRIPTION: Carved out of the side of a sagebrush covered hillside, Mahoney Creek airstrip sits 360 feet above the Middle Fork of the Salmon. The 30-foot-wide surface is irregular and looks like a two-track jeep road. Improvements in 1992 have included runway end markers and surface improvements. The approach is generally upstream over a sage covered plateau which drops away steeply to the river immediately before the approach end of the runway. Overfly the runway before landing to check for mud holes and animal damage.

CAMPING: Not recommended...but possible. This is our least favorite campsite on the Middle Fork. There are no facilities and access to the river is difficult due to the high bluff where the strip is sitting. There is, however, considerable traffic here during hunting season.

A preferred camping area is located across the river on Mahoney Flats. This requires wading the river which is impossible most of the year. During the summer, you might try to hitch a ride across the river with a passing boater.

HISTORY: Mahoney Creek was named after **Ray Mahoney** who grew a large orchard on the flat above the river. His fresh fruit commanded a fine price at all the mining locations along the Middle Fork.

One of the pioneers of this area was a man named **Charlie Norton.** He was described in his obituary as "A man of nerve", and that was no exaggeration. In his earlier days he was a bear hunter and one day, about 60 miles from Challis, he took aim at a bear and dropped him while at the same instant a big silvertip rose right beside him and struck a blow, crushing his face.

The story gets a little "grisly" from here, so read on at your own risk. Some time later, Charlie's companion found him, made him as comfortable as possible and struck out toward Challis for help.

Meanwhile, the flies found Norton's face. By the time his partner got back

and before they could take him into camp, they took a quart of maggots from his head. A litter was slung between two horses and off they went to Challis.

The doctor despaired and said he couldn't do anything for him, but tried anyway. Charlie lost his entire lower jaw but lived to tell the story. After a while it was realized his face would not heal because it tore every time he was fed. So a hole was cut in his neck for a feeding tube. His face healed, but then they couldn't heal the hole in his neck.

Elk Camp at Mahoney.

It took a trip to Salt Lake City to sew the hole up with silver wire. This healed up and then the contractions of the muscles in his face clamped his mouth shut so that he was unable to eat. His mouth was cut open time and time again.

Charlie, still courageous at this point, still refused to take ether or any other anaesthetic. Following many surgeries, Charlie went prospecting and his mouth grew shut again. The men in his party could not bring themselves to cut his mouth open as he pleaded for them to do.

He found a rock, whetted his knife, propped up a pocket mirror on a stump and cut his own mouth open. Once again he could eat, and he was happy. Then, cancer developed on his face and he endured four surgeries in five years...again with no anaesthetic.

Before his last operation he met Abe Pierce and told him he had to go in again for another operation. At the end of his story he remarked, "and, do you know Abe, I am getting to be a damned baby. I kind of flinch when I think about it." After all the suffering and innumerable operations, he kept his will to the end. He died like thousands of pioneers of the West, a county charge and long forgotten by his relatives whose addresses he had forgotten.

But Charlie Norton, a man of nerve, will never be forgotten as his "grisly" tale is passed from campfire to campfire in the Middle Fork wilderness.

Elk Camp at Mahoney.

HUNTING & FISHING: The **Cougar Ranch** provides outfitted hunts in the area and uses Mahoney Creek as its drop off point. For more information contact: Donald "Buck" Wood, P.O. Box 56, Big Arm, MT 59910; (406)849-5007. They offer guided hunts for elk, deer, goat, sheep, bear, cougar, predators, forest grouse. Fishing, Trailrides. Unit 27.

MAPS, LOCAL CONDITIONS, AND INFORMATION:

Maps and information: Middle fork Ranger District, Box 337, Challis, Idaho 83226 (208)879-4321.

Local charter pilot with current airport conditions: Bob Plummer, Bob's Aircraft, Challis, Idaho 83226 (208)879-2364.

MEMALOOSE

HIGHLIGHT ✈ *Oregon airstrip on rim of Hells Canyon. An incredible on-top-of-the-world view. Ancient Indian burial ground.*

- - - - -

AIRPORT DESCRIPTION: Memaloose is precariously perched on the Oregon rim of the Hells Canyon, overlooking the Snake River 5000 feet below. The approach end of runway 36 drops off sharply. The runway is well defined with runway markers and has a windsock. Horses always seem to be present.

The Forest Service has used the Memaloose Guard Station to base a helitack fire suppression crew for years. Several unoccupied buildings remain on the site after the helitack crew was relocated.

CAMPING: ***Memaloose** - There are no camping facilities located on the airstrip but wilderness camping is allowed.

The ****Saddle Creek Overlook** is situated on the canyon rim 3 miles south of the airstrip. It has 7 improved campsites with picnic tables, fire rings, and pit toilets. From the airstrip, follow Hwy. 4240 southwest toward Imnaha.

**Hat Point Overlook - 2.2 miles from the airstrip, offers a spectacular 360 degree view of Hells Canyon from the 100 foot fire tower. The campground located near the base of the tower offers 6 improved campsites with picnic tables, fire rings, and pit toilets. From the airstrip, follow Hwy. 4240 northeast to its junction with Hwy. 315.

The ***Sacajawea Campground**, located within a half mile of Hat Point, had 7 improved campsites with picnic tables, fire rings, and pit toilets. However, after a forest fire raced through the campground, the ambiance just isn't the same.

EXPLORING MEMALOOSE: The **Hat Creek Lookout** was constructed by the Forest Service in 1931. All the material was packed in by horse. In 1948 it was replaced with the present 100-foot high structure. The tower is wood, historic, and very small at its pinnacle - not the kind of thing for large crowds of people, but 5000 visitors a year climb the narrow winding stairs for a view that will never be forgotten.

HISTORY: The name Memaloose is Chinook jargon for death or mysteriously dead.

On the lower Columbia River, the name was used in conjunction with Indian burial grounds. The peoples indigenous to Hells Canyon were Nez Perce, but regional trading among the diverse Indian tribes led to certain words common to the languages of many tribes. It is thought that Memaloose may indeed be one of these shared words.

When trappers and settlers explored the area in the early 1800s, the local Indians referred to this area as Memaloose Meadows, but, unfortunately, the significance of the name Memaloose, in relation to this specific site, has been lost.

In distinct contrast with the numerous village sites in the bottom of Hells Canyon, Memaloose shows little sign of prehistoric habitation. To add to the mystery, an early day Forest Service employee based in the Hat Creek Lookout, discovered a single Indian grave in the vicinity of the Lookout. The amateur archaeologist opened the grave and discovered a number of stone tools and artifacts indicating this was quite possibly the grave of a prominent person.

Hat Creek Lookout.

Since the Indians lived primarily along the river, and were typically buried in the immediate vicinity of their villages, it would have taken significant effort and reason for the burial party to climb the mile deep canyon wall to bury this lone Indian. Therefore, the indicators point to a very well respected and/or powerful person buried here.

Memaloose, being the highest point of the surrounding terrain, and overlooking the mile deep canyon directly below its rim, has a hauntingly ethereal quality about it. Your instincts tell you that this has been and still is a significant place. The New Age folks may refer to the area as an energy vortex, while the local cowboys don't talk much about the hair rising on the back of their necks as they ride their horses, reverently silent, through Memaloose Meadows.

ORIGIN OF NAME HAT CREEK - Two different versions of the origin of the name Hat Creek exist. One version claims that in the 1890s, **Alex Warnock's** horse began bucking and knocked Alex's hat off near the creek. The hat couldn't be found for quite some time. Eventually Alex's stepfather found it and hung it on a tree where it remained for over a year.

A more plausible story claims that a rancher with the initials H.A.T. marked the boundaries of his ranch by carving his initials on trees. Subsequently, it became known as Hat Creek.

HUNTING & FISHING: The Memaloose area is well known for its fine elk hunting. One or more outfitters use Memaloose as their base. For more information, contact:

Oregon Department of Fish and Wildlife
Box 59
Portland, Oregon 97207
(503)229-5403

MAPS, LOCAL CONDITIONS, AND INFORMATION:

Airport Information:
Forest Air Officer
60131 Pierce Road
La Grande, Oregon 97850
(503)963-7171

Maps and forest information:
Wallowa-Whitman National Forest
Box 907
Baker City, Oregon 97814
(503)523-6391

For more information, refer to the Hells Canyon overview on page I-3.

MIDWAY

HIGHLIGHT ✈ *An Idaho boom town on the decline; but unlike those based on gold fever, Midway's boom and bust was based on the splitting of the atom.*

AIRPORT DESCRIPTION:
The Midway runway has something for everyone. The east end starts out with gray round river gravel, (presumably left over from the decomposed pavement). The gray gravel gives way to red volcanic cinders from a nearby crater, and this turns into off-white decomposed volcanic

Main Street Atomic City, Idaho, 1993.

ash at the western end. The west end looks like it could be a real mudhole if it were wet. All in all though, the runway is in reasonably good shape.

The tiedowns exist but are difficult to find due to overgrown grasses and tumbleweeds. They are on the south side of the strip, past the windsock, about where the red section of the runway begins.

SERVICES & LODGING: Fackrell's Texaco, downtown Atomic City, is a combination post office, bar, store, gas station, motel, and trailer park. In their spare time the owners also operate the town well and turn irrigation pivots on and off. They don't offer cooked meals, but have a good supply of jerkey, Twinkies, and assorted chips and soft drinks. For years, this has been the watering hole of workers from the nearby Idaho National Engineering Laboratory. However, after the road from Arco to Blackfoot (hence the name "Midway" between two towns) was relocated to bypass the town, ongoing layoffs at the INEL have caused the town's population to go from 500 people to about 25.

Lodging is available through Fackrell's Motel for a reasonable $50 per week.

For information and reservations, contact Fackrell's Texaco, Box 71, Atomic City, Idaho 83215 (208)684-4037.

EXPLORING ATOMIC CITY: From the southwest end (the off-white volcanic ash end), follow a dirt road to the south west 1/4 mile until it connects with the old paved highway. Turn left and follow it 1/4 mile into Midway. A small grassy park with a hitching rack is on the left side of the street. **Fackrell's Texaco** is on the right. A few other buildings and mobile homes are scattered around town. Stop in, say "Howdy", and have a cool sarsaparilla.

HISTORY: There was a large influx of settlers to the area during 1910 to 1920, as "locators" rushed in to claim the rich volcanic farm lands. But by 1920, a period of wet weather reverted to its normal desert climate and without water the farms were abandoned. Later, discovery of water in 600 feet deep wells allowed marginally successful farming in the area.

The town was listed on a 1930s map as **Furey.** One report links the "fury" of the desert wind to the origin of the name. However, it's likely the town was named after **Charles H. Furey,** one of the early pioneers of the Lost River. In the harsh

winter of 1889-1890, a heavy snow caused the loss of 60 of Furey's 106 cattle.

In the 1940s, the name of the town was changed to Midway, to reflect its location midway between Arco and Black- foot. In the 1950s, the Atomic Energy Commission brought rapid growth to the town as the Atomic Energy Site was

Fackrells Texaco · combination post office, bar, store, gas station, motel, and trailer park.

being developed. The town grew to 500 people during this period. It was also during this period that the name was changed from Midway to Atomic City.

HUNTING & FISHING: The surrounding desert holds good populations of sage hens, antelope and elk. No hunting is allowed on the adjoining INEL, so make sure you know where you are or you may become the hunted.

MAPS, LOCAL CONDITIONS, AND INFORMATION:

Airport information: Division of Aeronautics, 3483 Rickenbacker St., Boise, Idaho 83705, (208)334-8775.

Local conditions: Fackrell's Texaco, Box 71, Atomic City, ID 83215 (208)684-4037.

For more information, refer to the Arco-Kimama overview on page I-1.

MILE HI

HIGHLIGHT ✈ *Probably the most hazardous mountain airstrip in Idaho and possibly the U.S., Mile Hi sports some of the most beautiful country and best elk hunting imaginable. Don't even consider landing here without a local professional pilot and even then, be damn choosey!*

- - - - -

AIRPORT DESCRIPTION: Mile Hi is situated on the hill directly north of Vines, about a mile up Garden Creek. A large old barn, near the approach end, is still visible. The runway has no markings, windsock, or tiedowns. The Idaho Fish and Game now owns the ranch and the Forest Service owns the airstrip. Maintenance appears to be non-existent.

HISTORY: The **Elliot Brothers** (Joe, Roy, Bert, and Hardrock) were nephews of **"Auntie" Garden** (see Vines). The brothers put in a lot of hard work on the place. They raised cattle, grew vegetables, and built a sawmill to supply the Snowshoe Mine. After the death of their uncle **Kid Garden** in 1918, the Elliot brothers discontinued running cattle on the ranch, but Joe went ahead and homesteaded the place in 1920.

All the brothers eventually left except Hardrock, who lived here until his death from spotted fever in May, 1934. He is buried on a knoll above the buildings. The ranch was then sold to **Lafe and Emma Cox.**

The Coxes built a hunting lodge on the ranch in the 1940s in order to guide hunting and fishing parties. For years, Lafe supplemented his income with the Clover mail route. They built an airstrip on the ranch to accommodate their guests but the strip was and is short, mountainous, and dangerous. Remains of airplanes are scattered over the area. Story has it, that a Ford Tri-motor was successfully taken in and out of Mile Hi. It gives one a great appreciation for the talents of the early day backcountry pilots. The airstrip is currently seeing some use by backcountry charter services.

The Coxes sold the Mile Hi Ranch to the Idaho Fish and Game in the 1950s and it is used as a winter game range.

Payette Forest Air Officer, Box 1026, McCall, Idaho 83638 (208)634-0746.

(Above) Big Game Hunting out of the Mile Hi Ranch. Circa 1940.
Courtesy: Idaho County Free Press.
(Below) Lafe and Emma Cox's Mile Hi Ranch. Circa 1940.
Courtesy: Idaho County Free Press.

MOOSE CREEK

HIGHLIGHT ✈ *A Selway-Bitterroot Wilderness gem. Don't miss Moose Creek for the finest wilderness airplane camping and fishing for native cutthroat.*

- - - - -

AIRPORT DESCRIPTION: The Moose Creek airstrip lies deep in a narrow canyon within the Selway-Bitterroot Wilderness at the confluence of the Selway River and Moose Creek. Due to the confines of the canyon walls, the Division of Aeronautics suggests an approach that maximizes the turn-around areas. However, much of the approach is in the blind and it's necessary to announce your position and intentions on 122.9. Summer temperatures can exceed 100 degrees. Under these conditions, the effects of density altitude on aircraft performance become profound. Plan your arrival and departure for early morning or late evening. Tiedowns are located near the Ranger Station and the campsites.

This is one of our favorite backcountry destinations. The runways are well manicured turf, with RWY 1-19 being relatively long (4100' X 250'), by Idaho backcountry standards.

CAMPING: The **Moose Creek Campground** is situated high on a bluff overlooking the river confluence below, adjacent to the southwest edge of RWY 4. Potable water can be found at the Guard Station and five well spaced campsites offer picnic tables, barbecue grills, and pit toilets.

The Forest Service is currently (1993) undertaking an environment analysis to determine the future of the Moose Creek Airstrip camping facilities and the maintenance thereof. We hope a cooperative maintenance effort between the U.S. Forest Service and general aviation volunteers can restore the luster to this beautiful wilderness strip.

EXPLORING MOOSE CREEK: Airplane camping season comes early to Moose Creek due to its low elevation. While the rest of Idaho is still under snow, early birds can call the airport manager and check conditions. You just might have the place to yourself.

Nearby towering cedars provide a dense canopy and ample cool shade, an ideal spot for pulling up the plane. A short excursion from the southwest end of the airstrip off the bluff, takes you down to two suspension bridges, one crossing Moose Creek and the other crossing the Selway.

An interesting description of the area and the men that made it that way is accounted for at the Guard Station historical exhibit.

The horses are corralled by electrical fences, so use caution when crossing. If you happen to plan a short trip out for supplies, you might ask the Forest Service employees at the Guard Station if they could use a cold drink. The only supplies they receive come in by way of a 22 mile packtrain.

HUNTING & FISHING: Fishing regulations around these parts might sound a little confusing, but in the long run, a small price to pay. As if the beautiful clear tumbling waters of the granitic streams aren't themselves a treasure, lurking in the quiet pools behind the river's boulders is the Western Slope Cutthroat.

He lives in the abundantly food rich waters of Eastern Idaho, Western Wyoming, and Southern Montana. He may decide today that the only morsel that will do will be the emerging green drakes, between the sizes of three and four millimeters. And, only a certain hue will do.

On the other hand, the Western Slope Cutthroat often takes the first meal that comes along, because it may be his last. In short, he is a survivor. Unfortunately, his aggressiveness has earned him the reputation of being "dumb" and the fishing pressure has taken its toll.

Attempts to transplant the Yellowstone Cutthroat to Western Slope environment failed miserably. The Yellowstone simply starved to death while his "dumb" cousin survived.

Thus, policies of catch and release and slot limits are enforced to prevent harvesting of sexually active fish and to ultimately restore the populations of the fish most suited to the environment, the wild Western Slope Cutthroat.

MAPS, LOCAL CONDITIONS, AND INFORMATION:

Nez Perce Forest Air Officer, 319 E. Main Street, Grangeville, Idaho 83530 (208)983-1964.

Moose Creek Ranger District, Box 464, Grangeville, Idaho 83530 (208)983-2712.

Selway Bitterroot Wilderness Map ($2.00), Selway Bitterroot Primer ($2.00) are both available from Moose Creek Ranger District.

MURPHY HOT SPRINGS

HIGHLIGHT ✈ *1940s desert resort based around natural hot springs. Pool and private hot baths. Lodging with Restaurant/bar/gas station.*

- - - - -

AIRPORT DESCRIPTION: This north/south turf covered runway sits on a high plateau and straddles the Idaho/Nevada border. It is well marked with a windsock and the tiedowns are at the south end. To the north you can see miles and miles of the flat, indistinguishable Bruneau desert leading to the deep scar of the Jarbidge River.

TRANSPORTATION: Harry Showalter at the **Murphy Hot Springs Resort,** will pick you up at the airport if you call in advance (208)857-2233 or give him a low buzz (not recommended). A mountain bike gives you a 2.5 mile exhilarating experience racing down the steep canyon road. Harry will offer to give the less athletic a ride back up the road to the airport.

SERVICES & LODGING: Murphy Hot Springs Resort - originally known as **"Kitty's Hot Hole"**, is the only game in town. Murphy is dead and gone but his name lives on. When 80 year old **Harry Showalter** went fishing one day, he took a wrong turn and ended up at Murphy Hot Springs - 70 miles from his original destination. He liked it so much he bought it.

The resort centers around a natural hot water swimming pool and several private hot pools (available for $3.00 per day-unlimited usage).

Harry Showalter, manager of the Murphy Hot Springs Resort.

Nine "miners" cabins (no plumbing) and four trailers range in price from $21.40 to $34.78 a night. There is also a restaurant/bar/gas station, the gathering place for visitors and local cowboys for miles around.

The **Tsawhawbitts Ranch** is 17 miles away in Nevada...in the mountain ghost town of **Jarbidge** at an elevation of 6,200 feet. This spot carries the distinction of having the last stagecoach robbery in the United States. A canyon with mountains on all sides, Jarbidge is surrounded by the Humbolt National Forest and bordered by a river of the same name.

The beautifully landscaped ranch consists of the main lodge, two cabins, and breathtaking panoramic views.

Recreation includes hunting, fishing, pack trips, kayaking, trail biking, jeep touring, exploring for Indian treasures, gold hunting, and gambling. For information, reservations, and guest airport shuttle, contact Krinn McCoy (702)488-2338.

EXPLORING MURPHY HOT SPRINGS: Soaking up the hot sun and relaxing in the natural spring water was the main attraction for us. Easy does it out here where Idaho's working cowboys provide authenticity that the Old West is alive and well. The Tsawhabitts Ranch provides the opportunity for roughing it in style.

HISTORY: **Jarbidge** is a strange name. Its origin is even stranger. Jarbidge is the twisted spelling and pronouncing of Jahabich (Jah-Hah-Bitch) and the word is also a confused way of saying Tsawhawbitts (Tuh-Saw-Haw-Bits).

Main Street Jarbidge, Nevada. Circa 1908. Courtesy: Idaho State Historical Society.

Tsawhawbitts was the name of an evil cannibalistic giant who, according to local Indian legend, roamed the mountains and valleys capturing people, putting them into a basket, then returning to Jarbidge Canyon to eat them.

G-134

There is archaeological evidence of Indians having lived in nearby mountain and valley areas. There is no evidence of their presence in the canyon proper.

Lost Sheepherder Mine - In the 1880s a sheepherder claimed he found gold in the Jarbidge Canyon, guarded by a skeleton with a pick and rifle. When he and his boss tried to return to the place, one of them became very ill and turned

Jarbidge, Nevada tent town during gold strike.
Circa 1908. Courtesy: Idaho State Historical Society.

back while the other went on alone. He also became sick and barely made it to the lost mine. He picked up a few handfuls of gold samples and returned to Mountain Home where he died. The surviving prospector could not be persuaded to go back to the canyon. There is still controversy as to whether or not the "Lost Sheepherder Mine" was ever found again.

Jarbidge Gold Rush - In the spring of 1909, Dave Bourne and companions located a very rich outcropping of gold ore on the side of a gulch. By the end of the year, 71 claims had been filed and the camp's population swelled to 1,500 people. Bourne was quoted by newspapers as claiming that $27 billion of gold was in sight! But when the reality of the situation became apparent, all but 300 men abandoned the town.

The gold ore was of a type that made it difficult for the small operator to do any good. However, during 1913 to 1937, two large mining companies were successful in recovering gold where the small miner had failed. The Elkoro and the Elko Prince Mining companies removed, by today's prices, $155 billion dollars in gold and silver from 90,000 feet of underground tunnels.

LAST HORSE DRAWN STAGE ROBBERY IN THE NATION: In a snowstorm on December 5, 1916, townspeople went out looking for an overdue mail stage. When the stage was found on the outskirts of town, the searchers also discovered the dead body of driver Fred Searcy. Almost three thousand dollars were missing. A massive manhunt began.

Ben Kuhl and Ed "Cut-Lip Swede" Beck were arrested and convicted of the crime. Kuhl, a petty criminal and horse thief, was convicted by a bloody palm print found on a slashed mail bag. It was the first time a palm print had been admissible evidence leading to a conviction. Kuhl served 28 years in prison, and his cohort "Cut-Lip Swede" served six years.

Restaurant/gas station at Murphy Hot Springs Resort - watering hole for some of America's few remaining cowboys.

HUNTING & FISHING:

Information on hunting and fishing in Nevada: Nevada Department of Wildlife, Box 30040, Reno, Nevada 89520-3040, (702)688-1500.

Information on hunting and fishing in Idaho:, Idaho Department of Fish and Game, Box 25, Boise, Idaho 83707, (208)334-3700.

MAPS, LOCAL CONDITIONS, AND INFORMATION:

Airport conditions: Division of Aeronautics, (208)334-8775.

Lodging and accommodations:, Tsawhawbitts Ranch Bed & Breakfast, Krinn & Chuck McCoy, Box 90, Jarbidge, Nevada 89826 (702)488-2338. Murphy Hot Springs, Anita & Harry Showalter, Rogerson, Idaho 83302 (208)857-2233.

OROGRANDE

HIGHLIGHT ✈ *Historic mining community. A long neglected airstrip that may soon be renovated as a wilderness reliever airstrip. Check for future recreational improvements.*

- - - - -

AIRPORT DESCRIPTION: This airstrip has been located here for a long time but has seen limited use in recent years. The Forest Service is presently (summer 1993) working with the Idaho Aviation Association and the State of Idaho towards developing a restoration/management plan for this strip. New growth pines have encroached on the edges of the runway and narrowed its width to approximately 50 feet. Cable tie downs are located on the south end of the airstrip but ropes are missing.

Proposed plans include restoring the original dimensions of the strip, replacing the windsock, installing vehicle barriers, raking rocks, and installing a vault toilet near the existing tie down area. Further site development, including picnic tables and fire rings, might occur in the future if use would warrant.

Looking north toward the Buffalo Hump.
Courtesy: Idaho Historical Society.

CAMPING: There are presently no designated camp sites on the airstrip, but as noted above, that could change in the future.

The Forest Service has a **vacation cabin**, located at the south end of the airstrip that they rent out in the $20-$25 a night range. For cabin information and reservations, contact: Elk Creek Ranger Station, Box 416, Elk City, Idaho 83525 (208)842-2245.

Five Mile Recreation Site is located 1 mile south of the airstrip on Crooked Creek. It has four campsites with pit toilets, picnic tables, and fire rings. Potable water is not available.

HISTORY: The name "Orogrande" is spanish for "coarse gold". Unfortunately, no one is quite sure why this name was applied to this settlement. The same name has also been applied to a settlement in Upper Loon Creek and one near Pierce, Idaho.

Buffalo Lake and an old miner's cabin in foreground. Circa 1944.
Courtesy: Idaho State Historical Society.

The first gold strike at this Orogrande was attributed to a Frenchman who went by the name of Pete Johnson (universally presumed to have had another name) some time around 1894. Johnson built a cabin on Fish Lake in 1913 and disappeared two years later while on a hunting trip. After several years, a skeleton and rusty rifle were found and identified as Johnson's. His friends then put up a sign on his abandoned cabin, stating it was all right to stay there as long as you left more than you took.

Boasting a population of about 50, Orogrande became the trading center for the Buffalo Hump mining district in the early 1900s. Three two story hotels provided lodging for the miners. An open pit mine and a dredge were in operation during the 1930s and 1940s. Even today, the scars from the dredge are left behind on the valley floor.

The Orogrande airstrip was originally constructed by private individuals (holders of unpatented mining claims) in 1959 or 1960. The Strip is located adjacent to the Crooked River on old dredge tailings.

HUNTING & FISHING: Orogrande is the gateway to 25 mountain lakes in the **Gospel Hump** area. Fish Lake (not to be confused with Fish Lake Airport) and Rainbow Lake, both located in the headwaters of Crooked River, were the only two lakes in the Buffalo Hump country that were naturally stocked with fish. All other lakes were barren.

The early knowledge of the abundance of fish in nearby Fish Lake was well known. An 1899 newspaper account reported large catches of trout were being made daily at Fish Lake.

MAPS, LOCAL CONDITIONS, AND INFORMATION:

Elk City Ranger District, Box 416, Elk City, Idaho 83525 (208)842-2245.

Mail Stage coming into Buffalo Hump.
Horses are using snowshoes in about nine feet of snow.
Circa 1900. Courtesy: Idaho State Historical Society.

PINE

HIGHLIGHT ✈ *A lakeside airstrip featuring fishing, boating, waterskiing, and local resorts. Fly in for banana cream pie and the Pine Lodge will come pick you up.*

- - - - -

AIRPORT DESCRIPTION: The approach to 34 is directly over Anderson Ranch Reservoir, as the runway parallels the shore line. The surface is turf and gravel. The runway is often depicted and described as having a dogleg in the north end. However, the runway has since been straightened.

TRANSPORTATION: There is no courtesy car available. If you plan on enjoying the services of the local resorts and lodges, you can call ahead for a pickup. Call in advance though, because there are no phones at the airstrip. A mountain bike is the preferred mode of transportation around the lake and resort.

SERVICES & LODGING: Pine Resort is the classic Idaho cafe/bar. Located 1.3 miles north of the airstrip windsock, the owners, Ken and Gloria DeThorne go out of their way to make visitors comfortable. Ken and staff at the Pine Lodge provide a wealth of local information which they share freely...a great place to visit and get oriented after you first arrive. The long hardwood bar, satellite tv, cushioned bar stools, and subdued lighting offer a haven from the rigors of fishing, water skiing, swimming, etc.

Awaiting all weary recreationists is the DeThorne's fabulous banana cream pie. Bob Hannah, from Hannah Field in Caldwell, flies his Super Cub here just for this indulgence. For information (or ordering pies) contact: Ken & Gloria DeThorne, Pine Resort, HC-87, Box 200, Pine, Idaho 83647. (208)653-2323.

Nester's Mountain Mart is located just north of the Pine Resort and has all the items that you forgot to bring and a few you probably wouldn't want to bring. They have gas, groceries, ice cold beverages, t-shirts, sweatshirts, hunting and fishing licenses and supplies, liquor store, copy and fax service. They also have a private campground on the river (see Camping) and two cabins. Open 7 days a week, (208)653-2222.

Deer Creek Lodge is located on the east shore of the reservoir, 3.4 miles from the airstrip. They have rooms available for $29.00 per night, a cafe and bar, R.V. parking, tent campsites, and a boat dock. The fish sandwich I had for lunch was about as good as I've had in long time. The new owners are were very hospitable and anxious to please. Deer Creek Lodge, Howard & Audrey McKinney, (208)653-2454.

Main Street Pine, Idaho. Circa 1900. Courtesy: Idaho State Historical Society.

Fall Creek Resort & Marina is on the Fall Creek inlet to Anderson Ranch Reservoir, about 10 miles from the airport. It is a 10 room hotel with restaurant/lounge. You can enjoy dining and your favorite beverage on the deck overlooking the Cove. They offer 30 RV spaces, 10 rooms, health club and showers. Sixteen foot fishing boats with motors are available to rent for $50 a day. They specialize in individual and small group functions, club or company parties, reunions, seminars, weddings and receptions. Rooms start at $45 a night. For information and reservations call: (208)653-2242.

CAMPING: Many options present themselves, for the camping sites are plentiful.

**Pine Campground is located 0.7 miles south of the airstrip windsock on the Anderson Ranch Reservoir shore line. It is in an open setting and has 7 campsites with shaded picnic tables, fire rings, pit toilets, a boat ramp, two piers, and garbage service. Drinking water is not available. It is jointly provided by Elmore County Waterways Commission and the USDA Forest Service.

**Nester's Campground is a private campground in a lovely timbered setting along the river's inlet to the reservoir. From the airstrip windsock, go north 1.5 miles. The road passes the one room school house (no longer in service) at 0.9 miles and the cemetery at 1.0 mile. The Pine Resort is 1.3 miles, continue on north for another 0.2 miles to the Nester's Mountain Mart for camping information. It has all the amenities plus showers for $4.50 per night. For more information contact Nester's Mountain Mart (208)653-2222.

Deer Creek Lodge Campground is a private campground located on the east side of the reservoir. From the airstrip, it is visible directly across the water. Follow the road to the north around the shore line 3.4 miles or call ahead and arrange a pickup from the airstrip. They have all the amenities plus showers, cafe, bar, boat dock, motel, (see Services & Lodging) and some camping supplies. Campsites are $4.50 per night.

Pine Campground on the shore of Anderson Ranch Reservoir.

Dog Creek Campground is located about 6 miles north of the airstrip (past Pine Resort on FH61). This is a Forest Service Campground and a fee is charged. There are 12 campsites with tables, fire pits, drinking water, and pit toilets in a timbered setting along the river.

Elks Flat Campground is just past the Dog Creek Campground. It is a Forest Service Campground and a fee is charged. It requires a reservation and has drinking water and pit toilets. It is along the river in an open setting with fishing, floating, rafting, kayaking, and swimming. Reservations can be made by calling MISTIX (800)283-2267.

EXPLORING PINE: Most of the land lies within the Idaho Batholith, a large and highly erosive geologic formation. Through uplift, faulting, and subsequent dissection by stream-cutting action, a mountainous landscape has developed. The average precipitation ranges from 15 inches at lower elevations to 70 inches at higher elevations.

This land supports an evergreen forest that includes pure or mixed stands of ponderosa pine, Douglas-fir, Engelmann spruce, lodgepole pine and subalpine fir. Brush grass or grass are found in the non timbered areas. There are many different animal species and places for animals to live. The forest contains large areas of summer range for big game species, such as mule deer and Rocky Mountain elk. Trout are native to most streams and lakes.

The Anderson Ranch Dam, completed in 1950, was once the largest earth-filled dam in the world with a structural height of 456 feet. The backwaters of the dam form the Anderson Ranch Reservoir, 17 miles long, with 50 miles of shore line.

Water skiing is a popular sport on the reservoir because of the ideal water temperatures and the calm water in the mornings and late summer evenings. Fishing is the overriding attraction to Anderson with numerous species and large fish.

The Trinity Mountain area, about 20 miles northwest of Pine, is a beautiful alpine area with numerous lakes and streams for fishing. It also has hiking trails and a lookout perched atop the mountain which offers spectacular views. No motorized boats are allowed on the lakes and the fishing is great with brook trout being the mainstay of the lakes. The area also has well maintained trails for hiking and mountain bike riding.

HUNTING & FISHING: The reservoir is open to fishing year-round and near-record smallmouth bass, rainbow trout, kamloop, dolly varden, chinook, and kokanee salmon have been taken. Fish can successfully be taken from the bank or by lake trolling. Excellent stream fishing exists above and below the reservoir. Fishing boats can be rented from the Fall Creek Lodge & Marina.

To maximize your fishing time, you might talk to one of the retired locals. They seem anxious to share their wealth of fishing lore and may even invite you along to share their success. The owners of Pine Resort or Deer Creek Lodge may be able to put you into contact with one of these "fishing gurus".

After you catch that once in a lifetime lunker, take it to the Pine Resort or Deer Creek Lodge and have it weighed. They have an ongoing fishing contest with monthly and annual prizes awarded for the best fish. There is no entry fee for the contest.

MAPS, LOCAL CONDITIONS, AND INFORMATION:

Airport Conditions: Division of Aeronautics, 3483 Rickenbacker St., Boise, Idaho 83705 (208)334-8775.

Maps and Forest/Camping information: Forest Supervisor, Boise National Forest, 1750 Front Street, Boise, Idaho 83702 (208)364-4100.

PITTSBURG

HIGHLIGHT → *Hells Canyon airstrip on the banks of the Snake River. Improved campsites across the river if you can hitch a ride on a passing boat.*

- - - - -

AIRPORT DESCRIPTION: The landing strip is located on the Oregon side of the Snake River across from Pittsburg Landing. The intersecting runways and relative openness of the canyon make Pittsburg one of the better airstrips in the canyon. However, both runways are quite short and require special skills and aircraft. An administrative building, surrounded by trees, is located at the north end of the bar.

There is no windsock or runway markings. Use caution for animals on the runway. Check with the Wallowa-Whitman National Forest for current availability of the airstrip for public use. Call (509)758-0616.

CAMPING: There are presently no developed camp sites on the airstrip, but primitive camping is permitted. Potable water and a pit toilet are available at the administrative building. **Fishtrap Bar**, located 1/2 mile upstream, is listed as having toilets and campsites.

***Pittsburg Landing, on the Idaho side of the river, is under development with 28 campsites, toilets, potable water, picnic tables, fire rings, and sun shades. Unfortunately, getting across the river is a problem. Using your most courteous efforts (or offers of cold beverages), you can usually hitch a ride across the river from a passing boater.

HISTORY: Story has it the name "Pittsburg" came from a sternwheel riverboat that ran upriver from Lewiston during the highwater of the spring of 1877. The boat was carrying troops to intercept the fleeing Nez Perce Indians. While waiting for the Indians to show up, the water subsided and grounded the riverboat. Supposedly, the boat remained here for a year until the next spring runoff. In the meantime, the troops constructed a road over the saddle to the Salmon River to bring in supplies.

G-144

However, this boat story doesn't hold water because the Nez Perce War of 1877 is well documented, and General Howard made no mention of this incident. I don't blame him. I wouldn't either.

Another version of the origin of the name Pittsburg comes from the reference to local mining investment money which came from Pittsburgh, Pennsylvania.

A thin vein of coal found in the area and the association of coal with Pittsburgh, Pennsylvania offers another plausible version.

In 1900, a wagon road was built from Whitebird over Pittsburg Saddle to Pittsburg Landing and the Thomason ferry. This road and ferry system led to the filing of 21 homestead entries in the vicinity. The ferry operated until 1933.

Steamboat "Imnaha" at Eureka on the Oregon side of Snake River, near the junction of the Imnaha and Snake River. The "Imnaha" was wrecked later in 1903. Courtesy: Idaho State Historical Society.

At one time, there were 61 people living in the Pittsburg area. The Forest Service eventually acquired the private holdings as part of the Hells Canyon National Recreation Area.

HUNTING & FISHING: Because the airstrip sits on the Oregon side of the river, it requires an Oregon fishing license to fish from the bank. Even if you wade into the water, and you're standing on the bottom, you need an Oregon license. However, if you are fishing from a boat on the Oregon side, an Idaho license will work.

MAPS, LOCAL CONDITIONS, AND INFORMATION:

Pittsburg Airstrip & Oregon side camping information: Hells Canyon National Recreation Area, Clarkston, Washington (509)758-0616.

Pittsburg Landing camping information (Idaho side): Hells Canyon National Recreation Area , Box 832, Riggins, Idaho 83549 (208)628-3916.

Oregon Hunting & Fishing Information: Oregon Dept. of Fish & Wildlife, Box 59, Portland, OR 97207-0059 (503-229-5403.

For more information, refer to the Hells Canyon overview on page I-3.

PRIEST LAKE

HIGHLIGHT ✦ *Access to several first class lake resorts and shore line campsites. Huge catchable trout lurk in these deep panhandle lakes. Scenic beyond belief.*

- - - - -

AIRPORT DESCRIPTION: Located two miles west of Kalispell Bay on Priest Lake, and three miles south of Nordman, the US Forest Service Priest Lake Airport provides recreational access to the western side of Priest Lake. Tiedowns are provided. Be sure and call for current runway conditions. The runway turf becomes quite soft after it rains.

TRANSPORTATION: Provided for guests of Grandview Resort (208)443-2433, 6 mi.; guests of Hills Resort call (208)443-2551, 5 mi.

SERVICES & LODGING: Elkins on Priest Lake - HCO 1, Box 40, Nordman, ID, 83848, (208)443-2432. Two miles east of Nordman, halfway up the west side of Priest Lake. 28 cabins, $70-180, LH, R, P, CU, CC, AB.

Grandview Lodge & Resort - HCO 1, Box 48, Nordman, ID, 83848, (208)443-2433. 36 units, $69-145, LH, R, CU, TV, SP, CC, AB, MR(25).

Hill's Resort - HCR 5, Box 168A, (208)443-2551. On Luby Bay. 52 units, $80-225, P, TV, AB, R, CU, CC, MR(125), PH.

Kaniksu Resort - HCO 1, Box 152, Nordman, ID, (208)443-2609. On the west shore of Priest Lake. 77 camp sites, 14 units, $10.50 - 100, LH, R, P, CU, TV, CC, AB, L/R, L, HU, DS, SH, MM.

Outlet Bay Resort - HC 5, Box 138, Priest Lake, ID, 83586, (208)443-2444. 7 units, $45-150, LH, R, CU, CC, AB.

Showboat Lodge - Box 11, Coolin, ID 83821 (208)443-2191. On southeast shore of Priest Lake at Coolin. 5 campsites, 9 units, $14-45, HA, R, P, CU, TV, CC, AB, MR, HU, DS.

CAMPING: There are no camping facilities at the Priest Lake Airport but there are several public campgrounds on the lake itself. Listed are four of the closest public campgrounds to the airstrip. For additional camping and hiking information, visit the Forest Service Guard Station at the airport or the visitor center at Luby Bay.

**Kalispel Island - From the airstrip, go south on Highway 57 about 1/4 mile and turn left on USFS Road 1338. Kalispell Bay lies less than a mile ahead. Kalispel Island is directly off shore and accessible only by boat. It has 31 units in five camping areas, with picnic tables and pit toilets. Potable water is not available. No fee is charged.

Priest Lake, Idaho. Courtesy: Idaho State Historical Society.

**Luby Bay Campground is along the shoreline south of Kalispel Bay. Follow the directions to Kalispel Island and turn right (south) to Luby Bay. A fee is charged and reservations can be made by calling MISTIX at (800)283-2267. User fees and a service charge are paid via major credit card or check. 52 campsites are available with toilets, picnic tables, stoves, and potable water. A visitor information center is also located here.

Osprey and ****Outlet Campgrounds - From Luby Bay Campground, continue along the shore line another mile to Osprey and then Outlet Campgrounds. Osprey has 17 campsites with drinking water, toilets, picnic tables, and stoves. Outlet has 28 campsites also with drinking water, toilets, picnic tables, and stoves. Both areas are non-reservation fee-charged campgrounds.

EXPLORING PRIEST LAKE: This 25-mile long lake is actually two lakes, connected by a scenic and slow moving 2.5 mile river called the Thorofare. The 26,000 acres of clear, pure, sparkling water makes this lake one of the most spectacular in the world. Eighty miles of shoreline surround the lake.

Tall majestic trees cover the hills, surrounding the lake. Logging is one of the area's most important industries. The Selkirk Mountains, including jagged Chimney Rock, can be seen from the shore of Priest Lake.

There are excellent beaches for picnickers and swimmers and it is perfect for water sports. Many well-marked hiking trails lead to acres of luscious wild huckleberries. During the spring, summer, and fall mushrooms abound.

Nell Shipman, silent screen star, made movies in the Priest Lake area during the 1920s. Shipman Point, on the lake, is named in her honor.
Courtesy: Idaho Historical Society.

The **Priest Lake Museum/Visitor Center** is housed in a log cabin built by the CCC in 1935 and has exhibits on local history. Open daily Memorial Day-Labor Day from 10-4. For information contact the Priest Lake Museum/Visitor Center, Box 44, Coolin, Idaho 83821 (208)443-2676.

HISTORY: **Nel Shipman**, famous silent screen star, novelist, and script writer moved her entourage of thirty persons to Priest Lake in the 1920s and filmed several classic movies here. Her movie camp, Lionhead Lodge, was located on a promontory known today as Shipman Point.

The grounds served as corral for two dog teams, a herd of horses, and a menagerie of other assorted animals. Most of the supplies and animals were brought across the lake from Coolin by steam barge. Dog sleds were used in the winter.

During the four year production stay (1923-1926), the film company made several movies on location. Among them were *White Water, The Grubstake, Trail of the North Wind, The Light on the Lookout,* and *Love Tree.*

Shipman's director got gangrene from frost-bitten toes, then suffered a mental breakdown. The creditors moved in. Nell had to kill the horses to feed her dogs and zoo animals. Finally the San Diego Zoo agreed to take the surviving animals, and paid transportation costs to ship them South.

The Atlantic Monthly serialized the story of the movie-making hardships in a May-July, 1925 series titled *"The Movie That Could Not Be Screened."* Nell Shipman died in 1970.

HUNTING & FISHING: Priest Lake has become famous as a producer of United States record fish caught on rod and reel. The U.S. record Mackinaw lake trout weighed 57 lbs. 8 oz. and the U.S. record Kokanee weighed 6 lbs. 9 3/4 oz. Other species of fish in the lake are Dolly Varden and cutthroat and in the streams one may find rainbow trout and eastern brook.

Kokanee populations have dropped in recent years so no longer does Priest Lake produce 50 lb. Macks but it does produce great numbers of fish in the 4-8 lb. range, with lunkers coming in at up to 30 lbs. Surface lines in the spring and fall will catch the smaller fish, but the real big fish normally succumb to deeply trolled lures.

MAPS, LOCAL CONDITIONS, AND INFORMATION:

Airport information: Panhandle Forest Air Officer, Coeur d'Alene Dispatch, US Forest Service, 11403 Airport Drive, Hayden Lake, Idaho 83835.

Hiking and camping information and detailed maps: Priest Lake Ranger District, HCR 5, Box 207, Priest River, Idaho 83856 (208)443-2512.

SALMON BAR

HIGHLIGHT ✈ *Hells Canyon airstrip on the Oregon shore at the confluence of the Salmon and Snake Rivers.*

- - - - -

AIRPORT DESCRIPTION: Salmon Bar sits on the Oregon side of the Snake River across from the mouth of the Salmon River. A hazardous depression exists on the east edge of the runway. It may or may not be marked. The Forest Service plans on doing some maintenance on this strip to make it easier to identify, e.g., runway end markers, mowing, brush removal, etc.

As John Plummer and I were doing the aerial photography of Salmon Bar, we were unable to identify where the runway was. Thanks to the help of **Ken Hessel**, USFS, and **Darell and Rusty Bentz**, we have identified on the aerial photographs the approximate location of the runway.

CAMPING: Camping is limited to some unimproved sites on the river beaches downstream from the airstrip. Be aware of the widely fluctuating water levels of the river and don't camp below the high water mark. There is a pit toilet in the vicinity.

HISTORY: Owned by successful businessman and Oregon State Congressman, **Jay Dobbin**, Salmon Bar was used as a sheep shearing ranch in the 1920s. Large wooden shearing sheds were used by Basque sheepherders to shear thousands of sheep. The wool was then shipped downriver by boat.

The **Pullman Mine** is located on the banks of the Salmon River just upstream from the confluence of the Salmon and Snake River. The mine shipped a few loads of copper ore to Lewiston in the 1920s. Today, the mine tailings and some old equipment are still visible.

Eureka Bar, located two miles upstream from Salmon Bar, was the center of much mining activity in 1903. 150 men were working here building a smelter, a sawmill, a two story hotel, a grocery store, and post office. A nearby saloon up Eureka Creek led to the following story:

Chieftain, July 16, 1903

The magnificently rugged Hells Canyon. Courtesy: Idaho State Historical Society.

Lewiston Tribune - "A report reached here last night stating that the tent saloon on Deer Creek (later known as Eureka Creek) in the Imnaha district, had been blown up with dynamite by some cowboys, who believed they had a grievance against the proprietor, who is known amongst the miners as 'Shorty'. The place was first established at Imnaha, but the boys became tired of it last fall and placing a box of dynamite under the joint suddenly started it skyward.

This was enough to convince "Shorty" that he was not wanted there so he moved to Deer Creek, where he has since been running his place. The men who have patronized the place say that only the vilest kind of liquor was handled and that it was the custom to fill a man up on the poison and then take his money away from him. The night the place was blown up there was a miner there who had drawn his wages that day and when he returned to the mine that night he had neither money or watch, nor had he any recollection of what had become of his belongings.

As told by an eye witness, the place was running as usual when, without warning, in walked two masked cowboys and ordered everybody to leave the tent. Soon after the tent was vacated there was a loud report that was heard for miles and there was not enough left of the joint to tell what it had been. Cigars, tobacco, broken bottles, and all kinds of canned goods were scattered over the hillside, but the wily booze seller had been so badly scared that he did not stop to see what he could save, but hurried to a place of safety and has not yet returned. It is understood that the miners will not tolerate any institution that will rob them of their wages and give them nothing in return."

MAPS, LOCAL CONDITIONS, AND INFORMATION:

Hells Canyon Natl. Recreation Area, Box 699, 2535 Riverside Drive, Clarkston, WA 99403 (509)758-0616.

For more information, refer to the Hells Canyon overview on page I-3.

Salmon Bar work party. Courtesy: Ken Hessel.

SHEARER

HIGHLIGHT ✈ *Wilderness airstrip on the banks of the Selway River. Secluded, private, and difficult strip with great native cutthroat fishing.*

· · · · ·

AIRPORT DESCRIPTION: Lying deep within the 1.2 million acre Selway Bitterroot Wilderness, the Shearer airstrip is the epitome of the wilderness flying experience. The 2000' airstrip sits adjacent to the Selway River. Take a good look at the strip from above and memorize the approach and where you need to touch down, as the river makes a pretty good jog on the approach end, obscuring the view until the last minute. White painted rocks identify the runway ends, but are not easily visible when low. The approach end of RWY 18 is displaced due to rough terrain. Don't land short. Don't land long.

The runway surface is mostly covered with grasses - about ankle deep in June. The runway has a good rise at the south end which helps slow the ground roll on landing and accelerates you on takeoff.

Tiedowns are located at the south end near the windsock. This area is used as a loading area. If you park on the hill, make sure to turn your fuel selector valve to a position that doesn't allow the fuel to drain from the high wing to the low wing and out the vent onto the ground. And be doubly sure to return the fuel selector valve to the correct position before takeoff.

The departure route proves to be equally interesting. Climbing terrain at the departure end prevents many airplanes from doing a straight out departure. However, it appears as if the trees have been trimmed to facilitate such a departure.

The alternative is to peel out over the river after lift off and negotiate the abrupt turn in the river channel - low and slow - never an ideal situation.

I would recommend discussing the approach and departure procedures with a professional local pilot and factor in the specific variables of pilot proficiency, airplane performance, density altitude, weather, and loading.

CAMPING: The *Shearer Camp sits on the bank of the Selway River. It is a wilderness camp with no amenities. A portable stove avoids the cooking/wood

gathering/scorched ground-debris problem. Avoid open fires and fire rings. If you must have a fire, build it in a metal fire pan and pack out the debris. This pristine area shows no signs of previous campers. Leave it that way or better.

A small sandy beach on the bank of the river creates a private idyllic setting, only to be disturbed by an occasional passing raft. Tall cedars, Englemann spruce, and Douglas fir are intermixed with open areas of hawthorne, elderberries, and mock orange shrubbery. The grassy meadows are havens for hungry elk.

Setting up camp along the banks of the Selway. "Now let's see, the "A" pole's connected to the "C" pole, or is it the "C" flange?"

EXPLORING SHEARER: If you haven't surmised by now, the Selway is one of my favorite haunts. Perhaps less known than the Middle Fork of the Salmon, it offers exceptional fishing and rafting opportunities.

Of the three main whitewater rivers in Idaho - the Snake, the Salmon, and the Selway, the Selway is the extreme for limited access and wilderness. Dropping 29 feet per mile, the rapids can be mean and tricky. During high water, the waves and holes approach epic proportions.

A permit system for floating the river is in place and is limited to 62 private permits a year. The odds of drawing a permit are slim, but well worth the effort.

For those wishing to take a guided float trip on the Selway, contact: Northwest River Company, Box 403, Boise, Idaho 83701 (208)344-7119.

HUNTING & FISHING: With the ever present threats of acid rain, oil spills, and ground water contamination around the world, it's hard to imagine that an area still exists that is so remote as to have mountain water so pure that its clarity can distort depth perception. What appears to be knee deep water often overflows the tops of your hip boots.

It is this pristine habitat that provides home to the Westslope Cutthroat. Declining water quality has reduced this native trout's historic range by 90 %, and the famous Lochsa (pronounced lock-saw)-Selway river system is one of the remaining strongholds for this fragile and vulnerable fish. This subspecies is predominantly small headed and deep girthed, and is almost too eager to tackle a well-placed lure or fly. The cutthroat average 12"-14" in length with some approaching 22".

Dolly Varden or bull trout and mountain whitefish also are commonly caught on the Selway. For starters, try a

Shearer Camp along the Selway River.

Renegade, Western Coachman, Elk Hair Caddis, Humpy, or my all time favorite, a Brown Hackle/Peacock/Yellow Tail in sizes 12 to 16.

When conditions are right, the fishing is simply phenomenal. Some stretches of water yield trout on every cast. This probably wouldn't be possible without catch and release regulations.

Each of us is responsible for the continued preservation and protection of this very special river. When the time comes to stand up and defend this river, let's not shirk our duty.

MAPS, LOCAL CONDITIONS, AND INFORMATION:

Maps: Nez Perce Forest Headquarters, Route 2, Box 475, Grangeville, Idaho 83530 (208)983-1950.

Airstrip information and local conditions: Moose Creek Ranger District, Box 464, Grangeville, Idaho 83539 (208)983-2712.

Selway River float permits: West Fork Ranger District, Darby, MT 59829 (406)821-3269.

Shearer's grassy meadows tantalize the area's elk.

SIMONDS

HIGHLIGHT ✈ *Very difficult airstrip requiring prior instruction. Used primarily for supplying outfitters during hunting season.*

- - - - -

AIRPORT DESCRIPTION: Simonds Airstrip lies on **Monumental Creek**, about 10 miles upstream from from its confluence with Big Creek. It is on the east side of Monumental Creek at the mouth of Copper Creek. This is a very short, difficult airstrip and demands the guidance of a local charter pilot. It is used frequently during the fall as a drop off/pick up spot for guided hunts.

HISTORY: In 1890, **Claude and Elsie Taylor** located a placer mine here. For 50 years, Taylor and his wife farmed, hunted, and mined here. In 1945, Taylor sold his ranch to **Leon "Cy" Simonds.** Simonds lived here with his wife, Ursula, for 18 years. Simonds had Lafe Cox (See Mile Hi) construct the airstrip with a bulldozer brought down Monumental Creek from Thunder Mountain.

Slim Clark located a mining claim .7 mile downstream from Simonds in the 1930s. Slim built a cabin and stamp mill on the site and sold mining shares on his claim. In the 1960s, Slim was shot to death by the son of one of the stock holders, which ended the mining venture.

MAPS, LOCAL CONDITIONS, AND INFORMATION:

Payette Forest Air Officer, Box 1026, McCall, Idaho 83638 (208)634-0746.

SLATE CREEK

HIGHLIGHT ✈ *Lower Salmon River airstrip known for good steelhead fishing. Historic town known as Freedom was saved from an Indian attack by Nez Perce woman.*

- - - - -

AIRPORT DESCRIPTION: Distinctive because it is the only public airstrip on the Salmon River, Slate Creek is located about 20 miles south of Riggins. The turf covered runway closely parallels the highway and is separated by a power line. However, the grass on the first of July was knee deep. The extra power gained from the relatively low elevation is welcome on takeoff.

The canyon walls begin to open up here to large grass-covered hills. There is farming on some of the more level hillsides. Fields of large round straw bales surround the airstrip before the terrain drops off to the river below. Tiedowns are found near the windsock.

CAMPING: It is just as well that no camping is available at the airport, since it is adjacent to the noisy highway. There is, however, a rest area located 1/4 mile downstream from the airstrip. Shade trees provide a nice setting along the Salmon River for the picnic tables, restrooms, and a boat ramp. RVs often camp here for the river access. Tent camping, while not ideal, is permissible.

EXPLORING SLATE CREEK: Slate Creek Museum - Visitors are invited and welcome to look at many historical items on display at the log cabin museum located in front of the Slate Creek Ranger Station along Highway 95 between White Bird and Riggins.

The two story log cabin was built in 1909 in the Salmon River Canyon. It served as district headquarters until 1917. It then was used as a guard station for fire and trail crews and road crews until 1959. The museum is open 7:30 - 4:00 weekdays.

HISTORY: Slate Creek is a large tributary of the Salmon River. The origin of the name refers to a large "slate bluff" projecting into a bend of the Salmon River, just below the Slate Creek/Salmon River confluence. Though it looks like slate, it is

actually the end of a lava flow containing schist. Mining records refer to the name Slate Creek as early as 1861. The area was favored by early day packers as a wintering place for their horses.

A post office was established in 1870 and named **"Freedom"**, presumably in reference to the freeing of the slaves after the Civil War. The names of Slate Creek and Freedom were apparently used interchangeably through 1875.

The land near the mouth of Slate Creek was purchased by **Charley Cone** in 1874 and used as a way station. Cone established a good relationship with the Nez Perce Indians who patronized his store.

Freedom Post Office at what is now known as Slate Creek.
Courtesy: Idaho State Historical Society.

At the outbreak of the Nez Perce War in 1877, three Nez Perce Indians - **Swan Necklace, Red Moccasin Tops,** and **Shore Crossing** warned the Slate Creek people of the impending battle and advised them to take cover so the Wallowa Indians who didn't know them wouldn't kill them.

Thirty Slate Creek families immediately dug a trench around the Post Office and stood logs on end around it forming a stockade. A Nez Perce Indian woman, **Tolo,** rode all night to Florence to warn the miners of the threat. Twenty-five men left Florence and sought shelter in the newly constructed fort at Slate Creek. The owners of the store distributed $2000 worth of goods to those seeking shelter.

During the War, Nez Perce Indians would appear in force at Slate Creek, but showed no hostilities. In fact, they even appeared under a flag of truce to settle their charge accounts at the store. On one such visitation, Tolo came out of the fort to reprimand the warriors for killing her friend Mrs. Manuel. The warriors responded that this murder was committed by one who was "full of bad whiskey". Tolo told the Indians that she and her sister would stay with the whites as they were her friends, and she refused to go with them.

Tolo's real name was Alblemot, but because of her great addiction to gambling, she was called "Tolo" (Chinook jargon for "wager") by the white settlers. She was universally loved and respected by the whites, and after the war, as a token of gratitude, Tolo was given a land allotment about two miles North of Slate Creek. She was not required to live on the reservation.

In the 1930s, Slate Creek was used as a C.C.C. camp and later as the U.S. Forest Service Slate Creek Ranger Station.

HUNTING & FISHING:

BIG GAME HUNTING - Surrounded by wilderness, national forests, and steep mountain terrain, Salmon River country offers some of the best big game hunting in the United States. Hunt for trophy elk, mule deer, whitetail deer, cougar, black bear, moose, big horn sheep, or mountain goat.

Remote rugged forests provide vast wildlife habitat. Large blocks of public lands offer easy access to prime hunting areas. Do it yourself, or hire the professional expertise of the area's outfitters and guides.

BIRD HUNTING - Upland game bird hunting includes chukar, Hungarian partridge, pheasant, and grouse. Because of the low elevation of the river corridors and perfect habitat, chukar populations thrive. Hunting them from float boats and jetboats provides access to the steep and rocky terrain they love. The lower Salmon River has the earliest opening season for game birds in the country.

View from the Slate Creek Airstrip.

STEELHEAD FISHING - Steelhead fishing here is as good as the hunting. This large anadromous rainbow trout challenges tackle and skill. These hard fighting fish travel 800 miles to get up the Snake and Salmon Rivers. Seasons generally run from September through March.

Fishing for smallmouth bass and trout is also very good in the rivers and streams.

WHITEWATER RAFTING AND JET BOATING - Several outfitters provide jet boat rides, fishing trips, drift boat fishing, and whitewater float trips. For a complete guide contact the North Central Idaho Travel Association, (800)473-3543.

MAPS, LOCAL CONDITIONS, AND INFORMATION:

For airport information: Division of Aeronautics (208)337-8775.

For maps: Hells Canyon National Recreation Area, Box 382, Riggins, Idaho 83549 (208)628-3916.

For information on jet boat trips, drift boat fishing, whitewater float trips, and big game hunting, one of the many outfitters is: Cook's Idaho Outfitters, Box 232, Riggins, Idaho 83549.

During an Indian uprising in 1877, Tolo, a Nez Perce woman, rode from Slate Creek to the mining camp at Florence to warn the miners. Circa 1890. Courtesy: Idaho State Historical Society.

SMILEY CREEK

HIGHLIGHT ✈ *High mountain valley airstrip with manicured turf and a full time caretaker. Nearby restaurant and lodging. Two ghost towns. Airplane camping at its best. Nearby mountain lakes set in the Sawtooth Mountains.*

AIRPORT DESCRIPTION: Smiley Creek sits in the high open valley of the headwaters of the River of No Return; the Salmon River. The incredibly rugged Sawtooth Mountains line the western edge of the valley, with mountain tops exceeding 10,000'. The beautiful White Cloud Mountains line the eastern edge. Galena Summit, located immediately south of the airstrip, separates the Salmon River drainage from the Wood River drainage.

The Bureau of Aeronautics maintains this as a level 6 airstrip, its highest standard. It has tiedowns, two windsocks, fences, irrigation, a full time caretaker, and golf course-like turf.

"Our boyfriend's back, and your're gonna be in trouble..." l. to r. M.J. Leventhal, Mary Jameson, and Ross Leventhal (posing as the bear).

TRANSPORTATION: The caretaker will sign you up for the state maintained courtesy car.

SERVICES & LODGING: The **Smiley Creek Lodge** is located 500 yards west of the airstrip and serves biscuits and gravy that are well worth the trip. Supplies can be obtained in the small store in the lodge. They also have rustic cabins available at $25 a night with a community shower and lodge rooms available for $50 a night with a private bath. A trail leads from the airport across a footbridge to the lodge.

CAMPING: The ***Smiley Creek Airport Campground** provides picnic tables, stoves, hot showers, potable water, and very clean rest rooms with flush toilets. The beautiful sod camping area has recently been renovated and has yet to see much use. Some flying clubs utilize Smiley Creek for their fly-ins, but you can generally be assured of privacy.

(Above) Smiley Creek Lodge, near the headwaters of the Salmon River.
(Below) Site of Vienna, Idaho, now a ghost town.

EXPLORING SMILEY CREEK:

MOUNTAIN BIKE OR CAR TRIP TO VIENNA - 15.8 mile roundtrip.

The abandoned mining townsite is on Smiley Creek, one of the streams forming the drainage of the upper Sawtooth Valley. From the airstrip, go south on Highway 75, 1.4 miles and turn right on the Smiley Creek Road. Continue on for 6.5 miles, and a 300' elevation climb, to the interpretive sign marking the townsite.

The dirt road is usable by regular automobiles as far as the townsite, though it is rather rough. The ride is very scenic, following tree-lined Smiley Creek, with many undesignated campsites along the way.

The rather open valley of Smiley Creek, with scattered meadows along the bottoms, provides a pleasant setting for the Vienna townsite. The location of this former town is on sloping, partly wooded, partly grassy ground on the west side of the canyon.

The only visible remains of the once-flourishing settlement are the remains of the log walls of a few cabins scattered over the townsite, a few cellar holes or refuse dumps, and a number of mine dumps and structures farther up the canyon.

The road that continues past Vienna to the Webfoot, Vienna, and Solace Mines is on private property and posted with NO TRESPASSING-GUARD ON DUTY signs. Without a written invitation, limit your exploration to the Vienna townsite and the surrounding Forest Service land.

Remnants of the old mill site, Vienna, Idaho.

MOUNTAIN BIKE OR CAR TRIP TO SAWTOOTH CITY
- 6.4 miles roundtrip.

This abandoned mining townsite is on the west bank of Beaver Creek, a tributary of the Salmon River, in the upper Sawtooth Valley. From the airstrip, proceed north on Highway 75, 1.4 miles to the marked turn-off on the left. The site begins 2.2 miles from the highway and extends upstream for about 0.2 miles. A half mile upstream from the townsite is the site of the mill for the Silver King Mine.

The townsite occupies a long, sparsely wooded flat in the open valley of Beaver Creek. The cabins have deteriorated to such an extent, that none are left standing on their own. Only the foundations of the Silver King Mill are evident one-half mile upstream.

MOUNTAIN BIKE OR CAR TRIP TO HISTORIC POLE CREEK RANGER STATION
- 6.4 miles roundtrip.

This early day Forest Service ranger station is situated on Pole Creek, in the upper end of Sawtooth Valley. From the airstrip, proceed south on Highway 75, 0.5 miles to the marked turnoff on the left. Continue 2.7 miles up the gravel road to the parking area.

This picturesque log cabin is one of the oldest administrative structures left on the Sawtooth National Forest. It was built in 1909 as the first headquarters of the Pole Creek Assistant Ranger District. Its first occupant was colorful **William**

H. Horton, who spent the remainder of his long Forest Service career here.

The site consists of the small, chinked-log ranger cabin, a lodgepole flag pole, interpretive signs, toilet, and parking area. The setting, on a rolling, grassy bottom near the banks of Pole Creek with the rugged peaks of the White Cloud Mountains forming a backdrop to the east, is magnificent.

MOUNTAIN BIKE OR CAR TRIP TO ALTURAS LAKE - 12.8 miles roundtrip.

***Alturas Lake** is one of several deeply glaciated lakes lying at the eastern base of the Sawtooth Mountains. Alturas is somewhat smaller than nearby Redfish Lake and gets less usage. 60 campsites, discreetly hidden in the trees along the shore, feature picnic tables, fire rings, stoves, pit toilets, fishing, boating, and swimming.

Shown on late 1800 maps as **Atlanta Lake** or **Lake Tahoma**, it was well known by **Vienna** and **Sawtooth City** miners as a reliable source of fish. The Alturas Lake Trail was built in 1879 to allow miners to carry ore over the mountains from Sawtooth City to the Buffalo Mill in Atlanta. A formidable hike today, it illustrates the determination of these early day miners.

Alturas Lake, known in the 1800s as Atlanta Lake or Lake Tahoma, was on the pack trail leading over the rugged Sawtooth Mountains to the mills in Atlanta.

HISTORY: In September 1824, **Alexander Ross,** led a group of 40 Hudson Bay Company trappers and Iroquois Indian trappers from the Wood River Valley over the 8700' pass (Galena Summit) into the Sawtooth Valley - the headwaters of the Salmon River. They are believed to have been the first white men to see this spectacular country.

In May 1878, **Levi Smiley** discovered a quartz vein at the head of Smiley Creek. But, due to the Bannock War on Camas Prairie, he retreated to Challis to sit out the skirmish. In October of that year he returned with T.B. Mulkey to locate a number of lode claims. Early in the spring of 1879, Smiley led an anxious group of miners back to the area and the towns of Sawtooth City and Vienna quickly sprung up after rich silver ore augmented with gold was discovered.

Vienna, located up Smiley Creek, was the larger of the two towns with a population in excess of 800 people. It was in existence from 1879 until 1892. It boasted nearly two hundred buildings with three general stores, six restaurants, two meat markets, a bank, a hotel, two livery stables, fourteen saloons, and its own newspaper.

Sawtooth City was located on Beaver Creek to accommodate the mineral discoveries north of the Vienna Mine. The city had a population of close to 600 people with three saloons, a general store, a meat market, two restaurants, a Chinese laundry, a blacksmith shop, and an assay office. It survived until 1889.

A pack trail led over the mountains and down Mattingly Creek to haul the ore to the Buffalo Mill in Atlanta. A toll road was built over Galena Summit to haul high grade ore to the Philadelphia Smelter in Ketchum.

Several unsuccessful attempts were made in the early 1900s to start up the mines but the extreme isolation and technological problems of ore recovery led to failure. The cumulative metal production for Vienna and Sawtooth City was about $800,000.

LOST TREASURE OF VIENNA: After Vienna met its demise, the last person to leave the town was a bartender (naturally). He gathered all the silver coins and plates, wrapped them, and placed them in a barrel and buried them for safekeeping until he could return the next spring. The bartender died that winter without disclosing the location of the buried treasure. It is yet to be discovered.

COWBOY JO: Cowboy Jo was the toast of every mining camp of the West. Her real name was Amanda, and that was as far as it went. Coming from Iowa, where she had spent six years in a Catholic Convent, she was a young woman when she rode into Sawtooth City in 1879. From there she went to Bonanza, one of the first women to enter the Yankee Fork country. The men had not seen a woman in months, and work came to a standstill as they flocked around the beautiful auburn haired stranger.

Cowboy Jo yearned for respect, but it was not hers to have. She was never known to raise her voice or become boisterous, but she laughed and drank with any man who had the price.

She had a big heart and was regarded as an angel of mercy. Any time news came to her of a prospector being ill or in need, she would pack food and medicine into her saddle bags and ride over the treacherous mountain trails to his cabin. She would nurse him, scrub the cabin clean and mend his clothes until he was on his feet again. In her was an uncontrollable restlessness, and she was never content to stay with any one man or any one place very long.

One man, who considered her as "his woman", lost her to another prospector in a poker game. Out of money, with the stakes raised from $50, he was so sure he held high hand with a straight club flush, that he put her up to cover the raise. His opponent held a royal heart flush, ace high.

After several years, Cowboy Jo married and went to live in the Loon Creek area, where she continued to help the needy whenever she could. Her grave in the Challis cemetery is unmarked, alone and forgotten by the world from which she came.

HUNTING & FISHING:

PIONEER MOUNTAIN OUTFITTERS - Tom & Deb Proctor, Route 2, 3321 Michigan Ave., Twin Falls, ID 83301 (208)734-3679 winter, (208)774-3737 summer. Hunting: Elk, Deer, Sheep, Bear, Cougar, Predators, Forest Grouse. Fishing, Trailrides, Backpacking.

VALLEY RANCH OUTFITTERS - Randall G. Baugh, Summer: HC64, Box 9946, Stanley, ID 83278 (208)774-3470. Winter: 121 Hurst Lane, Bellevue, ID 83313 (208)778-9517. Hunting: Elk, Deer, Goat, Bear, Cougar, Predators. Fishing, Wagon Rides, Sleigh Rides, Trailrides.

WHITE CLOUD OUTFITTERS - Michael Scott, Box 217, Challis, ID 83226 (208)879-4574. Hunting: Elk, Deer, Goat, Bear, Cougar, Sheep, Antelope. Fishing, Trailrides, and Backpacking. Float Boating and Steelhead Fishing.

MAPS, LOCAL CONDITIONS, AND INFORMATION:

Airport information: Division of Aeronautics, 3483 Rickenbacker Street, Boise, Idaho 83705 (208)334-8775.

Forest information: Sawtooth National Recreation Area, Headquarters Office, Star Route (Highway 75), Ketchum, Idaho 83340 (208)726-8291.

Sheep wagons and Basque sheep herders are still common sights in Sawtooth Valley.
Courtesy: Idaho Historical Society.

SMITH'S PRAIRIE

HIGHLIGHT ✈ *Very large turf covered airstrip on the edge of the prairie. Small ranch community ignoring the 20th Century and doing quite well. Whitewater rafting and superb fishing.*

· · · · ·

AIRPORT DESCRIPTION: Notable for its size, Smith's Prairie airstrip is 5,400 long and 125 feet wide, just about three times the length of most of Idaho's backcountry strips. Turf covered, Smith's Prairie lies one mile east of the town of Prairie.

About 50 square miles of private agricultural land surround the town of Prairie and that in turn is surrounded by the Boise National Forest. The area is sparsely settled because most of the land is held by a few large landowners who have held out against the tide of subdividing.

The South Fork of the Boise River bounds the area on three sides. The Danskin Mountains lie to the southwest across the river with Rattlesnake and Lava Mountain to the north. Names with negative connotations such as Washboard Creek, Deadhorse Creek, and Little Rattlesnake Creek have probably contributed to the area's isolation, but don't be misled. It's a beautiful, beautiful area and the locals would like to keep it that way.

Prairie store, Pairie, Idaho 1993.

TRANSPORTATION: There are no courtesy cars, rental cars or a telephone available at Smith's Prairie Airstrip. However, it is sometimes possible to prearrange transportation with the following: Conny Carrico, Boise River Canyon Shuttle Service, Prairie, Idaho 83647, (208)868-3255. Prairie Store, Prairie, Idaho 83647, (208)868-3222.

SERVICES & LODGING: The **Prairie Store** is located 1.6 miles west of the airstrip on Forest Route 159. Continue

west on the road past the Prairie turnoff for about a 0.6 mile. The store is the social gathering place for whitewater rafters, hunters, loggers, and local ranchers. They offer a saloon, store, cafe, and RV park. (208)868-3222.

CAMPING: There are no designated camping areas at Smith's Prairie. However, due to its spaciousness, visitors often pitch tents adjacent to the runway. The more adventurous may want to take a mountain bike along and head five miles in any direction to primitive camping on public national forest land.

EXPLORING SMITH'S PRAIRIE: The aerial view of the South Fork of the Boise River Canyon is spectacular. Volcanic activity has interspersed layers of basalt with granite to create huge multi-level benches along the course of the river. The volcanic ash has created fertile fields and pastures.

Basalt lava tubes are visible from the air. They are hollow inside because molten lava flowed out from beneath an already solid outer crust, leaving large parts of the flow an empty shell. The hollows commonly form long tubes that wind on and on, natural tunnels within the flow. Some of these lava tubes continue for miles.

Prairie Free Library, Prairie, Idaho 1993.

The roof of these underground hollows eventually fall, filling the hollow with broken rubble and often opening a sinkhole on the surface. As lava tubes collapse, they first become a series of holes in the surface of the flow, and eventually became a long depression.

Canyon Filling Lavas - The Boise River drainage was established in the granitic batholith (a large igneous body of rock with an exposed surface area of at least 40 square miles) more than four million years ago. The rivers have carved their paths deep into this batholith forming the steep walled canyons.

About 400,000 years ago, lava flows from nearby volcanos filled the canyon bottom with basalt (a dark volcanic rock with fine-grained texture). As the river began its erosive descent through the basalt, spectacular terraces with vertical walls were left behind on the canyon walls as the river again reached its previous batholithic bottom. This cycle of filling the canyon with basalt and the river eroding it away has been repeated several times. The wedge shaped terraces are simply the remnants of previous lava flows.

The fresh white paint of the Prairie School gives the impression that residents are proud of this (what appears to be) two-room school house. I understand the enrollment is eight students. I would be willing to bet they are getting quite an education.

The Community Center building, also known as the **"Doin's Hall"**, is a classic board and batten building with an open front porch and a wood latch on the front door. Any "doin's," a wedding, birthday, a funeral are held here in the Doin's Hall.

I noticed only one chimney and less than air tight construction on the building and asked if winter-time functions got a little cold. "Not really," was the answer. "Quite a bit of heat is generated by 135 dancin' people". Dances are held three times a year at Doin's Hall. I also suspect that some of the old boys might step outside occasionally for a nip from the old jug...strictly speculation however.

Doin's Hall, Prairie, Idaho 1993.

On an early summer visit in 1993, I was doing what everybody else does; sitting on a barstool in the Prairie Store chattin' and sippin' (sarsaparilla, that is), and, in general, enjoying myself. Loggers were in town to salvage the burned timber from the Foothills Fire of 1992. The 20 RVs out back, which housed the men, probably broke a record for campers in town.

At the end of the bar, a small color TV was entertaining the customers with afternoon cartoons. A couple fellows were shooting pool and just about everybody was enjoying a cold one. Then it happened.

Across the bottom of the screen of the 13" RCA, came superimposed the white letters of: STORM WARNING- 50 mile an hour winds, marble sized hail, thunderstorms with lightning and rain - TAKE SHELTER IMMEDIATELY.

I glanced up through the open doorway to see the biggest, blackest, meanest looking clouds I'd ever seen. They were coming my way, rumbling with thunder and flashing with lightning.

I really didn't like the idea of a huge hail storm having its way with my 182, and ultimately having its way with me as I frantically rode my bicycle down the dirt road getting beat up by these marbles falling from the sky. Old 400DH had seen me through some tough times and I wasn't about to leave her stranded. I barely out-pedaled the clouds coming from the west as I pedaled eastward.

Delta Hotel and I were glad to see each other. I threw the chains off and she started on the first crank. We did a frisky back taxi with a runup on the roll. Taking off into the wind, we were able to turn crosswind at midfield. She climbed the ridge to the east at 1500 feet per minute. As we passed over the ridge, I turned to see where the storm was. There it was, hot on our tail with an appendage coming around to the south of us.

We picked up a tail wind and our ground speed was up to 154 knots on the Loran. Ten minutes later, I could see that we were slowly pulling ahead of the storm. Another 20 minutes and we were taxiing into the hangar and closing the door. She was happy to be home, out of danger, and so was I.

As I pulled away in my ragtop '72 CJ5, the winds picked up and the clouds peeked over the west ridge. Let her come...we're ready for it now! And it did! Winds and rain, thunder and lightning.

The old gal still had it in her. When the chips were down, she had run like a race horse and gotten me out of a pack of trouble.

I thought, after dinner, I'd run down to the hangar and see if she'd like a quart of Aeroshell 50 weight for a job well done, as the dissipated and disappointed storm continued to drizzle through the evening.

WHITEWATER RAFTING: The nearby South Fork of the Boise River provides excellent whitewater rafting opportunities with a 17 mile float through some class III water. There is presently not a permit system in place and guides are not required for experienced rafters.

The trip can be done in one or two days with camping areas at the put-in site and along the river itself.

The **Boise River Canyon Shuttle Service** can provide shuttle service from Smith's Prairie airstrip for airplane/rafters. You can bring your own equipment or rent it from the Shuttle Service. For more information and reservations contact:

Conny Carrico, Boise River Canyon Shuttle Service, Prairie, Idaho 83647, (208)868-3255.

HISTORY: 1992 Foothills Fire - A lightning strike from a dry thunderstorm, on the afternoon of August 19, 1992, led to one of the largest fires in Idaho, known as the Foothills Fire, 10 miles west of Prairie. Seven years of drought and near zero humidity had created a tinderbox waiting for a spark. The spark hit, not only here but across the state.

3121 Forest Service fire fighters were called in from Minnesota, Texas, South Carolina, Florida, North Carolina, Nevada, Montana, South Dakota, Wisconsin, New Jersey, Georgia, Michigan, Wyoming, Pennsylvania, Maryland, and Colorado. The U.S. Air Force, Fish & Wildlife Service, National Wildlife Service, and Elmore and Boise County Sheriff's Departments also provided support.

The Smith's Prairie airstrip was used as one of the aerial support bases for the 24 helicopters and 4 airtankers used on the fire. High winds, heavy fuels, low humidity, and rough remote terrain hampered efforts in controlling the fire.

As the fire jumped the river on its way toward Prairie, orders were given for its inhabitants to evacuate. Some did and some didn't. As the fire continued its relentless pace towards town, the ablebodied civilians manned the firelines, fighting a losing battle to save their homes. At 2:00 in the morning, from a nearby hill on the outskirts of town, the hopeless inhabitants gathered to watch as the encroaching fire burned toward their homes.

Almost miraculously, it was as if a hand had reached down and snuffed the breath from the fire. What had only moments earlier been a certain conflagration of homes and lives now gave hope to the fire fighters of saving the homes. The fire diverted around Prairie to continue its path of destruction.

When one of the mothers that had watched this miracle from the hill, recounted the story to her son who had been on the fire line, her son reported that when all looked lost on the fire line, the fire fighters had gathered for a prayer - at 2:00 that morning.

Prairie was saved and the Foothills Fire was contained six weeks later after 127 miles of fire line were built, 257,600 acres were burned and $10,000,000 was spent.

HUNTING & FISHING: The South Fork of the Boise River, below Anderson Ranch Dam, is considered by Idaho Fish and Game as a blue ribbon fishery. The road following the river towards Prairie gives access to several launching areas.

Smith Creek and Spring Creek, near Prairie, also have excellent trout fishing.

MAPS, LOCAL CONDITIONS, AND INFORMATION:

Division of Aeronautics, 3483 Rickenbacker St., Boise, Idaho 83705 (208)334-8775.

Geological description paraphrased from *Roadside Geology of Idaho*, David D. Alt, Donald W. Hyndman, Mountain Press Publishing Co., Box 2399, Missoula, Montana 59806.

SOLDIER BAR

HIGHLIGHT ✈ *Very difficult wilderness airstrip on Big Creek. Gravesite of casualty from the Sheepeater War. Gets moderate use during hunting season.*

- - - - -

AIRPORT DESCRIPTION: Do not attempt to land here without an experienced pilot showing you the approach (see appendix). On the approach, the airstrip is not visible until the last 1/4 mile, and by then the altitude and air speed corrections need to be minor ones. Go-arounds can be executed early in the approach but become impractical and then impossible as the approach progresses.

RWY 25 climbs steeply. A major bump lies 450' from the threshold and a second major bump lies 905' from the threshold. Then a dogleg turns to the right. It invariably requires additional power to pull the airplane up to the end of the runway.

The IAFD lists the length of the runway as 1600'. However, on takeoff, only about 1200' are practical to use due to the bump at 905'. Accelerating at full throttle from the end of runway 7 on takeoff can damage the airplane's undercarriage on the 905' bump. Full throttle too soon may also cause difficulty in making the left turn dogleg just before the 905' bump.

Soldier Bar is located on Big Creek, 4 miles upstream from its confluence with the Middle Fork of the Salmon. The airstrip is located on a high grassy bench overlooking Big Creek. The approach end of runway 25 has a very steep dropoff into Big Creek several hundred feet below.

CAMPING: ***Soldier Bar Campground** sits off the end of RWY 25. There is a flat grassy area to park your airplane and pitch a tent near Private Eagan's monument. A pit toilet is conveniently located here. Eagan Creek and a spring provide water for the camp. Be sure to boil your water or use a filter. This camp gets a fair amount of use during the fall hunting season but is not heavily used during the spring and summer. Bring your own tiedown stakes and rope.

When Johnson Creek fills up with airplane campers, privacy at Soldier Bar can almost be guaranteed. Again, be forewarned. Unless you want a final resting place next to Private Eagan (see Exploring below), don't take your first trip in without an experienced pilot by your side.

EXPLORING SOLDIER BAR: Near the east end of the airstrip you will find the burial site of **Pvt. Harry Eagan,** the only known fatality in the Sheepeater War. One of Lt. Catley's men, he was wounded in a nearby ambush on August 20, 1879. Because both legs were shot through, the doctor gave Eagan chloroform and amputated one leg. The doctor lost his patient only a few minutes later.

The troops wrapped his body in blankets and buried him. No shot was fired and no word was spoken, but he was left to rest as peacefully as if there had been pomp and ceremony. "No more, old Comrade, will you be called to fat bacon and bean soup, to climb mountains nor damned by civilians for a lazy lout."

HISTORY: Cougar Dave Lewis was a Union Soldier in the Civil War. He served with Wild Bill Hickock in the siege of Vicksburg and was also an Indian War veteran, having scouted for Captain Benteen. He arrived at the Little Big Horn shortly after Custer's massacre.

Cougar Dave Lewis, a Civil War soldier and Indian fighter, built a cabin near Soldier Bar in 1894. He claimed to have killed 600 cougars before his departure in 1935 at the age of 93. Courtesy: Idaho Cty. Free Press.

He was in charge of the ammunition train (two mules), when he accompanied Captain Bernard on Big Creek when the Sheepeaters ambushed the troops.

In 1894, Lewis returned to Big Creek and built the first cabin at the mouth of Goat Creek, just upstream from Soldier Bar. He later moved to Soldier Bar and made a living by packing supplies for the Thunder Mountain gold rush and later by outfitting, blacksmithing, and hunting cougar.

With a state bounty of $15 for a cougar, Lewis claimed to have taken more than 600 pelts. He received some notoriety in 1927 by having his picture, along with his pack of hounds, appear in the *New York Times*.

But by 1935, Lewis felt the outside world closing in on him and complained to his nearest neighbor (who lived five miles away) that "a man don't have no privacy no more!" After selling his ranch, he left Big Creek for Cascade in a rain storm. He caught pneumonia and died at the age of 93.

Ambush at Soldier Bar

Captain Bernard's Umatilla Indian Scouts discovered an Indian Village of 12 wickiups on Soldier's Bar on August 18, 1879. Some of the loot from **Lieutenant Catley's** earlier retreat was recovered along with 35 horses and the village was burned. The supplies and packers were left at Soldier Bar as the troops were drawn down Big Creek Gorge in search of the escaping Indians.

A family of Sheepeater Indians. Courtesy: Idaho Historical Society.

The Indians, however, circled back and hid in the rocks and brush of the hillside overlooking the burned out village. The Indians waited until the packers had all but one animal loaded up and commenced to open fire on the guards and packers.

It was a good plan, for by driving the guard and packers away the Indians would have made a haul of rations, blankets, and other much needed supplies. But the guards were "old Indian fighters" and did not run. Lieutenant Catley, who had been sent back to the South Fork to pick up supplies earlier in the day, heard the shooting and returned to the camp.

When the bullets began to fly, one brave soldier who had been in service for 18 years, ran behind a bluff along the creek and was not seen until evening. Fearing desertion from Catley's men, a couple of Cavalry men drew their revolvers and threatened to shoot anyone who ran during the skirmish.

This is where Pvt. Harry Eagan was shot. Also, a horse was killed, three other men wounded, and a mule was poisoned. The soldiers continued to pursue the Indians down Big Creek but ultimately lost track of them in the "The Impassable Canyon" on the Middle Fork.

MAPS, LOCAL CONDITIONS, AND INFORMATION:

Challis Forest Air Officer, Box 247, Challis, Idaho 83226.

STANLEY

HIGHLIGHT → *Gateway to the Sawtooth Mountains. Lodging and restaurants. Whitewater rafting, hiking, and mountains comparable to the Swiss Alps.*

- - - - -

AIRPORT DESCRIPTION: This dirt and sod surface airstrip sits above the tiny town of Stanley, on a sage covered bench. The Division of Aeronautics does not charge landing or tiedown fees.

Fog and low clouds will sometimes cover the valley floor in the mornings, but it generally burns off by noon. When Stanley is fogged in, Smiley Creek serves as a reliable alternate, due to its higher elevation.

Some confusion exists over the CTAF. It was changed from Unicom 122.8 to Multicom 122.9. Announce your intentions on 122.9 and keep an eye out for airplanes on the wrong frequency.

TRANSPORTATION: There is no guarantee of availability, but **National Car Rental**, located in the Mountain Village Lodge, is a drop off point for rental cars. They can be reached at (208)774-3661 or (800)843-5475. Their Boise number is (800)227-7368.

SERVICES & LODGING: During peak summer months, it is a good idea to bring your own tiedowns; other times several are available. Stanley Air Taxi is located on the field and will sell aviation fuel if available. Its best to call ahead of time to confirm availability. A pay phone is located at the north end of the strip near the airplane tiedowns.

Lodging is available within walking distance of the airport. From the north end of the airport, climb the fence, and a trail leads 300 yards downhill to Upper Stanley.

Creekside Lodge, Box 110, Stanley, Idaho 83278, (800)523-0733, (208)774-2213. On the banks of Valley Creek, west end of Stanley. 14 units, $60-$100.

Danner's Log Cabin Motel, Box 196, Stanley, Idaho 83278, (208)523-3539. 9 cabins, $35-$45.

Mountain Village Lodge, Box 150, Stanley, Idaho 83278, (208)774-3661. 60 units, $42-$110.

Sawtooth Hotel, Box 52, Stanley, Idaho 83278, (208)774-9947. 18 units, $21.50-$50.00.

Rod & Gun Club Saloon & Cafe - With a reputation reaching far and wide, this saloon actually made it on the cover of National Geographic Magazine. The "Stanley Stomp", a dance you'll do if you go there on a Saturday night, was what attracted the magazine. Casanova Jack's brother is in charge of drinks and music and promises a fun evening of cowboy adventure.

Six Hailey men with fish caught from Red Fish Lake. Date unknown.
Courtesy: Idaho State Historical Society.

The saloon was once the watering hole of loggers, Basque sheepherders, ranchers, miners, and other ne'er do wells. But in recent years, the crowd has been homogenized by the whitewater rafting crowd of lycra clad, plastic water bottle packing, new-age outdoor yuppies. Not quite as many bar room brawls these days, and you hardly ever hear of a gun fight any more. (208)774-9920.

The Mountain Village Restaurant & Saloon features homestyle breakfast, lunch and dinner. Open year 'round, 7 days a week. (208)774-3317, (208)774-3680.

Stanley Kasino Club - The menu features a garden fresh salad bar, nightly pasta specials and Idaho's finest beef, lamb, pork and poultry. Fresh seafood when available. #21 Ace of Diamonds Ave., Downtown Stanley. (208)774-3516.

CAMPING: This tiny town serves as the gateway to the pristine and somewhat undiscovered Sawtooth Wilderness Area, the Frank Church River of No Return Wilderness and the White Clouds. Most of the camping is free and all of it boasts some of the most beautiful scenery you could hope to find anywhere.

Because of the many options, it is a good idea to stop first at the **Stanley Ranger Station,** located two miles south of the airstrip. This is an excellent resource for wilderness information, camping and hiking locations. (208)774-3681. There is no camping at the airstrip.

Redfish Lake.

This area is very popular, and generally the trend of this book has been to guide visitors to areas "off the beaten path". However, the high scenic values of Redfish and Stanley Lakes offset the lack of seclusion and the book would be remiss in omitting them.

***Redfish Lake is located 3 miles south of Stanley off Highway 75. There are approximately 10 campgrounds on or near the lake containing more than 200 campsites, amphitheater, sailboating, waterskiing, and wilderness trail heads. The special features are fishing, river, lake, boat ramp, drinking water, toilets, camping, picnicking, boat rental, swimming, marina, store, and restaurant. Redfish is well known and campgrounds are consistently full in July and August.

Daily use fees are charged. A campsite reservation system is available by calling MISTIX, (800)283-2267. The operators will take a reservation for a specific site or help any customers find a site to their liking that is in the reservation program. User fees and a service charge are paid to MISTIX via major credit card or check.

***Stanley Lake. Drive 4.75 miles west of Stanley on Highway 21. Turn left on the Stanley Lake Road and travel 3.5 miles to Stanley Lake. Four campgrounds with 38 units are located on the lake. The area offers fishing, camping, picnicking, boat launches, drinking water, toilets, boating, and trailheads. This is a non-reservation fee area, and does not receive the pressure that Redfish Lake does. The views of McGown Peak reflected in the mirrored surface of the lake are an unforgotten image of tranquility.

EXPLORING STANLEY: When it comes to scenery, the 99 residents of Stanley could be the richest people in the world. Often compared to the Swiss Alps, the rugged and majestic Sawtooth Mountains act as a backdrop for the Stanley Basin, respected and appreciated for its yet unspoiled beauty.

Although the population soars in the summer months, the area does not carry National Park status and likewise does not have entrance fees, guided walks, handout litter bags, restroom lines, sterilized park food, and in general no "people funnels" whatsoever. Hunting and fishing is a way of life here.

The Sawtooth Wilderness was established in 1972 as part of the Sawtooth National Recreation Area and is under the administration of the Sawtooth National Forest. This 216,000 acre wilderness contains jagged "sawtooth" mountain peaks, deep gorges, glacial basins, waterfalls, timbered slopes and lush grassy meadows.

Nestled among the Sawtooth's high peaks are more than 200 alpine lakes and headwaters of four impressive rivers: Middle and North Forks of the Boise River, South Fork of the Payette, and the Salmon River.

Stanley Lake - Sawtooth Mountains. Courtesy: Idaho State Historical Society.

A hiker's paradise, nearly 300 miles of trails offer a wide range of routes through the wilderness. Designated as "Trailless Areas," many of the highest lake basins have no constructed trails leading to them.

Wildlife abounds with populations of mountain goat, elk, mule deer, black bear and a variety of birds and smaller animals. Trout can be found in the numerous glacial cirque lakes. The Stanley Basin is most popular from mid July through August. Scheduling your visit around this time should almost insure privacy.

Sunbeam Hot Springs - Hot spring pools created at the edge of the Salmon River, where 170 degree water mixes with the cool river water for a delightful, soothing dip. Restrooms and dressing rooms on site. 12 miles north of Stanley on river side of HWY 75. Between mileposts 201 and 202.

Basin Creek Hot Springs - Unimproved natural hot springs flow out of the rocks and into the Salmon River. Users have piled rocks to create pools for soaking. Be cautious of the 170 degree water flowing into pools. 8.3 miles north of Stanley on river side of HWY 75. Highway junction between mileposts 197 and 198.

Kelly Creek Road - Much wildlife in the area for viewing in mornings and evenings. Take a camera (allow 1 hour for trip). 5 miles west of Stanley, turn on Stanley Creek Road opposite of Stanley Lake Road, proceed approximately 1 mile to junction to Basin Butte and turn right. Road winds into mountains and at top of summit several remains of old mining cabins and gold digs can be inspected. Further along, the road climbs again to provide fantastic Sawtooth views. Highway junction between mileposts 126 and 127.

WHITEWATER RAFTING: Stanley is the homebase for numerous whitewater rafting and kayaking outfitters. For a complete guide, call or write the Stanley-Sawtooth Chamber of Commerce.

Sevy Guide Service, Inc. - Float trips on the famous Middle Fork of the Salmon River, the legendary Main Salmon River and the scenic Owyhee and Bruneau Rivers. March and April Steelhead fishing from Stanley. Bob Sevy, Box 24, Stanley, Idaho 83278. (208)774-2200

Sun Valley Rivers Co. - Middle Fork of the Salmon river float/fishing trips. Oar/paddle/kayak option available. First Class quality. Owner accompanied. Fall chukar/fishing combination trips. Main Salmon Spring Steelhead fishing. Box 1776, Sun Valley, Idaho 83353 (208)726-7404.

Sawtooth Rentals - Complete float trip equipment packages, Middle Fork and Salmon Rivers. Inflatable kayaks, mountain bikes, jet skis, tents. Licensed and bonded outfitter, guided & unguided trips. Box 192, Stanley, Idaho 83278. (208)774-3409 or (208)734-4060.

HIKES: GOAT LAKE

General description: Goat Lake represents the essence of the Sawtooths. Its remote alpine grandeur is a Sawtooth Sampler. Snowfields cling to the steep surrounding terrain and cast ice chunks into the lake. Goat Lake is not a safe place to take children or inexperienced hikers, and sturdy boots are a must. Roundtrip hiking distance is 7 miles with an elevation gain of 1500'. Because of its cross country sections, it can be difficult. Access is limited to August and September, due to snow.

Finding the trailhead: Drive 2.6 miles west of Stanley on Highway 21. Turn left on Iron Creek Road and go 3.2 miles to Iron Creek Transfer Camp and park your car. The trail head is at the west end of the parking lot.

The Hike: At 1.25 miles, you will meet the Alpine Way Trail. Turn left and cross the foot bridge. At 2.75 miles the Alpine Way trail splits. Take the right fork to the southwest (unsigned trail).

At 2.9 miles, the trail splits again. The left fork descends to the base of Goat Falls and the right fork climbs steeply on a make shift trail to Goat Lake. Follow the tumbling stream uphill. You will be scrambling up loose sandy soil or slick granite boulders. Pick your way carefully and watch your footing as you climb. The trail fades in and out. Just keep going up.

Cross the creek well above the falls. The lake is at 3.5 miles. Enjoy the breathtaking scenery and perhaps a cold drink.

Mountain Bike - Elk Mountain Trail Loop. Many say it is one of the best trails they have tried. 5 miles west of Stanley, take Stanley Lake Road for 1.5 miles, then see sign for loop trail on right-hand side of road. Trail is of moderate difficulty and returns to HYW 21 about 7 miles west of Stanley, where riders can cross HYW 21 and return to point of origin by way of Cow Camp Road to Stanley Creek Road, cross HWY 21 again and ride in 1.5 miles on Stanley Lake Road to starting point. Highway junction between mileposts 126 and 127.

HISTORY: In 1862, a party of 23 miners led by Captain John Stanley, spent the summer prospecting around Florence, then moved on to Warrens's Diggings the following summer to spend the Fourth of July. From there they moved up to the headwaters of the Middle Fork of the Salmon.

Here they found thousands of salmon spawning in the shallow creeks and bears were everywhere. Hence, the name of Bear Valley. The party frequently saw signs of Indians , but failed to encounter any, and gold seemed just as scarce.

Eventually, a small placer deposit was discovered west of present day Stanley Basin and the area was named after Captain John Stanley.

By 1864, 200 men were working the creeks as a result of the discovery. Twenty years later, gold-quartz was discovered. A log cabin at the confluence of Valley Creek and the Salmon River, built in 1890 by Arthur and Della McGown, was

Stanley Basin with Mt. McGowan in background.
Courtesy: Idaho State Historical Society.

probably the first building in Upper Stanley. Here they sold beef to packers and miners and operated a saloon. But, it wasn't until 1919 that the town was surveyed, platted, and named Upper Stanley, often referred to as "Dogtown." Apparently, one of the families in town kept too many dogs.

In 1907, Lower Stanley was built in a picturesque setting on the banks of the Salmon River, and was the first town to use the name Stanley. It was also referred to as "Squawtown" because it seemed that the women did all the work.

Eventually, Upper Stanley took the post office and school from lower Stanley, which never really recovered from the setback.

Bill Harrah, of Harrah's Casino in Reno, Nevada, fell in love with Stanley in the '70s and contributed a grocery store, restaurant, lodging, and the airstrip. An authentic Stanley Steamer, from Harrah's Car Museum, was on display for many years.

Fishing Valley Creek. North end of the Sawtooth Mountain Range in background. Courtesy: Idaho State Historical Society.

ANNUAL EVENTS AND ACTIVITIES: Third Sunday in June, Braun Brothers Concert. Fathers Day, Cowboy Poetry. Third weekend in July, Sawtooth Mtn Mama's Arts & Crafts Fair. Third weekend in September, Quilt Festival.

HUNTING & FISHING: Ace of Diamonds St., in Upper Stanley, is the place to look for McCoys Gift & Tackle Shop, to find out what's biting...fabulous hunting and fishing in the area. Call (208)774-3377.

MAPS, LOCAL CONDITIONS, AND INFORMATION:

Maps and information on camping and hiking can be obtained from the Stanley Ranger Station located two miles south of Stanley off highway 75. Sawtooth NRA, Star Route, Ketchum, Idaho 83340, (208)726-8291. Stanley Ranger District, Sawtooth NRA, Stanley, Idaho 83278 (208)774-3681

For airport information, call the Division of Aeronautics in Boise at (208)334-8775. For local conditions, call Stanley Air Service at (208)774-2276.

For additional information on restaurants, lodging, and outfitters, contact: Stanley/ Sawtooth Chamber of Commerce, Box 8, Stanley, ID 83276 (208)774-3411.

SULPHUR CREEK

HIGHLIGHT ✈ *Private guest ranch offering overnight accomodations, trailrides, guided hunting and fishing trips, and the busiest breakfast spot in the backcountry. No landing fee.*

- - - - -

AIRPORT DESCRIPTION: This private guest ranch, in the Frank Church River of No Return Wilderness, is located four miles from the Middle Fork of the Salmon River. Just three miles southwest of the Morgan Ranch, you are likely to see horses, deer and elk grazing on the runway. It is a good idea to circle the strip to confirm it is clear. The runway surface is light turf/gravel with the east end grass covered and soft in the springtime, and the west end slopes uphill with quite a bit of loose gravel.

Sharon scrambles some eggs and bakes biscuits, but only Billy is allowed to prepare his own creation - "Cowboy Benedict."

TRANSPORTATION: The airstrip is located just steps from the guest ranch, so overnight guests will be met by a 4-wheel ATV to haul you and your baggage to your cabin. Although vehicles of any kind are prohibited in designated wilderness areas, you will see a couple of others. An old jeep pickup and a Ford tractor beat the wilderness designation to Sulphur Creek, but are now confined to the ranch.

SERVICES & LODGING: The buzzword in the Idaho Backcountry is breakfast at Sulphur Creek. Served seven days a week from June 1 through August by managers Bill and Sharon Nichols, the meal guarantees your airplane's c.g. will shift aft.

Pancakes, eggs, bacon, ham, sausage, biscuits and gravy, and omelettes are

all on the menu along with Bill's very own creation, "Cowboy Benedict".

Reservations are appreciated but not necessary and can be made through the Boise office (see Maps, Local Conditions and Information). But after this story, you might think reservations are a pretty good idea.

Left to right, Gretchen Fraser, Lita West, Don Fraser, and Jim White enjoy breakfast at Sulphur Creek.

Last summer a group of pilots from Blaine County Pilots Association scheduled a fly-in breakfast at Sulphur Creek. That same morning, several unexpected drop-ins arrived from the 185 Club rendezvous at Johnson Creek. When breakfast was served it didn't go around, at least for the first seating.

Wise and cunning, long time guide at the Shepp Ranch and active Super Cub pilot, 80-year-old Ben Hurtig observed that there was a moose in the corral. Cameras and binoculars in hand, about half the group rushed for the door while Ben and his buddies sat down to breakfast.

It only took a couple of minutes to figure out the moose was a mule. An honest mistake? "What kind of eyesight do you expect from an 80-year-old?," Ben asked with a twinkle in his eye.

Lodging runs $75 per night per person and includes three meals and activities. Rustic cabins provide hot and cold running water, showers, and wood stoves.

EXPLORING SULPHUR CREEK: The center of activity at Sulphur Creek is the guest ranch house perched on this high mountain meadow in just the right spot to soak up as much sunshine as possible. Funky old lawn chairs just outside invite you to pause and reflect on the quiet setting.

Nighttime brings the sounds of horses galloping freely behind the cabins, coyotes singing at the moon, and owls hooting. The early morning wake up call may come in the form of an elk bugle, never to be forgotten.

After daybreak, the horses are put in the corrals, to eliminate interference with airplanes, where they kindly share their salt lick with deer, while elk and moose graze in the meadow. You may see an occasional black bear snooping around for a special morsel.

When making reservations; be sure to discuss what you would like to do while you are on the ranch, fishing in the pond, horseback riding, or overnight pack trips to high mountain lakes for excellent cutthroat and rainbow fishing.

HISTORY: Story has it that **Ed Parker** and his son **Roy** owned the ranch in the 1930s. They ran some cattle and put up the hay in the summer and trapped marten and fox in the winter.

Ed had a talent for brewing moonshine, which was put into service during prohibition. His son, Roy, would load up a pack string and provide much needed "drought relief" to the miners and ranchers in the back country. Whiskey Cabin, near Landmark, was appreciatively named by the grateful survivors of the "drought."

During WWII, the lodge and ranch were used as a retreat for the men stationed at Mountain Home Air Force Base. DC-3s were brought in with men to enjoy...what else but booze, gambling, and girls. Today the old wooden bar, a couple of slot machines, and the upstairs of the lodge partitioned off into many very small rooms, and remnants of an airplane in the trees, are left to remind us of its previous history.

HUNTING & FISHING: The Sulphur Creek Ranch provides guided hunting trips for elk, deer, bear, cougar. Fishing, trailrides, backpacking, (Guest Ranch). Fish and Game Units 27 and 34. Trophy elk and deer hunts range from $1250 to $2750 for week

"Jim," the hired hand, has spent most of his life in the Idaho Backcountry.

long hunts. They have 22 horses and a few mules. Never ridden a horse before? No problem, they have horses that have never been ridden before either.

MAPS, LOCAL CONDITIONS, AND INFORMATION: Sulphur Creek Ranch, Tom Allegrezza, 7153 W. Emerald, Boise, Idaho 83704 (208)377-1188.

THOMAS CREEK

HIGHLIGHT ✈ *Wilderness airstrip with two nearby natural hot springs. Take a hot bath while watching elk lick the natural mineral salts. Whitewater rafting and excellent fishing.*

- - - - -

AIRPORT DESCRIPTION: Thomas Creek lies within the heart of the Frank Church River of No Return Wilderness. The airstrip is situated on a plateau on the bank of the Middle Fork between Indian Creek and Mahoney. It is state owned and administered by the Division of Aeronautics.

CAMPING: *State Land Camp* - A spacious low bench with scattered ponderosa pines is located along the river adjacent to the airstrip. This is a wilderness camp with no facilities. The pit toilet has been removed. The camp is used heavily during fall hunting season.

Hood Ranch Camp - The Hood Ranch and Campground is named for Milt Hood, who at one time lived on the Thomas Creek Ranch (later Middle Fork Ranch). Hood built several outfitting cabins near the hot springs, with the idea of using the hot water as a source of heat for the cabins. The abandoned cabin and homestead still exists. This is a wilderness camp with no facilities. The pit toilet has been removed.

Sunflower Flat Campground <see Sunflower Flat Hotsprings Hike below>

Little Creek Campground - Follow the trail from the southeast end of the runway downstream to the packbridge. Cross the bridge and walk downstream, passing the Little Creek Guard Station and continue downstream. No facilities.

Jim Hash and his wife were the first residents at Little Creek. They ventured into the Middle Fork with 40 head of burros and earned a living packing supplies and equipment to the Thunder Mountain Mine. Their cabin still stands and is located about one-quarter mile below Little Creek.

Lost Oak Campground - From the southeast end of the airstrip, follow the trail upstream on the right bank 2.0 miles. It is located across the river from Sunflower Flat. It is a large camp on a timbered bench or terrace. No facilities.

EXPLORING THOMAS CREEK

Hood Ranch Hot Springs Hike: General description: From the tiedown area, this is an easy 1.8 mile round trip hike . This is a highly touted hot springs soaking pool at the river's edge. However, in May, after a winter's heavy use by elk and deer, the area smelled and looked like a winter feed lot for cattle. Fifty to

The hot springs at Sunflower Flats has been a gathering spot for backcountry adventurers for the last 7,000 years.

seventy elk had spent the previous evening wallowing in the mud baths and eating the minerals deposited by the natural hot springs. Several carcasses from elk were left from the harsh winter - not my idea of an idyllic soak. This is well worth a check later in the season after the elk move up to higher country and nature's predators have had a chance to clean up the area.

Finding the trailhead: From the tiedown area near the maintenance building at the airstrip, walk to the northeast end of the airstrip (downstream) and pick up the signed trail on the immediate end of the runway.

The hike: From the trailhead follow the trail downstream for 0.3 mile to Milt Hood's cabin. Several relics have been hung on the outside of the cabin. Old fruit trees, lilacs, and scattered clumps of rhubarb point to an earlier way of life on this isolated river bench.

Continue downstream another 0.2 miles until you come to several acres of dark earth that appears to have been overturned by rooting animals - only because it has. This is the source of the Hood Ranch Hot Springs and serves as a wallow and mineral source for wintering herds of deer and elk. A small stream of very hot water leads from the wallow over a small falls and continues down to the river. River rocks have been placed to make a small soaking pool. You can control the water temperature in the pool by adjusting the rocks and mixing in cold river water.

The creekbed of Sunflower Creek comes off the mountain and across the grassy flat meadow. During the peak of the spring runoff the creekbed was bone dry and appeared as if it had been for a few years. Also odd is the fact that there are no sunflowers in the area.

Sunflower Flats Hot Springs Hike: General description: This is an easy 3.5 mile round trip hike. This small but beautiful camp has several level campsites carved out of the hillside. Ponderosa pines and scattered birch trees provide shade and privacy.

Seven small soaking pools have been dammed up with varying temperatures from hot to hotter. From the last pool in the series, a hollowed section of log extends beyond the cliff's edge to create a 20' cascade of exquisite hot water to the river's edge.

Many stop here for this natural shower. The pit toilet has been removed to maintain the wilderness nature of the site. This is one of the most popular camps on the Middle Fork and sees a lot

Whitewater rafters on the Middle Fork.

of use. Pick your time to avoid the rafter rush, and it's all yours.

Finding the trailhead: The hike starts at the tiedown area on the airstrip.

The hike: From the tiedown area near the maintenance building follow the road upstream 0.9 miles to the packbridge. Be aware that property on the opposite end of the bridge is private property. The owners have graciously allowed the public to cross this corner of their property enroute to this hot springs.

The public has a myriad of reasons to knock on the door of the lodge or in one way or another make their presence known - DON'T! This is a good chance to utilize your skills at making yourself invisible. Respect the rights of the property owner.

Cross the bridge and take an immediate right across their hot springs and meadow. Use the gate at the far side of the meadow and be sure to close it.

This trail is not shown on Forest Service maps and is not regularly maintained but is in reasonably good condition. In a couple of areas, fallen trees and rock slides require a scramble around them. The trail follows the river upstream and has shady flats to stop and regale in the surrounding beauty.

After picking your way around the final dark outcropping of rock, the magnificent water shower becomes visible. Continue on the last 100 yards and camp-sites surround the springs. This has to be one of the prettiest places on the river.

HISTORY: The Buckskin Boys: Thomas Creek received its name from a placer miner in the area, in the late 1800s. Around 1900, **Jim Bollard** from England and **"Mac" McNerney**, possibly from Ireland, settled here. They did some mining up Thomas Creek and built a two story cabin and barn. They planted fruit trees and set up an irrigation system for their hay field. Because of the leather clothing they made and wore, they were often referred to as the "Buckskin Boys". By 1910, they sold the much improved ranch for $50,000.

A party of boaters has pulled into Sunflower Flat Hot Springs for a little R and R.

ELMER KEITH AND ZANE GREY: In 1931, noted outdoor writer and firearms designer, Elmer Keith booked a party led by novelist Zane Grey for a two month trip through the Middle Fork country. Zane Grey wanted background information for his novel *"Thunder Mountain"*.

Grey reported that they were "mountain people" and would travel light. However, when the party arrived in Salmon, they had three cars and a large truck loaded with gear. Keith used 57 horses and seven men to transport the party to the Middle Fork.

After delivering the party to their destination, two months later, Grey paid Elmer Keith with a series of checks, which bounced. Keith claims to have gotten a $100 saddle horse and enough money to pay his men but $1500 short of the original deal.

But, ultimately justice was served, as shown in the following excerpt from Keith's book, *Hell, I Was There!* "We had a beautiful camp across from the mouth of the Camas on the Middle Fork. One night we got a young cloudburst. It really soaked up the camp. There was a great puddle in front of Zane Grey's tent, and snow was on the mountains down several hundred feet from the top. Grey took a look through his big spotting scope at that and ordered his secretary to bring out his long handled underwear. She hunted and couldn't find them. Then Grey told me that my packers had stolen his underwear. I told him that they hadn't stolen anything. Everything he had was there. His secretary was dressed in Gokey boots, slacks, buckskin shirt, buckskin jacket, and a black hat with silver conchos with a band around it and flat topped crown. She got mad at Grey and she took one of his war bags and crawled into it head first. Finally out she came with his long-handled underwear. She was so mad she went in front of him and threw them in the middle of this pool of muddy water. She pulled his hat off his head, threw that in on top and jumped up and down on the whole works until she'd tromped it well into the mud with her big Gokey boots. Zane Grey never said a word."

Tom McCall: In 1938, Tom McCall purchased the ranch in hopes of turning it into a dude ranch and offer excellent hunting and fishing to his clients. In order to build the cabins and lodge necessary, McCall needed to construct a sawmill on the site. He flew in the materials piece by piece to build the sawmill.

He planned to use water power to run the operation. The steel pipe used to transfer water from Thomas Creek to the mill was brought from an abandoned hydraulic operation up Greyhound Creek. He hired a packer with six mules to carry the pipe down the trail to a point below Pistol Creek Rapid, where he figured on floating the pipe the rest of the way. Each 16 foot section of the heavy metal pipe was transported by two mules, the length of pipe suspended between them.

When all 21 sections were finally at the river's edge, Tom welded metal plates over the open ends of the pipe. He then brazed sections together to form the strongest raft ever built on the Middle Fork. The floating mass of metal was poled and lined to the Thomas Ranch nearly 13 miles downstream. When the raft finally reached its destination it was disassembled and the pipe was reassembled to supply the water necessary to power the hand built mill.

Bill Harrah: The Harrah Corporation, of Reno, Nevada purchased the resort in the 1970s. They turned the Middle Fork Lodge into a mountain retreat in the wilderness. The lodge and cabins had to be flown in piece by piece. Even the log fence surrounding the estate was air-freighted in to the site. All day long, trip after trip, the Twin Otters transported materials from Challis. One crew worked to load the Otter and another unloaded the plane at Thomas Creek. The Harrah

Corporation completely wore out one Otter building their Middle Fork Lodge. Several antique cars and even an old bus were flown into the resort by helicopter. These old relics were used to drive guests and dignitaries back and forth from the airstrip. The mecca was constructed just for Harrah Club entertainers and guests.

After the death of Bill Harrah in 1978, the Middle Fork Lodge was owned briefly by the Holiday Inn and then by the Nature Conservancy.

John McCaw: John McCaw, of Seattle based McCaw Communications, is the present owner of the Middle Fork Ranch and uses it as a private retreat for family and friends. It is not open to the general public.

HUNTING & FISHING: Wonderful catch and release fishing for rainbow, cutthroat, brook trout, and Dolly Varden exists in the Middle Fork. Special regulations require the use of single barbless hooks to facilitate the release of fish. Fish from some tributaries to the Middle Fork and mountain lakes may be kept. Check current regulations first.

MAPS, LOCAL CONDITIONS, AND INFORMATION:

Airport conditions & information: Division of Aeronautics, 3483 Rickenbacker Street, Boise, Idaho 83705 (208)334-8775.

Forest information: Middle Fork Ranger District, Challis National Forest, Box 337, Challis, Idaho 83226 (208)879-4321.

TWIN BRIDGES

HIGHLIGHT → *Nearby lodge offers trailrides, hunting, fishing, and overnight accomodations.*

- - - - -

AIRPORT DESCRIPTION: Roaming cattle frequently enjoy dust baths on this runway which runs parallel to the Trail Creek Road, connecting Sun Valley and Mackay. Also, watch for antelope and deer.

Twin Bridges is located near the junction of Copper Basin Road and is surrounded by Bureau of Land Management and U.S. Forest Service public land. The East Fork of the Big Lost River joins the main Big Lost River here to form what used to be some of Idaho's finest trout fishing. You will see the apparent effects of mountain glaciation, high arid desert covered with sage and cheat grass leading to high timbered mountains.

The windsock and boundary markers are in good condition. Tiedowns are located at the southwest end of the strip.

TRANSPORTATION: Other than prearranged transportation for guests of the nearby Wild Horse Creek Ranch, a mountain bike or shoe leather are the modus transporti.

SERVICES/LODGING: The **Wildhorse Creek Ranch**, previously known as the Devil's Bedstead Ranch is nestled in the beautiful Pioneer Mountains near the headwaters of the Big Lost River, three miles southeast of the airstrip. The 6,900 foot elevation provides forty high mountain lakes within immediate proximity of the ranch. The numerous creeks in the area have been rated as one of Idaho's "blue ribbon" trout fisheries.

John and Shelly Thompson, the new resident managers, offer private ranch rooms and bunkhouse accommodations, along with sumptuous meals for overnight guests.

The native materials and vaulted open beam ceilings relate the lodge to its natural surroundings, while a huge wall of glass separates the harshness of the environment from the very coddled luxuries of the lodge...an oasis in the wilderness.

For information and reservations for accommodations and guided packtrips, contact Wildhorse Creek Ranch, Box 398, Mackay, Idaho 83251, (208)588-2575.

CAMPING: There are presently no camping facilities on the airstrip. This airport is awaiting adoption under a volunteer program established by the Division of Aeronautics at which time such improvements would be made.

**Deep Creek Campground is located 0.5 miles south of the airstrip on the Big Lost River. It has two campsites with pit toilets, picnic tables, and fire rings. Potable water is not available.

Twin Bridges Airstrip.

**Garden Creek Campground is located 3.5 miles downstream from the airstrip. It also sits on the Big Lost River and has three campsites with pit toilets, picnic tables, and fire rings. Potable water is not available.

EXPLORING TWIN BRIDGES: This country is awesome. What never ceases to amaze us is the diversity of the land. You name the terrain and you will find it in this vicinity. High mountain lakes make majestic hiking destinations, rivers and streams provide good spots for fishing and picnics and the great open valleys stretch for miles.

LOST TRAIL CREEK SILVER - In the 1890s , a hitch of freight wagons (See Copper Basin History) tipped over while coming down the Mattie Grade, a portion of the Trail Creek toll road. The skinner sent a message to Ketchum for help which soon arrived, for the cargo was 100 pound silver ingots. The men of the Lewis Fast Freight Co. worked feverishly throughout the night to recover this valuable load. When morning came the wagons were righted, the teams hitched, and the ingots loaded; all except six, which were never found.

Jim Herbert fishing Twin Bridges Creek.

A 100 pound silver ingot was found near Twin Bridges on this same toll road. It had apparently been thrown off a freight wagon, as it crossed the lower bridge, by some dishonest freighter in hopes of a later recovery. It was found in 1961 and bore the stamp of Salmon River Silver company.

If this ingot were indeed one of the missing six, there's five more left to be discovered by some lucky person.

TWIN BRIDGES CREEK HIKE: From the north end of the runway, a dirt road leads up Twin Bridges Creek Canyon. After 30 years of passing by this canyon in search of new places to fish, Jim Herbert and I literally stumbled across this little hideaway.

After about 1-1/2 miles, the canyon opens up to reveal the remnants of an old homestead. The willow lined meandering creek refused to yield any fish on this trip (which corresponded to the spring runoff) but shows promise. Jim, however, was rewarded for his efforts by recovering a moose horn, shed during the previous winter.

For the athletically inclined, the Twin Bridges Creek continues 10 trailless miles upstream to 10,010 ft. Jerry Peak. I haven't been there and have no immediate intentions of going, so you are on your own. If you decide to try the hike to Jerry Peak however, keep an eye out for the author along the creek; I need to do a little further fish sampling research...purely business.

HISTORY: See Copper Basin History.

HUNTING & FISHING: Wildhorse Creek Ranch has recently reorganized. For current information on guided adventures, contact: Wildhorse Creek Ranch, Box 398, Mackay, Idaho 83251 (208)588-2575.

Tom Jarvis provides guided hunting trips for elk, deer, goat, antelope, bear, cougar, predators, and forest grouse as well as guided fishing trips, trailrides, and backpacking in Units 36A and 50. He will meet you at either Twin Bridges Airport or Copper Basin Airport to begin your adventure. For more information contact Tom Jarvis, Box 1117, Challis, Idaho, 83226, (208)879-4230.

The North Fork of the Big Lost River has excellent fishing for smaller rainbow and brook trout. As a general rule in this area, the larger the water, the larger the fish. As the East Fork and North Fork join the main Big Lost near Twin Bridges, sufficient water forms deep enough holes to hold large lunkers running upstream from Mackay Reservoir. In the heat of the summer, the larger fish lie hidden in shady pools and beneath undercut banks. The smaller fish are allowed to actively feed on the surface and accept the risk of predators; after sundown, however, the lunkers move the smaller fish out of the prime feeding areas and become quite aggressive feeders.

Fishing Kane Creek with Mount Hyndman in the background.
Courtesy: Idaho Historical Society.

MAPS, LOCAL CONDITIONS, AND INFORMATION:

Maps and camping/hiking information:, Challis Ranger District, Box 337, Challis, Idaho 83226, (208)879-4321. Salmon District Office, Bureau of Land Management, Box 430, Salmon, Idaho 83467 (208)756-5400.

Airport Conditions: Division of Aeronautics, 5483 Rickenbacker, Boise, Idaho 83705 (208)334-8775.

UPPER LOON CREEK

HIGHLIGHT → *Site of historic ghost town responsible for the start of the Sheepeater War. Nearby campground. Hike to hot springs. Beautiful mountain setting.*

- - - - -

AIRPORT DESCRIPTION: This airstrip lies in the narrow upper valley of Loon Creek. We are always amazed at the fresh pine smell that greets you upon arrival. Nearby Loon Creek provides good fishing and camping opportunities.

The runway lacks distinguishing runway end markers but the turf/dirt surface easily stands out against the surrounding sage and conifers. The upstream approach has a very memorable granite outcropping on the left hand side of Loon Creek to gauge your approach.

TRANSPORTATION: None...but primo mountain biking opportunities on the road. The road leading to and from Loon Creek exists as a corridor through the Frank Church River of No Return Wilderness. The Wilderness Rules apply immediately upon leaving the roadway. No motorized vehicles, no bicycles, no carts, no wheeled game carriers, no motorized tools or equipment such as chain saws, generators, or pumps are allowed.

This is a perfect place to use a mountain bike, but stay on the road and resist the temptation to use it on a trail! Refer to Wilderness Rules & Camping Etiquette in the appendix.

The Loon Creek Library - bring your own Sears catalog.

SERVICES & LODGING: The **Diamond D. Ranch** is a guest ranch that sits about three miles upstream from the Upper Loon Creek Airstrip.

11 units, $400-$645/week, R, P, C/M, SP, HT, MR (32).

For information and reservations contact: Diamond D Ranch, Box 1 Clayton, Idaho 83227, or Box 1555, Boise, Idaho 83702 (208)336-9772.

Hunting season brings ice to the upper reaches of Loon Creek.

CAMPING: ****Tin Cup Campground** lies one half mile downstream from the air strip. It has improved campsites, picnic tables, pit toilets, and overlooks Loon Creek. Bring your own drinking water or water filter. Tin Cup also has sites for rec- reational vehicles. Expect to see RV's, but not many due to the long, rough road.

    *Loon Creek Campground lies 2 1/4 miles upstream. It's an unimproved campground used as a trailhead for Trail 115 leading up Salt Creek. It has pit toilets but not drinking water.

EXPLORING UPPER LOON CREEK - HIKES: Oro Grande & Casto Historical Sites General description: 4.25 mile round trip hike from the Southwest end of the airstrip. Finding the trailhead: From the airstrip intercept the road and follow it upstream. The Hike: This is an easy hike along the backcountry road 007. At 0.5 miles is the site of the historic mining town of Oro Grande. At 2.125 miles is the historic site of Casto.

Miners abandoned this crane near the gold fields of Upper Loon.

Upper Loon Creek Hot Springs General description: 11.5 mile round trip hike from the trailhead at Phillips Creek Transfer Camp. A series of hot springs with varying degrees of batheability and temperature, from tolerable to exquisite. Finding the trailhead: From the airstrip proceed downstream on the road, approximately 1 1/4 mile. Pass Tin Cup Campground and find the Trailhead at the **Phillips Creek Transfer Camp** The hike: Loon Creek Trail 101 follows Loon Creek down stream through talus slopes and rock out croppings. At three miles a pack bridge crosses the stream. At five miles, you will come across the remains of an old log cabin hidden in the brush near the creek. Just around the bend, below the cabin, are waterfalls from two hot springs plunging over 20 foot cliffs into Loon Creek. An idyllic natural soaking pool exists at the base of the pool. Use river rocks to allow more or less cold river water into the pool to adjust the temperature.

Upper Loon Creek Airstrip is as pretty as they come.

HISTORY: Oro Grande was the center of gold rush activity in the Loon Creek drainage. In May of 1869, **Nathan Smith** discovered paying placers in Loon Creek. By mid summer, nearly 70 fortune were on their way from Leesburg. By August, the news hit Idaho City, and miners, merchants, tradesmen, and packers from the Boise Basin were on their way. The excitement even reached Montana, resulting in a population of 2500 by the end of the month.

The placers were difficult to mine due to the gold bearing gravel bars which were covered with six feet of large boulders. However, the gold was second only to Kootenai gold and highly regarded.

By spring of 1870, Oro Grande boasted log cabins, canvas houses, seven stores, seven saloons, one butcher shop, three boarding houses, two express offices, and 30 more buildings under construction. All of Loon Creek was diverted into a wooden flume and used for placering near Oro Grande.

It took only a year for the claims to become low grade, poor paying and rejected as worthless by white miners. Many claims were subsequently sold to incoming Chinese. By 1872, half the local population was Chinese (60 to 70), and shortly thereafter, the population was 100% Chinese.

By February 12, 1879, only five Chinese miners remained and they were reportedly massacred by Sheepeater Indians, although controversy exists today as to whether or not the Sheepeaters were actually to blame.

For some time, white settlers and miners encouraged the army to go after the Indians. They stood to profit from the sale of supplies to the military. However, it was not unthinkable to consider that the whites murdered the Chinese for their gold (as happened seven years later in Hells Canyon when Indians were blamed for the murder of 29 Chinese). Evidence has never been discovered to prove Indians were at fault.

Regardless, the army spent five months rounding up the Sheepeaters in 1879. They took them as prisoners to Vancouver Barracks in Washington. As a result of the campaign 51 Indians, 15 classified as "warriors" surrendered. A confiscated Indian arsenal totalled only eight guns.

HUNTING & FISHING: Diamond D Ranch, Inc., Thomas Demorest, May-Oct.: Box 1, Clayton, Idaho 83227 (no phone); Nov.-Apr.: Box 1555, Boise, Idaho 83701; (208)336-9772 offers guided hunting trips for elk, deer, goat, sheep, bear, cougar, and predators. Fishing, Trailrides, Backpacking, (Guest Ranch) in Unit 27.

MAPS, LOCAL CONDITIONS, AND INFORMATION:

Yankee Fork Ranger District
HC 67, Box 650, Clayton, Idaho 83227 (208)838-2201

Hunting Camp on Upper Loon.

VINES

HIGHLIGHT ✈ *Original homestead of "Kid" Garden, a.k.a. the "Yellowstone Kid", a reputed outlaw from Montana. Now mostly overgrown and very difficult, still sees some use by local charter pilots.*

- - - - -

AIRPORT DESCRIPTION: Vines Airstrip lies in the bottom of Big Creek at the mouth of Garden Creek about three miles upstream from the confluence of Cabin and Big Creek. The runway is on the south side of Big Creek on a flat bar created by a jog in the stream. Trees have grown up on the approach and require a steep glide slope to clear them. The runway has a 4% upslope and has a rough surface. There are no runway markings, windsock, or tiedowns.

HISTORY: **Arthur (Kid)** and **Viola (Auntie) Garden** homesteaded here in 1913. "Kid" Garden was an outlaw from Montana known there as the "Yellowstone Kid." His wife "Auntie" was a preacher's daughter. Auntie was best known for her special cougar recipes. Garden Creek, to the north of the Vines Ranch, was named for this pioneer family. The creek leads to Towhead Basin and the MileHi Ranch.

In 1914, the Clover Post Office was established in Kid and Auntie's home on the south side of the creek (where the airstrip presently is). It was the east terminal on the trail from Warrens, by way of Elk Summit and the mail arrived by horse, foot, and dogsled. In 1929, the post office was moved to the Mile Hi Ranch (see Mile Hi) and later to Cabin Creek. The post office got its name from the native clover found in the area.

Kid left the ranch in 1918 to get two bulls and was caught in an early winter storm. Upon getting wet and sick, he returned to Old Town Meadows to get treatment but died in the hotel. Auntie then sold the ranch to Edward Osborne, who in turn sold it to Art and Margaret Francis.

John Vines owned the ranch from 1930 to 1960. Rex Lanham (see Cabin Creek) built the airstrip for Vines with his bulldozer. The treads were so uneven, the runway surface was quite rough and dangerous. It has since deteriorated further.

In the 1950s, Vines hired two men to build a cabin for him. One of the men got so mad at Vines, he hit him over the head with a sledge hammer. Vines recovered, but the cabin didn't. It was left unfinished.

MAPS, LOCAL CONDITIONS, AND INFORMATION:

Payette Forest Air Officer, Box 1026, McCall, Idaho 83638 (208)634-0600.

Kid Garden's ranch and the Clover Post Office on the banks of Big Creek. Circa 1915. Courtesy: Idaho County Free Press.

WARM SPRINGS

HIGHLIGHT ✈ *Nearby communal hot springs. Nice turf airstrip.
Good airplane camping.*

- - - - -

AIRPORT DESCRIPTION: Warm Springs Airport sits in the South Fork of the Payette River Valley 13 miles east of Lowman. The airport was originally used by the Forest Service for fire suppression. The strip sits on a bench above and out of sight of the river and highway. The grass on the runway is a sight to behold. Tiedowns are located on the southeast side of the strip near the campground.

CAMPING: The ****Warm Springs Airport Campground** has three campsites with tables, stoves, drinking water, and a pit toilet. The first camper in the spring needs to prime the hand pump. Four tiedowns are located adjoining the camping area. The Ponderosa Flying Club, with the Division of Aeronautics and pilots across the state, have done a commendable job of constructing and maintaining this beautiful strip and camping area.

The U.S. Forest Service maintains a campground at the trailhead to Bonneville Hot Springs (see HIKES). This area gets a lot of drive in use from campers wanting to use the nearby hot springs and is not as private as the campground at the airport. In the event that the Warm Springs Airport Campground is full, this would be a good alternative. It has picnic tables, stoves, and pit toilets.

EXPLORING WARM SPRINGS: As with most of the backcountry, the hiking and hunting opportunities are plentiful, however, hunting takes a bit of a twist here (see hunting/fishing).

HIKES: Bonneville Hot Springs: General description - This is an easy 2.3 mile round trip hike to the natural hot springs. You may bathe privately in a bath house containing an old enamel tub or soak in one of the communal pools next to the creek. Ponderosa pines and the tumbling Warm Springs Creek make the canyon a beautiful peaceful setting for camping and relaxing. The springs are located 1/4 mile from a heavily used family campground, so take swimwear with you. Remember - no soap.

Finding the trailhead: Start from the Warm Springs Airport Campground.

The hike: From the campground located on the airstrip, follow the dirt road around the northeast end of the strip. As the road turns back to the southwest, abandon following it and proceed straight ahead across the open meadow uphill. At 0.4 miles from the start, look for a single ponderosa pine with a sign that says W.S. Trail and Link Trail, with arrows pointing left. Turn right and follow the trail downhill, intercept the Warm Spring Road, and follow it left to the Warm Springs Campground at 0.9 miles. The road terminates in a parking lot at the campground. Follow the trail upstream for 0.25 miles to the hot springs. Enjoy.

Bonneville Hot Springs.

HISTORY: Lowman - In 1907, **Nathaniel W. Lowman** settled about 10 miles downstream from the Warm Springs Airstrip. Four years later, when he started a post office in his large log house, the community was named for him.

Only a few scattered settlers lived here then. Lowman got all its supplies once a year from a large freight wagon over a state road built in 1894. Eventually, a one-room schoolhouse was moved here from Garden Valley. It still serves Lowman.

HUNTING & FISHING: Hunting the elusive Morel Mushrooms - The recent forest fires in the Lowman Ranger District have resulted in a tremendous loss of timber and habitat. The current attitude is that this is a natural cycle of environmental rebirth. To some of us old time fire fighters, the jury is still out on this issue.

However, out of the ashes of the burned forest rises one of natures greatest culinary prizes, the morel mushroom, the most highly prized of all edible mushrooms. It is found in May and June in recently burned areas. Following the Lowman fires of 1990, the mushrooms appeared in such quantity that the Forest Service was required to issue mushroom picking permits. To alleviate conflicts between commercial and personal use pickers, picking areas are segregated. For information and permits, stop by the Lowman Ranger Station located 13 miles west of the airstrip.

*Springtime bathers enjoy the warm waters
of Bonneville Hot Springs.*

Our personal success in finding the morel in this area has been limited to the Morchella Angusticeps, or Narrow-Capped Morel. The cap has dull brown pits, with ridges darker gray-brown or slate gray, often becoming almost black with age, in the shape of a narrow cone with bluntly rounded tip, hollow, fastened by the lower edge to the stem but with pronounced groove before it touches the stem. Ridges between pits conspicuously in vertical lines, are connected by cross ridges, two to four inches tall, about an inch wide, sometimes narrower. The stem is dingy cream to buff, stout, often furrowed at the base, granular all over, shorter than the cap.

A few unfortunate individuals have a bad reaction to morels, so if you have never eaten them, try cautiously at first. For proper disposal of morel mushrooms, make immediate contact with the author.

A Giant Helvella, Gyromitra gigas, was found near the airstrip in early May. It is edible and considered excellent by most people. Care should be taken to distinguish it from the brain mushroom and the hooded helvella. In cooking the giant helvella, first parboil and throw away the water in which it was blanched, rinse the pieces, then proceed with the cooking. Eat only a small quantity on first trial.

For trailrides, packtrips, fishing trips, and guided hunting trips for elk, deer, moose, goat, bear, and cougar, Darl Allred with Sawtooth Wilderness Outfitters will pick you up at the Warm Springs Airport. Contact Darl and Kari Allred, Sawtooth Wilderness Outfitters, Box 81, Garden Valley, Idaho 83622. (208)462-3416 winter or (208)259-3408 summer.

MAPS, LOCAL CONDITIONS, AND INFORMATION:

For maps and area information: U.S. Forest Service, Lowman Ranger District, Highway 21, HC-77, Box 3020, Lowman, Idaho 83637 (208)259-3361.

For airport information: Division of Aeronautics, 3483 Rickenbacker St, Boise, Idaho 83705 (208)334-8775.

WARREN

HIGHLIGHT ✈ *Historic mining community that prides itself in its annual "Spotted Owl Shoot." Nearby lodging, dance hall, and restaurant. Hasn't changed much in last 100 years. See it before the 20th century ruins it.*

- - - - -

AIRPORT DESCRIPTION: If you have ever had a burning desire to land on Main Street, you can come pretty close in Warren. The strip is just a stone's throw from the center of town. About as close to a ghost town as you can get, Warren gives you the feeling that around a 100 years ago or so, the townsfolk just closed their doors and walked away. This is a great place to stop for lunch and explore.

The surface is primarily decomposed granite and is generally in good shape. Early spring can leave some soft spots, however.

Warren Hotel, Warren, Idaho, 1993.

A cabin with rail fence has been built across the northeast end of the runway. Little plastic brushes stick up through the runway surface, marking the property lines. Avoid crossing the markers and on takeoff don't blow dust and gravel on the house.

SERVICES & LODGING: The **Winter Inn**, located a stone's throw from the airstrip, is a restaurant/bar. They serve breakfast, lunch, and dinner. Rooms are also available across the street. Contact: Shirley Winter, The Winter Inn, Box 100, Warren, Idaho 83671. Radiotelephone: Arnold Aviation (208)382-4336.

CAMPING: This decision is up to you. I have seen people camped with their airplanes at the end of RWY 11, but would not recommend it. This really isn't a safe place to tie down your aircraft without interfering with landing planes, and there are no facilities.

(Above) Main Street Warren, 1993. (Below) Winter Inn, Warren, Idaho. 1993. Notice the spotted owl dangling from a hangman's noose in the upper left hand corner.

Due to the close proximity of the road leading from Warren (and local drinking establishment), one's tranquility may be in jeopardy.

EXPLORING WARREN: The population here is very small but it seems a good sense of humor is enjoyed by all. A big banner

strung over Main Street advertises the annual "Spotted Owl Shoot" over the Fourth of July. A hangman's noose gripped a plastic owl decoy swaying in the breeze below the banner. It was full of arrows. You really had to be there. Whether or not this was some kind of socio/ecological/economic statement, or just pokin' fun at the outside world, we're not sure.

The old dance hall still stands at the end of Main Street and a variety of cabins stand in various degrees of decay. You can't help but notice the dredging work in the area. After the placer mines ran out, the dredges crawled down Warren's Creek, wreaking destruction in their path. The once beautiful valley floor literally has been ingested and regurgitated. One rusting old dredge still stands as an ugly reminder of its reckless and devastating past. Another skeleton of a dredge, referred to by locals as "Noah's Ark" sits hidden in the trees about three miles west of town.

An interpretive center is on the east edge of town at the U.S. Forest Service.

HISTORY: A chap by the name of **James Warren** is credited with discovering gold here in 1862. A log cabin was erected at the mouth of Slaughter Creek (one mile east of the landing strip) and a village quickly sprung up around it.

Southern sympathizers in the Civil War named the village **Richmond** after the Confederate Capital.

Not to be outdone, the Unionist miners built their own town one mile downstream from Richmond and named it **Washington.**

Unfortunately for Richmond, the town was found to be located on a site favorable to placer mining. In 1866, they picked up the town and moved it a mile downstream to Washington so they could mine the town site. (So much for Confederate loyalties when gold fever struck.) Washington continued to grow, and by 1879 the name Warren came into popular acceptance.

Fisher Station was the first stage stop on the Warren Wagons Road from Upper Payette Lake to Warrens. Circa 1911. Courtesy: Idaho State Historical Society.

Like most early Idaho mining camps, Warren had its share of Chinese. By one account, as many as 1000 Chinese lived here at one time. The Orientals had their own store, saloon, gambling house and butcher shop.

They suffered severe discrimination at the hands of miners. Some camps passed laws prohibiting entrance of any Orientals, other times they were shot or robbed at the slightest provocation. The Territorial Legislature even passed a four dollar a month tax on alien miners.

The Orientals rarely got to work virgin placer claims due to the threat of reprisal from white miners. However, the white miner was always anxious to sell worn out mining claims to the Chinese. Through hard work and industriousness, the Chinese could rework "worn out claims" successfully. Later, they often became respected community members.

POLLY BEMIS - Lalu Nanthoy was thirteen years old. Her father called her his treasure, his 'thousand pieces of gold,' yet when famine struck northern China in 1871, he was forced to sell her. The price: two bags of soy beans.

G-208

By the time Lalu was eighteen, she had belonged to the madam of a Shanghai brothel, a slave merchant bound for America, and a saloon keeper in a gold-rush mining town (Warren). In time, she would be known as Polly Bemis. She would marry the man who won her in a poker game and gave her freedom. A woman of rare pluck and true courage, she would start a new life as a homesteader on the River of No Return, winning a place of respect and dignity among the pioneer women of the early American West." Bemis Point directly Northeast of Warren and Bemis Creek leading into Warren are named after Polly and Charlie Bemis. *Thousand Pieces of Gold*, Ruthanne Lum McCunn,

(Above) Charles and Polly Bemis in front of cabin, presumably near what is now the Shepp Ranch. Courtesy: Idaho State Historical Society.

Warren Tavern, Warren, Idaho, 1993.

Dell Publishing Co., Inc., 1 Dag Hammarskjold Plaza, NY, NY 10017.

HUNTING & FISHING: One of the few benefits resulting from the dredging of Warren Creek was the creation of several ponds with fish in them. Ask one of the locals for directions.

MAPS, LOCAL CONDITIONS, AND INFORMATION:

Airport Information: Payette Forest Air Officer, Box 1026, McCall, ID 83638 (208)634-8151.

Lodging: Winter Inn, Box 100, Warren, Idaho 83671 (208)382-4336 Arnold Aviation Radiotelephone.

WEATHERBY

HIGHLIGHT ✈ *Just a short hop downstream from Atlanta. If the fishing slows down there, try here. A good spot to try your hand at panning gold.*

- - - - -

AIRPORT DESCRIPTION: Weatherby Airstrip is located 9 miles downstream from the community of Atlanta on the Middle Fork of the Boise River. It is squeezed between the gravel road to Atlanta and the river. The valley floor shows the effects of gold dredging with mounds of round river rock upturned in the dredge's wake. It has a windsock and tiedowns.

CAMPING: I have seen people airplane camping here but am always a little puzzled as to why. A cloud of dust from the very near road seems to hang over the valley floor and when the summer heat wave hits, the exposed rocks from the dredging operation act as an oven. There are no camping facilities here.

HUNTING & FISHING: The fishing here is very good for pansized rainbows and cutthroat trout. The Middle Fork of the Boise River is clear cold trout water. I have often noticed that the water here has a peculiar uniqueness in its pale blue clarity even during high water. I suspect the Atlanta batholith and granitic geology contribute to this quality.

MAPS, LOCAL CONDITIONS, AND INFORMATION:

Maps: Boise National Forest, 1750 Front Street, Boise, Idaho 83702 (208)334-1516

Airport conditions: Boise Forest Air Officer, 1750 Front Street, Boise, Idaho 83702 (208)334-9800

*The rocker box or cradle was a common form of placer mining in early Idaho.
The lure of gold brought hardy independent individuals to Idaho's
most isolated areas. The gold may be gone but the real treasure was left behind
waiting to be discovered as you FLY IDAHO! Taken from the "Century Magazine,
January, 1883. Courtesy: Idaho State Historical Society.*

NOTES

NOTES

NOTES

NOTES

NOTES

INFO

ARCO-KIMAMA DESERT OVERVIEW

Located in South Central Idaho, lies the haunting Arco Desert. An area of contradiction - 4000 square miles of largely unexplored no man's land.

* water is practically non existent but the government provides training for nuclear submarines.

* people are outnumbered by jackrabbits 100 to 1 but a nearby cowboy town became the first town powered by nuclear energy.

* where the Big Lost River completely disappears into the desert.

* where barren lava fields burst into a springtime rush of color as wildflowers extract moisture from the melting snow.

* where summer temperatures soar into the hundreds in the daytime but cool to near freezing at night.

* where trophy mule deer can live a lifetime without seeing a human - let alone a hunter.

* where teepee rings of rocks from Indian hunting parties can still be found undisturbed.

* where underground caves are filled year round with ice in deference to the soaring temperatures above ground.

* where rattlesnakes are as common as grasshoppers.

* where plagues of locust, "Mormon Crickets", travel in such incredible numbers, that their collective chirps can be heard great distances, and when they cross one of the few highways, the road turns greasy as millions are smashed, but statistically having no effect on the wildebeest like migration.

* a landscape so bizarre that one early traveler dubbed it "a weird lunar landscape" and in fact the lunar astronauts came here to train.

The Arco Desert has been described as "an outdoor museum of volcanism," and "a desolate and awful waste". The Shoshone Indians never inhabited this area in large numbers, but they hunted here. Pioneers in covered wagons skirted the lava flows; later cattle ranchers avoided the place; and miners staked claims only nearby. But this odd landscape, showing our globe's awesome forces, eventually became an object of awe.

HISTORY

The Limbert Trek - Robert Limbert headed into the rugged lava beds north of Minidoka, Idaho, in 1920 with W.L. Cole and a dog.

For 28 miles the trio trekked torturous a'a lava, unable to sleep for lack of level ground. Cole's feet blistered; the dog's feet were so cut to shred they carried it. At last they got onto smoother pahoehoe flows, but the new problem was water. The porous lava allowed no water to remain on the surface.

In deep lava fissures they finally found snow to melt. Later, by following dove flights they found snowmelt water holes within Great Rift faults. The two men were awed by unique features and named many in descriptive terms. Limbert's reports of the expedition and his photographs were instrumental in securing national monument status for 85 square miles of the desert known as Crater's of the Moon.

WILDLIFE

Garnering livelihoods from this alien, moonlike landscape are no less than 2000 insect species, 148 birds, 47 mammals, 8 reptiles, and a lone amphibian, the western toad. Secretive predators, bobcats and great horned owls, hunt here. The prairie falcon preys on other birds and small mammals with lightning dives.

More than 200 species of plants are also native to this apparently desolate landscape. Big sagebrush, antelope bitterbrush, and rubber rabbitbrush are established on the older lava flows. On the younger flows mockorange and tanysbush may fill deeper crevices, where soil and organic matter have accumulated.

Wildflowers carpet the desert from early May until late August. The more delicate annuals bloom during late May and early June when snowmelt and occasional rains provide fair amounts of moisture. With summer's dryness the more drought resistant plants continue to grow and bloom.

THE AIRSTRIPS

The desert strips were built as emergency strips, probably during World War II. Apparently, they have been responsible for saving more than a few aircraft in the past.

Population in this area is sparse, to say the least. A few poorly maintained dirt roads connect the airports and a few isolated ranches with the outside world.

Surprisingly, the area does have a considerable number of grazing cattle and a few horse herds. They seem to enjoy grazing on the runways and leaving their hoof prints for nose gear to find.

Runway surface conditions can never be guaranteed. Look for rodent activity, badger holes, livestock, game animals, and deep ruts left by four wheel drive vehicles.

Survival equipment, along with lots of water, is a must while visiting the desert. Plan ahead that you will probably be stranded, so a flat tire or dead battery becomes an inconvenience - not a life and death situation. The decision to stay with the aircraft is generally a good one. Walking out of the desert from a stranded airplane is probably your worst choice of options, first try your ELT, the aircraft radio, a handheld radio, emergency markings on the ground, etc. etc.

For an "out of this world experience," visit these strips in May or June, and practice your soft and short field take-offs and landings in preparation for mountain flying later in the season.

HELLS CANYON OVERVIEW

DESCRIPTION

An 8000 foot drop from He Devil peak to the Snake River creates one of Mother Earth's most breathtaking scenes - the deepest gorge in North America - Hells Canyon. This national treasure covers 652,488 acres, including some of the most rugged spectacular wildlands on earth. The area straddles the wildest whitewater stretch of the mighty Snake River where it runs south to north on the Idaho-Oregon border.

About 67 miles of the Snake River inside the boundary is managed under the National Wild and Scenic River System.

Nearly 215,000 acres of the National Recreation Area, almost one-third, is managed as wilderness. No machines, motors, or vehicles (including bicycles) operate in the Hells Canyon Wilderness.

HISTORY

Researchers have identified over 700 archaeological sites in and around Hells Canyon, with evidence of human habitation going back over 7000 years. Sites with historical significance range from rock art and winter pithouse villages to pioneer cabins and homes of Chinese miners.

Far earlier than the keeping of records, Chief Joseph's band of Nez Perce Indians lived in Hells Canyon. They and the Shoshone-Bannock, Northern Paiute and Cayuse Indians, who were frequent visitors to the area, were drawn by relatively mild winters, lush forage and plentiful wildlife.

May 27, 1806 - three members of the Lewis and Clark expedition penetrated Hells Canyon by following the Salmon River while looking for a route to the Pacific Ocean. Unaware they were near an awe-inspiring canyon more than 7500 feet deep, the party turned back and rejoined the expedition near today's Kamiah, Idaho.

The first real exploration of Hells Canyon area was in 1811 when the Wilson Price Hunt expedition tried to find a shortcut through Hells Canyon to the Columbia River. They reached a point three miles upstream from the present site of Hells Canyon Dam, but hunger and freezing cold forced them back.

Other explorers soon followed with similar aspirations to search out new territories and find new passages, but most experienced similar results because of the canyon's legendary inaccessibility. Expedition journals reflect their attempts; however, little or no evidence of their endeavors remain in the canyon today.

CHIEF JOSEPH

The Nez Perce Treaty of 1855 reserved vast areas of land for the Nez Perce Indian Tribe. The land stretched from what is now central Idaho to the eastern edges of both Washington and Oregon. Tucked remotely away in the Oregon allotment was the beautiful and fertile Wallowa Valley. Here, amidst the picturesque setting and the superior hunting grounds, Chief Tu-eka-kas (Chief Joseph's father) and his band of Nez Perce lived peacefully. For unnumbered generations the Wallowa Valley had been the home of their ancestors.

Hostilities began when settlers and cattlemen increasingly trespassed upon the Indian's land. In 1861, when gold was discovered in Orofino, Idaho, 10,000 miners invaded their homeland in search of the precious mineral. The friendly Indians became restless.

In 1863, the U.S. Government offered a new treaty in an attempt to pacify the new settlers and give unobstructed access to the newly discovered mines. Chief Tu-eka-kas refused to sign the treaty because it totally excluded the Wallowa Valley and outlying areas from the Indian's land. However, a number of chiefs whose interests were not affected, signed the new treaty and the Government contended that all the Nez Perce were bound. Tu-eka-kas and his tribe were to leave the Wallowa Valley and move to the newly designated Lapwai reservation in Idaho.

Tu-eka-kas ignored the treaty, and despite grievances against the Government, skillfully maintained peace with the settlers. He and his people remained in the Wallowa Valley until his death.

With Tu-eka-kas now in his grave, the mantle of authority fell upon Joseph. His young braves were held in check in spite of the growing resentment felt at losing more land and horses to an increasing white population. The Government continued to urge Joseph to give up the land peacefully and move his people to the reservation.

Finally, in the spring of 1877, General Howard of the United States Army became impatient and notified Chief Joseph that he must move within 30 days or be driven out by soldiers. Joseph, realizing the unfavorable odds of a fight with the U.S. Army, reluctantly agreed to move.

The disappointed tribe dismantled their Wallowa Valley camp for the last time in late May of 1877, moving off toward the Snake River. Chief Joseph's band consisted of approximately 400 Indians, including about 64 braves, ages 16 and over. They took over 1,000 head of horses and cattle, leaving much of their stock behind.

After crossing the Snake River, Joseph's people joined with other bands of Nez Perce and a small group of Palouses. Thereafter, the historical Nez Perce War began, turning the peaceful journey into a flight for freedom and sanctuary in Canada.

Every mile of the retreat brought danger. Aided by Chief Joseph's surpassing military genius, the Nez Perce confused and outwitted the 2,000 regular troops of the United States Army. Though the warriors were encumbered with women, children and the elderly throughout their flight, they were able to outdistance the fresh troops continually appearing in their path.

Joseph and his people came to the end of their bloody trail in the Bear Paw Mountains of Montana, only 30 mils from the Canadian refuge. Hemmed in by winter snow the Indians were besieged by the U.S. Army and forced to surrender. After three months of unquestionable grief, anxiety and hardship, Joseph, in a pathetic, yet dramatic surrender, said: "From where the sun now shines, I shall fight no more forever."

WILDLIFE

Hells Canyon provides a home for over 375 species of animals including 29 species of fish. Of these animals, the Rocky Mountain elk is perhaps the best known. These elk, introduced in Hells Canyon in 1923, are now found through the entire area.

Native Rocky Mountain bighorn sheep disappeared when domestic sheep diseases decimated the local population. They have since been reintroduced successfully in both Idaho and Oregon.

Rocky Mountain goats inhabit the Seven Devils Mountains in Idaho. The most prevalent game bird is the chukar partridge, also an introduced species, which is found at lower elevations. The white sturgeon, America's largest freshwater fish, inhabits the Snake River. Anadromous salmon and steelhead are found in both the Snake and Imnaha River drainages. Both bald and golden eagles are fairly common here, as well as a number of species of hawks and falcons.

RIVER TRIPS

The Snake River in Hells Canyon offers a scenic float with some major rapids. The water flow is controlled by the Hells Canyon Dam. The river is floated by permit only and is recommended to only the experienced floater or with the services of a licensed outfitter. The Snake also offers great opportunities for those interested in jet boat activities. Day trips are available with licensed outfitters from Hells Canyon Dam or from Lewiston.

Float permits are required for all launches between Hells Canyon Dam and Rush Creek Rapids during the period beginning on the Friday preceding Memorial Day through September 15 (self issuance-permits are required for launches below Rush Creek). Reservations are made via a telephone confirmation system, (509)758-1957, which generally begins on the first weekend in February and continues through daytime business hours weekdays until all spots are taken.

LICENSED OUTFITTERS

Beamer's Landing
Box 1223
Lewiston, Idaho 83501
(800)522-6966, (208)743-4800

Hells Canyon Fishing Charters
Box 232
Riggins, Idaho 83549
(800)626-3714, (208)628-3714

River Adventures Ltd.
Box 518
Riggins, Idaho 83549
(208)628-3952

BIG GAME OUTFITTERS

Cook's Idaho Outfitters
Box 232
Riggins, Idaho 83549
(800)626-3714, (208)628-3714

Meadow Creek Outfitters
HC01 Box 80
White Bird, Idaho 83554
(208)839-2424

Whitten Guide Service
Box 498
Riggins, Idaho 83549
(208)328-3863

HORSE BACK TOURS

Sam Whitten
Box 82
Riggins, Idaho 83549
(208)628-3673

Dave Stucker
Seven Devils Outfitters
Box 172
Riggins, Idaho 83549
(208)628-3446

For a complete list of licensed outfitters and guides for this area, call:

North Central Idaho Travel Association (800)473-3543

For more information, maps, and descriptive literature on adventure in Hells Canyon contact:

Hells Canyon National Recreation Area
88401 Hwy 82
Enterprise, Oregon 97828
(503)426-4978

Hells Canyon National Recreation Area
2535 Riverside Drive, Box 699
Clarkston, Washington 99403
(509)758-0616

Hells Canyon National Recreation Area
Box 832
Riggins, Idaho 83549
(208)628-3916

INDIANS ON THE MIDDLE FORK OF THE SALMON

Caves and rock shelters along the Middle Fork and its tributaries hold artifacts that show native Americans used this area for 12,000 years. The two Indian groups that ranged this region most recently, the Nez Perce and Shoshone, left only yesterday in terms of archaeological time. Remnants of the Shoshone group called Sheepeaters avoided the military roundup of their people in 1879 and remained in isolated parts of this wild country until near the start of this century.

Those cultural resources related to Indians include stone and bone tools, remnants of clothing and basketry, remains of stone dams and weirs used in fish traps, depressions that were once pit houses, rocks stacked to form shelters, storage bins, and ambush sites for Indian hunters. Indian signs and symbols are chipped and painted on rock walls throughout this wild canyon country. Many remain undiscovered by professional archaeologists. Much that has been found is not well understood. Travelers in the area should remember that collection of artifacts by the general public is prohibited by the Antiquities Act.

Both the Shoshone and Nez Perce used a wide array of hunting and fishing strategies requiring highly specialized tools and skills. They fished with communal traps and weirs, and established semi-permanent platforms where migrating salmon were dipped out with long-handled nets. Hooks, spears, and seines were common. They knew how to formulate poisons both for stunning fish and for use on arrow or spear points. Hunters used decoys, blinds, snares, pits, and deadfalls. Elk were hunted on snowshoes when the snow was deep. Trained dogs were used for some pursuits.

THE SHEEPEATER WAR OF 1879

In 1879, the Sheepeater Indians were accused of murdering five Chinese miners on Loon Creek. There was no evidence that Indians were actually involved in the crime but it was convenient at the time to blame Indians for any unexplained violence against whites.

Brigadier General O.O. Howard, Commander of the Department of Columbia, ordered troops to the Middle Fork in 1879. Cavalry Captain Reuben F. Bernard was in charge of the field operation, but it is explained in much more detail in the diary of Private Edgar Hoffner, who rode with Bernard and his junior officers throughout the Sheepeater War.

Private Hoffner sums up the campaign as follows: "We marched (and rode) 1,258 miles through sections where no human beings had ever set foot before. A number of animals (horses and mules) were made useless and men badly used up."

Private Hoffner's diary also tells of pack mules tumbling over cliffs, saddle animals shot after they played out, food and blankets lost time and again when pack animals were swept downriver in the many dangerous crossings. The soldiers were often lost, frequently hungry, commonly wet and cold. The Indians they sought were as elusive as wolves-and just as much at home among the peaks and canyons that were always the major enemy of the military.

This "war" ended with two brief exchanges of fire between soldiers and Indians. One soldier, Private Harry Eagan, was killed and is buried in a marked grave on what is now named Soldier Bar on Big Creek. The Indians, who fired from ambush and moved on, were seldom seen and had no known casualties.

The Indians seemed puzzled, and finally bored, by the dogged pursuit. They eventually surrendered to Lieutenant Edward S. Farrow and his troop of Umatilla Indian scouts on October 1, 1879. They were eventually settled on the Ft. Hall Reservation in eastern Idaho. A few of their group missed the surrender gathering and remained in the mountains for many years.

General Howard felt much better about the Sheepeater War than did Private Hoffner. His letter to the Adjutant General in San Francisco says the expedition was "handsomely completed," with the forced surrender of the entire band and the capture of their camp, stores, and stock.

The soldiers, however their campaign is judged, left their marks and relics on the Middle Fork. They left Private Eagan buried on Soldier Bar, and they left mule packer Dave Lewis · later locally famous as Cougar Dave Lewis · alive and well as a new Middle Fork settler.

FLYING INFORMATION
MOUNTAIN FLYING TIPS

Prior to flying into the Backcountry, consider the following information on mountain flying. This information is based on years of successful mountain flying by experienced mountain pilots.

General

1. Do not consider flying the mountain country until you are proficient in slow flight. A check-out by an experienced mountain flying instructor is highly recommended.

2. Before flying into mountainous areas, practice short field landings power-on, upwind, downwind and crosswind. Be sure you can land on a fifty foot spot every time.

3. Carry enough fuel to make a complete round trip plus fifty percent.

4. Know your aircraft. Do not take an aircraft into mountain terrain that will not takeoff and land in a minimum distance. Most airports in this area are substandard in length and width and have associated high density altitude. It takes considerable experience to handle a high performance aircraft in the mountain environment.

5. Keep your aircraft weight as light as possible.

6. Know your planned destination airport. Check with experienced mountain pilots, if possible. Know the altitude, length, condition and approach/departure procedure at the airport. Many of these fields are one-way, and on some, a go-around is not possible once you have committed to land.

7. Check the weather frequently and stay out of doubtful or bad weather. Mountain weather changes rapidly and unexpectedly.

8. Plan your flight to arrive in the early morning hours. As a rule, the air begins to deteriorate around 10:00 a.m., grows steadily worse until about 4:00 p.m., then gradually improves until dark.

9. Stay out of the mountains if the wind is over 25 knots.

10. Route your trip over valleys whenever possible and study your charts thoroughly. Watch your compass heading to avoid getting lost.

11. Maintain a minimum of 2000' AGL while overflying the backcountry. Remember: others are in the mountains to enjoy a wilderness experience.

12. Approach all ridges at an angle so you can turn away if you encounter a downdraft. After crossing the ridge, head directly away from it.

13. Expect the wind to be changing constantly in the mountains. Do not rely on cloud shadows for wind direction. If you are unable to gain altitude on one side of a canyon, try the other side. If there is no improvement there, fly the

center. But do not under any circumstance fly up a canyon or valley without sufficient altitude and room to turn around. The grade of the canyon may climb faster than your aircraft.

14. Maintain flying speed in downdrafts. Do not panic; air does not go through the ground. A ground cushion of air will always be there unless below the top of the timber. The stronger the downdraft, the greater velocity it will have when it changes direction.

15. Remember, you will not have a horizon to check your aircraft attitude once you begin a let down in the mountains. Watch your airspeed and cross check your instruments.

16. Caution: traffic pattern terrain clearance is not standard at many mountain airports.

17. Above all, fly the aircraft every second, don't let it "fly you". You cannot make mistakes.

Heavy cold air goes downhill, while lighter warm air rises; therefore, under ordinary circumstances you can expect the wind to be blowing upstream in the late morning and afternoon as the air heats up, and downstream in the evening as it cools. The wind is affected by the topography. With a little analysis you can tell where the updrafts and downdrafts are likely to be. As a general rule, air follows the contour of the land it flows over. Use the updrafts to help you gain altitude. But do not fly an aircraft that does not have a ceiling sufficient to get you above the mountains without help from the updrafts.

Always remember your are flying in a sparsely populated area. If you have an accident, it may be a long time before anyone knows about it. Be sure you leave your itinerary with someone. You may be landing on airports where there is no one to help you in case of trouble, and it is a long walk out. Do not take chances. Equip yourself with proper clothing and at least minimum survival equipment on any flight into the mountainous areas. Make sure your ELT is in good working condition.

LANDINGS

Safety of flight dictates that each pilot transmit in-the-blind on 122.9 whenever approaching or departing a non-unicom equipped airport so as to advise other aircraft of your intentions.

You cannot maintain visual contact with the runway at many of the Backcountry airports. This situation will make it mandatory that you know the location and intentions of all other airport traffic. These airports receive considerable use when forest fires of similar emergency conditions exist. Make periodic position reports on 122.9 while flying over the Backcountry, giving your location, altitude and destination. This will keep other pilots advised of your intentions, and will greatly aid in any rescue effort that may be necessary.

1. Terrain and runway gradient usually dictates landing upstream. However, there are exceptions. Consult the airport directory for the preferred landing pattern. Maintain the recommended approach speed with power (see Pilot's Operating Handbook). If the aircraft is settling too fast, add power, but do not make power-off approaches: they are dangerous! When the landing is assured, reduce power for a controlled sink rate to the runway. Retract the flaps immediately after contact to permit the aircraft weight to settle on the gear to increase braking effectiveness.

2. Do not drag into mountain airports with a low approach. Under these conditions a downdraft has everything its way. If you have doubt about any approach, go around while you are still high and have room to maneuver safely.

3. Do not maneuver to land at low altitude. Go far enough from the field to turn so pattern execution can be made at a safe altitude. This allows time to stabilize your final approach speed and approach glide slope to the runway. If you find turbulent air when you let down in the canyons, return home. Turbulent air has no respect for you, regardless of your experience or ability. After landing, park your aircraft well clear of the useable runway surface.

TAKEOFFS

1. Remember that each thousand feet you are above sea level decreases aircraft performance. Temperature increases density altitude (that altitude the aircraft thinks it is at) so a 5000' airport elevation can be well above 8000' density altitude on a hot day. You should compute your takeoff roll using your Aircraft Operations Manual and other published guidelines. Also, compute your rate-of-climb to ensure you can maintain terrain clearance. If in doubt, do not take off.

2. Use common sense on takeoffs. If the air is turbulent, weather is marginal, or you have a tailwind, wait until conditions improve. Remember: most of these airports are not long enough to abort a takeoff attempt once airborne. Let the aircraft use as much runway as it needs, then it will be flying when it leaves the ground. Do not pull the aircraft off until you have gained proper flying speed.

3. You can shorten the takeoff distance by making your turn at the end of the runway at a good fast taxi speed, open the throttle as the aircraft swings around to line up with the runway. Practice the maneuver with an instructor on a good standard airport.

BACKCOUNTRY AIRSTRIPS

Pilots flying into Backcountry airstrips must keep in mind that most of these locations have few, if any, support facilities. Typically, resources such as aircraft maintenance, courtesy cars, telephones, lodging and dining, rest rooms, or even tiedown chains will not be available.

Due to the fact that these sites are unattended and receive limited maintenance, they are subject to deterioration caused by the weather, wild game, and other aircraft operations. Therefore, the airstrip may be rough enough to pose the problem of aircraft damage caused during landing. Each pilot intending to fly into the Backcountry must be prepared to operate within the limitations of the airstrips where landings are planned.

Each user of these facilities has a responsibility to ensure that fellow aviators will have the same opportunity to enjoy these remote environs. The delicate balance of nature and man's co-existence in the wilderness and other Backcountry airstrip areas are, for the most part, dependent on us meeting our obligation of use. Simply follow the basic rules! Don't use airstrips or any area for activities they aren't intended to support. Keep in mind that wilderness airports are allowed to exist in order to provide access for wilderness-dependent activities such as hunting, fishing, backpacking, etc. If you pack it in, pack it out. Finally, leave each area cleaner than you found it! Everyone likes a good neighbor.

DIRT STRIPS AND THE NEED FOR INSTRUCTION

The training required for obtaining a private pilot's license requires familiarization in short and soft field landing and takeoff techniques, airplane performance, and density altitude. These techniques are often taught from relatively long unobstructed paved runways. Whereas this is probably the appropriate spot to learn the techniques, it has little relevance in the real world of mountain flying.

To learn to fly the Backcountry, you must have qualified instruction and actual mountain flying experience. The FAA rating system does not appropriately identify individuals that are qualified for mountain flying instruction. In fact, I personally know of CFI's and CFII's who have made it through the ratings game without ever landing on an unpaved strip. I, in no way, mean to belittle their accomplishments, but simply want to point out the importance of finding local qualified mountain flying instructors and an FAA rating is not necessarily the best way to pre-qualify a mountain flying instructor.

In fact, the best mountain flying instruction I have ever had came from a fellow who has flown the Idaho Backcountry for 50 years. I doubt if he is a current CFI or for that matter he may never have been a CFI - to me, it really doesn't matter. I needed instruction on two airstrips (RHI 28 & 32) that I had never been in to and neither had go-arounds.

Under his instruction, the approaches to both these strips were as precise as the best ILS I had ever shot. The power settings and glide slope were a thing of beauty. It was a tightly choreographed dance as the airplane nimbly twisted and turned, as if on a convoluted VASI, to a gentle touchdown on the end of the runway like an autumn cottonwood leaf gently fluttering to the ground. The outcome was never in question.

OK, OK, How do I get local mountain flying instruction? Odd you should ask.

MOUNTAIN FLYING SEMINAR

Bob Plummer, of Bob's Aircraft, Inc., Challis, Idaho, has combined efforts with the Division of Aeronautics and the FAA to put on a three day mountain flying seminar for the past several years. The annual event has grown in popularity to such an extent that 1993 required three such seminars. The seminar is great!

Two and a half days of ground school are followed by personal instruction in your airplane on actual Backcountry airstrips. The instructors are frequently air charter pilots that fly the Backcountry for a living. Sign up early (i.e. January) as the classes quickly fill.

For information and reservations, contact:
Bob's Aircraft, Inc.
Box 525
Challis, Idaho 83226
(208)879-2364

CHEAP INSURANCE

I am not advocating carrying cheap hull coverage or liability. But rather, Bob Plummer's Mountain Flying Seminar, or personal instruction from a local mountain flying instructor is the "cheapest insurance" you can get to insure the safety of you and your family and your airplane.

FLIGHT PLANS

Flight plans in the Backcountry? Yea...right! you say. OK, I admit, it's not as easy to work the system in the Backcountry, but it's not impossible and can be well worth the time and effort. The basic problem with Backcountry Flight Plans is the lack of communication with FSS. Nine times out of ten, the FSS frequencies listed in standard airport directories, won't work from the ground in the Backcountry. Now what?

FLY-IDAHO! lists FSS frequencies that can be reached through line-of-sight VOR's. The catch is "line-of-sight". The only way you are going to be in line-of-sight is to be above the mountain tops, and in most cases that means 9500' and above. This requires one to close flight plans some time before landing...not great but better than nothing.

Another technique is to file a "round robin" flight plan when going into the Backcountry. If you don't return when you said you will, FSS will initiate a search for you. This doesn't give you much flexibility and if you have problems on your arrival, you are likely to sit there until FSS misses you on the round trip - which could be a few days later.

As you fly the Backcountry, you'll hear nearly constant chatter on 122.9 and 122.95 from the charter pilots. Everyone is reporting their position and destination and lots of chatter about the company Christmas Party, or whose turn it is to buy coffee, or the size of an elk taken out of Cold Meadows. These pilots are not frustrated CB radio operators but in this harsh environment where radar tracking is virtually non-existent, they are participating in an effective aircraft tracking system.

If a pilot gets into trouble and can get a call off before he drops too low, he can almost be assured of another pilot picking up his call. If he doesn't return to his office when expected, the jungle drums begin to sound. The pilots offer to buy coffee and last position report may very well be all that's necessary to narrow down the search.

WEATHER

The old time Backcountry charter pilots made their reputations on knowing the terrain well enough they could fly in any weather. Some made it but a lot didn't. There is still a high incidence of professional charter pilots that get caught in weather that closes in around them and don't make it.

As recreational pilots, we have it all over the charter pilots. We fly for fun. We can be very selective about when and where we fly. If the weather isn't nice, flying isn't fun and we don't do it (or shouldn't do it). There are a lot of really nice days, so there is no reason to fly the rotten days.

If you are in a position to own an airplane, you are also probably in a position to be somewhat flexible with your time, especially if it means risking your life. If the weather craps out on you, sit it out. Some of the best times of my life have been on the ground waiting for the weather to lift (at least it was better than being in the air).

The old timers claim that only fools and tourists predict the weather in Idaho. If you wait 15 minutes, the weather will change.

MECHANICAL ASSISTANCE

Well, it finally happened. You have just landed at Soldier Bar and blown a tire and you're all alone...now what? The passengers are all fine but the airplane won't make it off the ground with this flat. You need help.

Flight Service is almost impossible to reach on the ground anywhere in the Backcountry. But don't give up on the radio. I would recommend staying on 122.9 and trying to get a message to a passing airplane. Also try 122.95 and 122.75 as they are often used for aircraft to aircraft conversations and chit chat. It's an unwritten rule of the Backcountry - you help someone in need. If you can reach another airplane, they will generally help you any way they can.

But no one seems to be flying today and you haven't been able to reach anyone on 122.9, what now? Pull out your IFR enroute charts and try the appropriate Center Frequency for your sector. You won't reach Center, but you may contact an airliner flying overhead.

How about 121.5? Absolutely, use it. You may not be in a dire emergency now, but what happens if no one comes to rescue you for several days? Unfortunately, monitoring 121.5 is not as common as you might think in the Backcountry. Charter pilots usually have one radio on 122.9 and the second radio on 122.95 or some other frequency used by their office.

What if the battery goes dead and the radios are out of service? This is a great opportunity to use the portable handheld stuffed in the jockey box. You say you opted for the leather bomber's jacket instead of the handheld radio? Well, there is still hope. The ELT has its own self contained battery pack. This may be the time to manually trigger the ELT. But remember that most ELT's are trnsmitters only and do not receive.

No ELT? As a last resort, you might consider hiking to a Forest Service Guard Station or Lookout. This is rather risky. Many of the Lookouts are no longer manned and the Guard Stations are only seasonally manned. But the Forest Service uses a two way radio on the Backcountry Net and can get messages to the outside world. The ground section in this book mentions the availability of Forest Service Radio Communication when applicable. Remember, however, that most of the locations are manned only during the summer.

SURVIVAL SENSE

Any guide to flying would be remiss without including information on survival techniques. The following information is supplied by the Idaho Division of Aeronautics:

Key Survival Actions

1. Immediately after an emergency landing, exit the aircraft if at all possible. Check for injuries, but only give temporary first aid necessary to permit careful removal of casualties with serious injuries.

2. Stay away from the aircraft until engines have cooled and spilled gasoline has evaporated.

3. After occupants are all out and at a safe distance from the aircraft, re-evaluate injuries and administer first aid as necessary.

4. If the weather is adverse, make or find temporary shelter.

5. Evaluate your location dangers: fire, sliding, rockfall, avalanche, terrain and weather.

6. Stay near the aircraft if at all possible. It contains the basic ingredients for warmth, shelter and signaling materials.

7. Make sure that your ELT is on and working.

8. Signal for help. Do not neglect your aircraft radio. It may still be operational. Turn on squelch and volume and key the mike. If the results are positive, listen on a local or ATC frequency. When you hear a transmission transmit "MAYDAY-MAYDAY." If you should hear a jet, transmit on 121.5.

All airlines and military aircraft monitor 121.5. If you do not hear any transmissions go ahead and transmit in the blind on this frequency. Limit your transmissions to about one every fifteen minutes. Transmitting places considerably more drain on the battery than receiving. If both your ELT and radio are working, you will hear the ELT signal when listening on 121.5. It may be necessary to turn the ELT off when transmitting or listening on 121.5. (Don't forget to turn the ELT back on!)

9. If the weather is cold or wet do not spend too much time trying to signal. Your prime effort must be directed toward conserving the energy you have.

10. Wings, rudder, etc., all may be used to make a shelter. Keep this shelter as small as possible to lessen the area your body must heat. Insulate shelters with boughs, bark, tarps, maps, etc. Use anything to keep the rain from getting inside your shelter. Body heat loss is energy loss.

11. Your aircraft can fulfill most of your basic needs if you improvise. Think basic needs: shelter (cover), warmth (fabric), tools (metal). Maps, newspaper, engine cover and plastic tarps all make excellent emergency bedding.

12. Build a fire, if possible. Don't forget that the aircraft gasoline is a valuable resource in starting a fire when only wet wood is available. Caution must be used when using gasoline. Soak or pour gasoline on the wood but be sure the container is out of reach when igniting the wood. Paper such as charts can also aid in getting a fire started. However, do not burn your charts for firewood. Paper makes an excellent insulation for bedding, clothing and shelter.

13. In cold weather, insulation and upholstery from the craft make excellent material for overboots, sleeping bags, mittens, hats, and ground insulation. Sew them together with salvaged aircraft wire. Put plastic side out for better wetness protection.

14. If running water is not readily available melt snow or ice in an improvised pot, or squeegee dew drops from aircraft surfaces. Place a sheet of plastic flat on the ground so that it may collect dew or condensation. If it is raining, place plastic sheet in ground depression to collect water.

15. Keep your signal fire burning all the time. Smoke and fire light can be seen from great distances. Both air and ground searchers will be looking for them.

16. Aircraft should be made visible from the air if possible. Clear brush, cut trees, etc. Be prepared to make signals as aircraft approaches your area. Keep the mirror handy if the sun is shining. Practice its use.

17. Get your emergency signaling devices ready for immediate use. Every possible effort must be made to attract searchers to your location by signals—mirror, smoke, flares, color panels—and to sustain life and energy until assistance arrives.

18. Colored Panels can tell a message. Pile Brush in SOS. Stamp large, two-feet wide SOS letters in the snow. Fill stamped marks with boughs or small brush.

19. Clear windows make a fair emergency mirror. Signals make you effectively bigger.

PILOT'S SURVIVAL KIT

Compass, Tool Kit (small, light weight), First Aid Kit, Food (freeze dried, candy bars, etc.), Disposable Space Blankets, Saw, Matches (waterproof) & Fire Starter, Signaling Devices (flares, mirror, strobe light, etc), Knife, 50' 1/8" Nylon Rope, Garbage Sacks, Fish Hooks, Sinkers and Line, Can Opener, Sierra Cup. Seal contents in a container suitable to heat and store water, Winter Clothing & Sleeping Bag

For additional reading on survival techniques, I highly recommend reading and carrying in your survival kit, the excellent book - *Survival Sense for Pilots and Passengers* by Robert Stoffel and Patrick LaValla. Your brain, however, is your best survival tool. The first few hours of any wilderness survival emergency will be the most important. Decisions made during this period usually determine life or death.

GENERAL INFORMATION
NATURAL HAZARDS OF THE BACKCOUNTRY

Wilderness travel involves an element of risk. Wilderness travelers may be a long way from outside help if faced with an accident, sudden illness, or other emergency and should be prepared to be self reliant in such situations. The risk of serious injury can be reduced by:
- being supplied with proper equipment and clothing
- being armed with first-aid knowledge and supplies
- being aware of changing weather conditions and other natural hazards
In the event of a serious injury, the Forest Service may be contacted at the offices and Guard Stations, The Forest Service may take a temporary lead role in finding lost persons. The county sheriff will direct extensive search and rescue operations, with assistance provided by the Forest Service.

Following are some of the natural hazards present in the Backcountry:

Giardia: Giardia lamblia, an intestinal parasite that can, if ingested, cause diarrhea, abdominal cramps, bloating, fatigue, and weight loss, may be present in any surface water source in the Backcountry. The symptoms may take a few days or several weeks to develop. Relief usually requires prescribed medication from a physician. The ;most effective prevention measure is to treat all drinking water by boiling. Some commercially available filters may be effective in removing Giardia. Chlorine and Iodine are both effective in killing Giardia providing the proper dosage is used.

Ticks: Ticks are small insects that tenaciously cling to, and then burrow into, the skin or scalp. Ticks may transmit Rocky Mountain Spotted Fever and Colorado

Tick Fever, both serious diseases. Ticks are common early in the season. As summer progresses, the ticks become less common.

Poisonous Snakes: Rattlesnakes live in the Backcountry below about 5,000 feet elevation.

Poison Ivy: Poison ivy is common along the banks of the rivers, including the Middle Fork, Salmon, Selway, and Snake.

Hot Springs: Some of the hot springs are hot enough to cause burns. Caution should be exercised around hot water, especially if children are in the group.

Bears: There are few grizzly bears in Idaho. However, black bears are quite common but rarely seen. When encountering a human, black bears usually run away unless wounded or cornered. The exception is a female bear with cubs who may become aggressive if she feels her cubs are threatened, or bears who learn that human campsites are an easy place to find food.

WILDLIFE

The abundant and varied habits of the Backcountry provide homes for a broad diversity of fish and wildlife. Otters, coyotes, blue grouse, rainbow, steelhead, cutthroat trout, chinook salmon, golden-mantled ground squirrels, marmots, Canadian geese, and black-capped chickadees are just a few examples.

Some of the most spectacular animal residents are the big game species such as elk, moose, bear, deer, bighorn sheep, and mountain goat. Elk and deer can be found throughout the Wilderness in a variety of habitats with the exception of extremely rocky areas. Common places to see them are along the edge of forested and open areas, or near stream bottoms.

Bighorn sheep are sure-footed climbers who prefer cliffs and upland slopes near rocky areas where they can easily elude their enemies. During the winter they may be forced down to lower slopes, but will still try to stay close to rugged escape areas.

Mountain goats, one of the best rock climbers in the animal world, inhabit the most rugged and rocky terrain. Special adaptations allow them to thrive in this harsh environment. For example, their hooves act as "suction cups" that enable them to climb places where an experienced mountain climber would not dare to venture without a rope, and their white fur, conspicuous in summer, serves as excellent camouflage and insulation in the snow that covers these areas much of the year.

Wolves once ranged throughout nearly all of Idaho, but today they are only found in a few remaining isolated areas. Because of their decline and the small numbers of wolves remaining in Idaho and throughout the northern Rocky Mountains, the gray wolf has been classified as an endangered species.

Researchers in the mid-1980's estimate that there are less than 15 wolves remaining in central Idaho today. Unlike the wolves in Alaska and Canada who travel and hunt in packs, the wolves here have been seen primarily alone or in pairs, probably due to their low numbers, Elk, mule deer, and white-tail deer are their primary food, while Columbian ground squirrels, beavers, snowshoe hares, and grouse serve as alternate prey.

WILDERNESS DO'S AND DON'TS

The purpose of Wilderness, as stated in the Wilderness Act, is "to assure that an increasing population, accompanied by expanding settlement and growing mechanization, does not occupy and modify all areas within the United States." Further, land management agencies are charged with administering Wilderness "for the use and enjoyment of American people in such a manner as will leave them unimpaired for future use and enjoyment as Wilderness and to provide for the protection of these areas and the preservation of their Wilderness character."

WHAT'S ALLOWED IN THE WILDERNESS:
· River Running on the Salmon, Middle fork of the Salmon, and the Selway River systems under a permit system.
· Dayhiking, backpacking, and ski touring, with a maximum party size of 20.
· Horse riding and horse packing, with some restrictions on party size, camp location, and use of forage.
· Hunting and fishing under State regulations.
· Commercial guides and outfitters authorized by special use permits.
· Mining and prospecting for cobalt and related minerals in special mining zones, subject to certain restrictions.
· Jet boats on the Salmon and Snake.
· Continued use of established airfields.
· Access to private land.
· Reasonable access to valid mining claims or occupancies.
· Grazing of domestic livestock under permit.

WHAT'S NOT ALLOWED IN THE WILDERNESS:
· Timber harvesting.
· New permanent or temporary roads and new landing strips.
· Motorized or mechanized transport of any kind, including mountain bicycles, hang gliders, and wheeled carts (e.g. game carriers or wheelbarrows).
· Motorboats (except on sections of the Salmon and Snake Rivers).
· Dredge or placer mining in the Salmon, Middle Fork, and tributaries of the Middle Fork.
· Prospecting for minerals (except in the special mining zone).
· New permanent structures or installations.   (Existing structures may be maintained for administrative or historic purposes.)
· Commercial enterprises (other than guides and outfitters).

INSIGHT INTO LOCALS

Generally, you're not going to run into many locals in the Idaho Backcountry other than a few Forest Services employees, who thanks to our civil service selection program, aren't from Idaho anyway. Where do you find a local? What is a local?

Relax, they're out there. But they may not look like you would imagine. They often wear baseball caps with CAT across the front and bill facing forward. It's the tourists that wear the cowboy hats and new Justin boots. These are working men. They spend their days working in the woods as sawyers, undergound in hardrock gold mines, or on horseback wrangling cattle, or running jet boats on Idaho's whitewater, while their nights are spent in saloons unwinding from the day's hard toil. Some are educated, some aren't. Some are on a lam from the law. These are the same people that settled the west a hundred years ago...strong, hard working, independent people with little concern for the "outside" world.

DEMOGRAPHICS AND THE ZEN OF FLY-FISHING

A fish does not rate particularly high on the ladder of animal I.Q. · I would rate it somewhere down there with amoebas and doberman pincers. But unlike doberman pincers, fish make up for their lack of gray matter by relying extensively on instinct. Fish seem to be scared of everything while doberman aren't scared of anything.

I usually figure a fish will tolerate maybe three perfect casts before it will dart for cover. Then it zips its lips and refuses to eat even the most tasty morsel. Not a problem? You always make perfect casts? Well, they don't like shadows, either. Nor do they like vibrations from foot steps on the bank, nor loud noises. There are times when they can be boiling the water in a feeding frenzy...until you perfectly cast a size 22 when they have been feeding on only size 24's, and spook them into a mad fish dart as they zip their lips.

Fish are used to being picked on. Everything from otters, to birds, to bears, to homo sapiens has enjoyed catching and eating fish since day one. Since trout don't have the smarts to hold a summit conference and discuss their national defense, they boost their individual defense instinct to an incredible level.

Where is all this leading? Simple. Let's say I have spotted a hole in the river that I believe to hold a trout. I sit and watch...and soon spot little slurps at the head of the hole as a lunker sucks in passing midges. I quietly crawl on my hands and knees to the streams edge, trying my best not to spook this trophy. My concentration level rises to a point that I tune all other distractions out. It's me and you fish...let's get it on! My smarts against his instincts.

The first cast, gently placed three feet upstream from the fish, is politely ignored. I cast again, the same spot, and the water breaks free as the glistening red side of the rainbow rolls, short of my fly. Tension mounts. Will he give me one more chance or has he disappeared for the day?

As I prepare for what I expect will be my final cast, my concentration is interrupted as a rock from the far bank rolls into the river.

"Howdy", exclaims Gomer as he boisterously slides down the embankment followed by two wild eyed Munchkins. "How's fishin'?" he yells, as he and his two little disease carriers begin casting hardware in "my" hole.

"Just leaving", I say with as much politeness as I can muster. Fishing, more specifically fly-fishing, is a personal thing. It is not a group sport. Fly-fishing involves an understanding and appreciation of nature as well as the metaphysical. Norman Maclean, in *A River Runs Through It*, describes this peculiar synthesis as follows: "In our family, there was no clear line between religion and fly fishing. We lived at the junction of great trout waters in western Montana, and our father was a Presbyterian minister and a fly fisherman who tied his own flies and taught others. He told us about Christ's disciples being fishermen, and we were left to assume, as my brother and I did, that all first class fishermen on the Sea of Galilee were fly fishermen and that John, the favorite, was a dry-fly fisherman."

The urbanization of America has created a sociological quirk in human nature. Those individuals who have been living in relatively close proximity to one another (i.e. urban dwelling) have gone from being moderately gregarious to emphatically gregarious. This urbanized American is now uncomfortable in the absence of other people. And this is where conflicts between "locals" and "outsiders" arises.

While the "local" fellow derives pleasure and relaxation from his solitude while fishing, the "outsider" wants to go fishing with someone - they want to make a social event out of the affair.

The "local" will make a point of setting up his camp in an isolated private location, while the "outsider" will seek out an existing camp to pitch their tent nearby.

The "local" will pick a remote airstrip to enjoy a few days of tranquility while the "outsider" feels more comfortable in an group fly-in camp.

Don't get me wrong. I am not expounding the virtues of being either a "local" or an "outsider", and I am not sure that one life style is any better than the other. I am simply trying to give visitors a little insight into the Idaho people, much like I would appreciate a demographic briefing while visiting New York or Los Angeles.

I do not mean to imply that Idaho folks are unfriendly. Quite the contrary, they are generally the most outgoing, friendly people you will ever meet. But they have different space requirements than city folks.

If you spot a lone camp, don't ask the occupants if you can camp next to them, because they will probably yes, but would have preferred to say no.

Let them offer the space to you if they like.

The same is true of fishing. If you see someone fishing, keep your distance. It's not only their space you're intruding upon but also the space of the fish they are concentrating on. Don't ask to fish the same hole, as the polite "local" will obligingly say yes, but you will probably, unknowingly, have ruined his day. If he wants to share "his" hole with you, he will invite you. Leapfrog a good 1/4 mile up or downstream, out of sight, and maybe you will come to learn the "local's" appreciation for larger spaces.

We are blessed, here in Idaho, with an abundance of pure mountain streams thriving with trout. Take advantage of these larger spaces and when you discover your own special little section of stream, where you and the trout begin to understand each other, you are on the road to becoming a real fly-fisherman...and will also have gained some personal insight into the native population. Believe me, you'll know it when it happens!

AIRPLANE CAMPING

Its a strange human phenomenon that leads us from our warm shelters with electricity, cooking facilities, hot showers, comfortable beds, refrigeration, satellite TV, and hot tubs to move outdoors and leave all these wonderful conveniences behind. But it happens. Camping is one of America's favorite pastimes. And the airplane is the magic carpet that can lead to the country's finest camping opportunities.

People airplane camp for different reasons. While some consider it a challenge to make their camp as comfortable as their home with the use of generators, portable TV's, king size air mattresses, and fully stocked bars complete with blenders, others prefer the simplicity of primitive camping where creature comforts are limited to ones ingenuity.

Some people enjoy the camaraderie and social aspects of group camping while others seek the solitude of the Backcountry to escape the rigors of urban living. It is here that conflicts arise. While it is great fun to turn up the music and party into the night, it may not be the camping experience your neighbor was looking for. A little common courtesy and respect for the wilderness experience your neighbor might be seeking will make airplane camping pleasant for everyone.

Use *Fly Idaho!* to choose an airstrip that is compatible with what you are looking for in a camping experience. Obviously, don't expect the same level of peace and solitude at Johnson Creek that you may find at Bernard.

One of my pet peeves, while airplane camping, is the Gomer that gets up before sunrise (while frost is still on the wings) and fires up "old wonder bird". He insists on idling his engine until the defroster clears the windscreen and then taxis to the departure end where he faithfully runs the engine up and cycles the prop and then waits for the engine oil temperature to come up to normal before takeoff. The early morning air is so nice, Gomer decides it is a great time to practice his takeoffs and landings.

Meanwhile, every other camper is now wide awake. Two tents were blown over by the prop wash, a cloud of dust hangs over the camp from Gomer cycling his prop, (which now looks like it came off a tug boat going through a gravel bar), and watch out because here he comes to do it all again!

Plan an early morning flight the night before by parking your airplane where the early morning sun will hit it first. So while you are catching a few extra z-z-z's, you are utilizing free solar energy to preheat and deice "old wonder bird".

Now that you can see out the windscreen, preflight the airplane and start the engine (familiarize yourself with cold weather starting procedure). Taxi to takeoff. Use the lowest power setting possible to start the airplane moving, and then feed it in as necessary to keep rolling. This will do more to prevent rock damage to your prop than anything else.

If after years of having it drummed into you that you must cycle your prop before takeoff, do it while taxiing to takeoff. When you reach the end of the runway, your preflight should be done - make your departure call and take off.

What about my oil temperature? It's your oil pressure that you should be concerned with. The oil temperature will come up to normal in a short time in the air but idling on the ground won't do anything for you but create grumbling around the campfire.

But what about a few touch and go's? Don't even consider it. If it was that important to you to leave before sunup, don't come back and harass the late risers. The Mountain Backcountry is not the place to practice touch and go's. There are some excellent airstrips in the Desert Backcountry that one can practice touch and go's to their heart's content without disturbing anyone.

DERIVATION OF RELATIVE HAZARD INDEX

RELATIVE HAZARD INDEX (RHI) NUMBER

The RHI is a relative composite number with which current known physical hazards of airstrips can be compared. The purpose of the RHI number, as is the purpose of this book, is to give the pilot as much objective advance information about the airstrip as possible. Short final is not the place to realize you are in over your head.

As is true throughout aviation, the pilot has sole responsibility for his own safety. The RHI is simply one of several tools with which a pilot may use to factor in his go/no-go decisions.

The RHI does not take into consideration variable factors such as AIRCRAFT PERFORMANCE and CAPABILITIES (including STOL, turbocharging, type of landing gear, power/load ratios), PILOT PROFICIENCY (experience in high density altitudes, short/soft field techniques, currency in aircraft being flown - not type, mountain flying experience, and proficiency in non-standard patterns/approaches), nor POTENTIAL RISKS or VARIABLES (such as weather/wind, heavy traffic, lack of communication for emergency help, and threat of large animal collisions). The RHI only takes into consideration current known physical hazards.

RHI DERIVATION - As mentioned previously, the RHI is derived from three composite numbers.

The first composite number deals with current known hazards in the AIRPORT ENVIRONMENT (AE number). The AE number factors in the runway length, airport elevation, and the proximity to mountainous terrain exceeding 1000'.

The second composite number deals with the APPROACH/DEPARTURE ENVIRONMENT (A/D number). The A/D number factors in abrupt turns required on final, non-standard patterns, obstacles greater than 50 feet on approach, airstrip not being visible on 1/2 mile approach, over water approach, no go-around from landing flare, approach runway selection dictated by terrain not wind, abrupt turn required on departure, runway end not visible on departure, departure over an abrupt dropoff, and departure runway selection dictated by terrain not wind.

The third composite number deals with the current known RUNWAY SURFACE HAZARDS (RSH number). The RSH number factors in: runway markings, windsock, overgrown vegetation, loose gravel, soft sand, mud, erosion, standing water, surface deterioration due to large or small animals, dog legs, bumps, dips, adverse gradients, and others.

WHAT DOES ALL THIS MEAN TO ME? The Pilot's Experience and Proficiency (PEP) in the specific aircraft being flown plus the Aircraft Performance and Capabilities (APC) must exceed the RHI number plus the Variables (V). For those with a mathematical persuasion this can be expressed as:

$$PEP + APC > RHI + V \quad or \quad PEP + APC > (AE + A/D + RSH) + V$$

In summation, this means that if you as a pilot fly an airplane and get in over your head, your are going to be in Deep Do Do (DDD), and if your wife is along you will be in Real Deep Do Do (RDDD).

or: **You = DDD** or worse: **You = RDDD**

No real revelations here!

I-24

OK, OK! HOW DO I USE THE RHI (to stay out of DDD)? Let's say that you have been coming to Idaho for several years and airplane camping at Johnson Creek and that you are intimately familiar with your airplane and are current. Johnson Creek has an RHI of 14. Unfortunately, familiarity breeds contempt. Johnson Creek has become old hat and you are looking for a new adventure. You look over the RHI table and see that Big Creek has an RHI in the same range.

DOES THIS MEAN THAT IF I'VE BEEN FLYING INTO JOHNSON CREEK, I CAN SUCCESSFULLY FLY INTO BIG CREEK? Wait - not so fast! Not necessarily. Remember that the RHI is a composite of three numbers. Review the composite numbers to make sure you are not exceeding the capabilities of either you or your airplane in either the airport environment, approach/departure environment, or hazards on the runway surface. You must also take into consideration the Variables.

This is where you the pilot comes in. When calculating the Variables, take into consideration density altitude, wind conditions, incoming weather, moose on the runway, hangovers, and probably the biggest bugaboo - the FIRST time you have been there. The Variables list will change from day to day, hour to hour, and pilot to pilot. Only you can come up with this rating for yourself. And indeed, an inaccurate assessment of the Variables quite often leads to DDD.

DOES THIS MEAN THAT I SHOULD NEVER GO TO AN AIRSTRIP THAT HAS A HIGHER RHI THAN I AM USED TO? No, thank goodness, or Johnson Creek would become even more popular than it already is. You need to set personal thresholds for different actions.

For instance: I fly a Cessna 182 about 300 hours a year, most of it in the backcountry. My personal comfort level, taking into consideration low Variables, is an RHI of about the mid RHI-20's. In the high RHI-20's and low RHI-30's, I always take a professional local pilot with me on the first and sometimes second trip to familiarize myself with the approach. (It's the cheapest insurance money can buy.)

I currently don't have the airplane or the experience to attempt anything above about RHI-32. Nor am I willing to risk the damage to my airplane (or me) in landing at some of these more difficult strips. That could change as I progress to different airplanes and gain experience. Again, it's up to you to set your own thresholds of risk.

I'VE NEVER LANDED AT ANY OF THE STRIPS LISTED. HOW DO I COMPARE THE RHI NUMBERS WITH SOMETHING I AM FAMILIAR WITH? The RHI work sheet is listed in the appendix. I would suggest filling out an RHI Worksheet for an airstrip you are familiar with and using that RHI for comparison purposes.

I AM A 5000 HOUR PILOT AND I BENT MY PLANE ON AN RHI-4, WHAT GIVES? Many pilots get their training in environments much different from the Idaho

Backcountry. Without exception, all the strips listed in this book are unpaved and often unimproved airstrips. I have known CFII's and ATP's that have never landed off pavement. It's a different world.

The short field/soft field takeoffs and landings that are taught for the Private ticket are usually taught from the end of a 6000' paved runway. Good information...but it has limited application in the real world. If you are planning a trip to the Idaho Backcountry, and have not had recent experience in soft/short fields, get some training before you come.

The RHI numbers are relative numbers, not absolute numbers. An RHI-4 may give an impression of a strip that you could land on with your eyes closed. Not so. When applying the RHI rating system to public paved airports in Idaho, I have yet to find one that rated above a zero. Again, it doesn't mean that all paved public strips in Idaho are no-brainers, it simply means that the RHI rating system doesn't really apply to them, and that all of the strips listed in this book have current known hazards associated with them.

I'M AN ALASKA BUSH PILOT AND I THINK THIS RHI BUSINESS IS A LOT OF HOGWASH. Believe me, I know there are a lot of very skilled pilots out there and I have the utmost respect for them. The RHI rating system was not designed to intimidate pilots but simply to list current known hazards.

The flying skills needed in the Alaska Bush are differet from those needed in the Idaho Backcountry, or for that matter, the Los Angeles Basin. One type of flying is not necessarily more difficult than another but rather just different. Use the RHI as one of your tools to fly informed and fly safely.

I LANDED AT AN RHI-13 AND THOUGHT IT WAS MORE DIFFICULT THAN AN RHI-17. WHAT GIVES? Good for you! You have begun to develop your own personal RHI based upon your own experiences. Remember, the RHI was developed using current known existing hazards. Unfortunately, some of that information changes with the current conditions. (e.g. rodent activity, erosion, standing water on the runway, etc.). Mark up the book with your own RHI and notes.

APPENDIX

RHI WORKSHEET

Airport name:_____

AIRPORT ENVIORNMENT (AE)

RUNWAY LENGTH, choose 1:

	< 1000'	5
1000'	- 2000'	4
2000'	- 3000'	3
3000'	- 4000'	2
4000'	- 5000'	1
		subtotal_____

AIRPORT ELEVATION, choose 1:

	>7000'	5
6000'	- 7000'	4
5000'	- 6000'	3
4000'	- 5000'	2
3000'	- 4000'	1
		subtotal _____

MOUNTAIN PROXIMITY, choose 1:
(mountain defined as terrain exceeding 1000' above runway)

	< 1 mi.	5
1 mi.	- 3 mi.	3
3 mi.	- 5 mi.	1
		subtotal _____

AIRPORT ENVIORNMENT TOTAL (AE) _____*

Continued on back.

APPROACH/DEPARTURE ENVIRONMENT (A/D)

APPROACH, choose all that apply

abrupt turn req. on final .... 5_____

non-standard pattern required .... 3_____

airstrip not visible on 1/2 mile final .... 4_____

>50' obstacle on final .... 4_____

approach over water .... 3_____

no go around from flare .... 3_____

RWY selection dictated by terrain not wind .... 2_____

DEPARTURE, choose all that apply

abrupt turn req. on departure .... 5_____

end of runway not visible .... 1_____

departure over abrupt dropoff .... 2_____

RWY selection dictated by terrain not wind .... 2_____

APPROACH/DEPARTURE SUBTOTAL A/D) _____*

RUNWAY SURFACE HAZARDS (RSH)
(choose all that apply)

no runway markings .... 2_____

no windsock .... 2_____

overgrown grass .... 1_____

loose gravel .... 1_____

soft sand .... 2_____

mud   .... 2_____

deep erosion/water on runwater .... 2_____

deterioration due to rodents or large animals .... 1_____

dog leg   .... 1_____

bumps (1 pt. for each bump) @ .... 1_____

dips (1 pt. for each dip) @ .... 1_____

adverse gradient

(rwy runs uphill for takeoff or downhill for landing) .... 2_____

other   .... _____

RUNWAY SURFACE HAZARDS (RSH) TOTAL _____*

RHI = AE + A/D + RSH = total of * numbers _____

RHI AIRSTRIP LIST

RHI	AE-A/D-RSH	AIRPORT NAME	RHI	AE-A/D-RSH	AIRPORT NAME
3	01-00-02	Priest Lake	15	07-04-04	Lord Flat
4	03-00-01	Smith's Prairie	15	08-04-03	Sulphur Creek
4	03-00-01	Murphy Hot Springs	15	08-06-01	Indian Creek
5	02-03-00	Cavanaugh Bay	17	09-07-01	Warren
6	05-00-01	Magic Reservoir	18	08-03-07	Orogrande
6	05-00-01	Midway	18	08-04-06	Cayuse Creek
6	05-00-01	Bear Trap	18	09-06-03	Mackay Bar
6	06-00-00	Fairfield	19	07-12-00	Dixie USFS
7	05-00-02	Laidlaw Corrals	19	11-07-01	Atlanta
7	06-00-01	Grasmere	20	10-07-03	Weatherby
7	06-00-01	Cox's Well	20	11-04-05	Graham
7	06-00-01	Big Southern Butte	20	11-05-04	Cold Meadows
7	06-00-01	Stanley	21	10-10-01	Deadwood
7	06-00-01	Garden Valley	22	10-10-02	Bernard
7	06-00-01	Idaho City	22	10-12-00	Krassel
7	07-00-00	Smiley Creek	22	11-10-01	Upper Loon Creek
7	07-00-00	Antelope Valley	24	06-18-00	Moose Creek
8	06-00-02	Hollow Top	24	10-12-02	Thomas Creek
8	07-00-01	Copper Basin	26	11-10-05	Dixie Town
9	08-00-01	Warm Springs	26	11-10-05	Fish Lake
9	08-00-01	Henrys Lake	27	07-13-07	Dug Bar
9	08-00-01	Bruce Meadows	27	10-08-09	Pittsburg
10	03-06-01	Slate Creek	28	08-15-05	Shearer
10	06-02-02	Memaloose	28	09-11-08	Big Bar
10	09-00-01	Landmark	28	10-15-03	Mahoney Creek
11	08-00-03	Twin Bridges	28	11-13-04	Cabin Creek
12	07-03-02	Chamberlain	31	10-11-10	Salmon Bar
12	07-04-01	Magee	32	11-12-09	Soldier Bar
12	08-03-01	Pine	36	11-17-08	Vines
13	06-00-07	Elk City	37	13-14-10	Simonds
13	07-06-00	Flying B	42	12-25-05	Lower Loon
14	08-05-01	Big Creek	47	13-27-07	Dewey Moore
14	09-05-00	Johnson Creek	50	14-18-18	Mile Hi

AIR TAXIES SERVING THE IDAHO BACKCOUNTRY

BOISE, ID.
S.P. Aircraft
3180 Airport Way, Boise, Idaho 83705
(208)383-3323

Sawtooth Flying Service, Inc.
3815 Rickenbacker, Boise, Idaho
(208)342-7888

CASCADE, ID.
Arnold Aviation
Box 1094, Cascade, Idaho 83611
(208)382-4844

CHALLIS, ID.
Bob's Aircraft, Inc.
Box 525, Challis, Idaho 83226
(208)879-2364

GRANGEVILLE, ID.
Grangeville Air Service
Box 369, Grangeville, Idaho 82530
(208)983-0490

HAILEY, ID.
Pere-Air
Box 2025, Hailey, Idaho 83333
(208)788-9134

Sun Valley Aviation
Box 1085, Hailey, Idaho 83333
(208)788-9511

HAMILTON, MT.
North Star Aviation
Box 1264, Hamilton, Montana
(406)363-6471

LEWISTON, ID.
Hillcrest Aircraft Company
Box 504, Lewiston, Idaho 83501
(208)746-8271

McCALL, ID.
McCall & Wilderness Air
Box 771, McCall, Idaho 83638
(208)634-7137

Pioneer Aviation
Box 1983, McCall, Idaho 83638
(208)634-7127

NAMPA, ID.
Rocky Mountain
101 Municipal Drive, Nampa, Idaho
83687
(208)465-2249

SALMON, ID.
Salmon Air Taxi
Box 698, Salmon, Idaho 83467
(208)756-6211

STANLEY, ID.
Stanley Air Taxi
Box 30, Stanley, Idaho 85278
(208)774-2276

KOCH CHART

MODIFIED KOCH CHART FOR
ALTITUDE AND TEMPERATURE EFFECTS

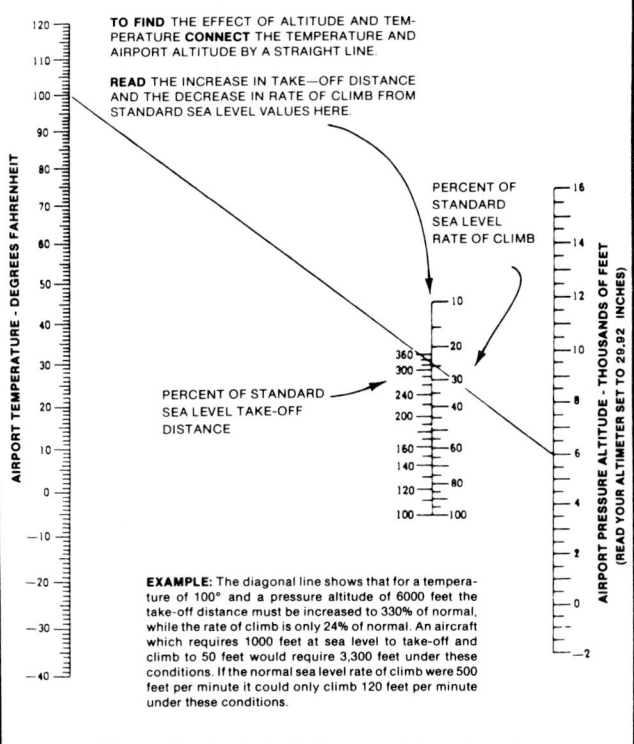

TO FIND THE EFFECT OF ALTITUDE AND TEMPERATURE **CONNECT** THE TEMPERATURE AND AIRPORT ALTITUDE BY A STRAIGHT LINE.

READ THE INCREASE IN TAKE—OFF DISTANCE AND THE DECREASE IN RATE OF CLIMB FROM STANDARD SEA LEVEL VALUES HERE.

PERCENT OF STANDARD SEA LEVEL RATE OF CLIMB

PERCENT OF STANDARD SEA LEVEL TAKE-OFF DISTANCE

AIRPORT TEMPERATURE - DEGREES FAHRENHEIT

AIRPORT PRESSURE ALTITUDE - THOUSANDS OF FEET
(READ YOUR ALTIMETER SET TO 29.92 INCHES)

EXAMPLE: The diagonal line shows that for a temperature of 100° and a pressure altitude of 6000 feet the take-off distance must be increased to 330% of normal, while the rate of climb is only 24% of normal. An aircraft which requires 1000 feet at sea level to take-off and climb to 50 feet would require 3,300 feet under these conditions. If the normal sea level rate of climb were 500 feet per minute it could only climb 120 feet per minute under these conditions.

This chart indicates typical representative values for "personal" airplanes.

For exact values consult your airplane flight manual.

The chart may be conservative for airplanes with supercharged engines.

Also remember that long grass, sand, mud or deep snow can easily double your take-off distance.

CROSSWIND COMPONENT CHART

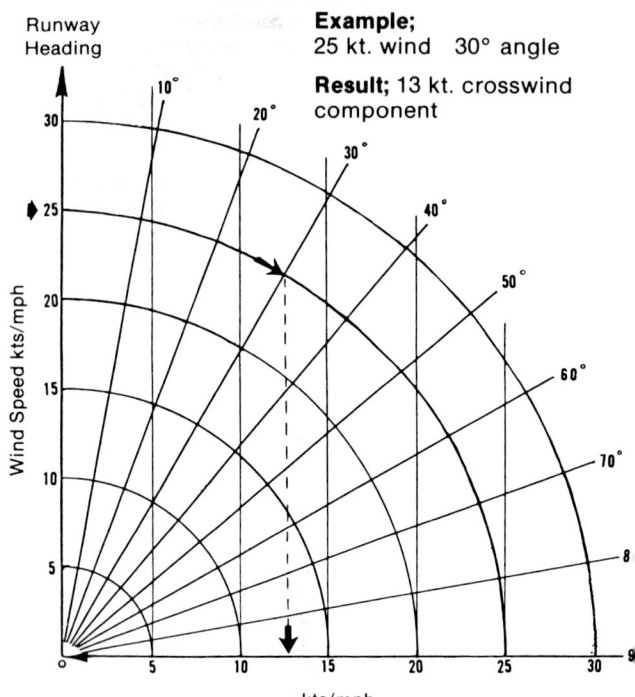

Example;
25 kt. wind 30° angle

Result; 13 kt. crosswind component

Runway Heading

Wind Speed kts/mph

kts/mph

Instructions For Use

The crosswind component chart is very useful and handy for ready reference. To use the Chart you must know runway heading, surface wind velocity and direction, and the maximum crosswind component allowed for the aircraft you are operating. Whenever wind conditions are gusty, it is suggested that the peak value be applied, and when wind direction is variable apply the greatest angle. Enter the chart at the wind speed scale, proceed to the right along the arc until it intersects the wind direction angle off the runway heading. At this point proceed straight down to the wind component scale and read the value. If the component is greater than that allowed for your aircraft, check for a runway that will offer less of a crosswind component, or land at a different airport where conditions will be more favorable.

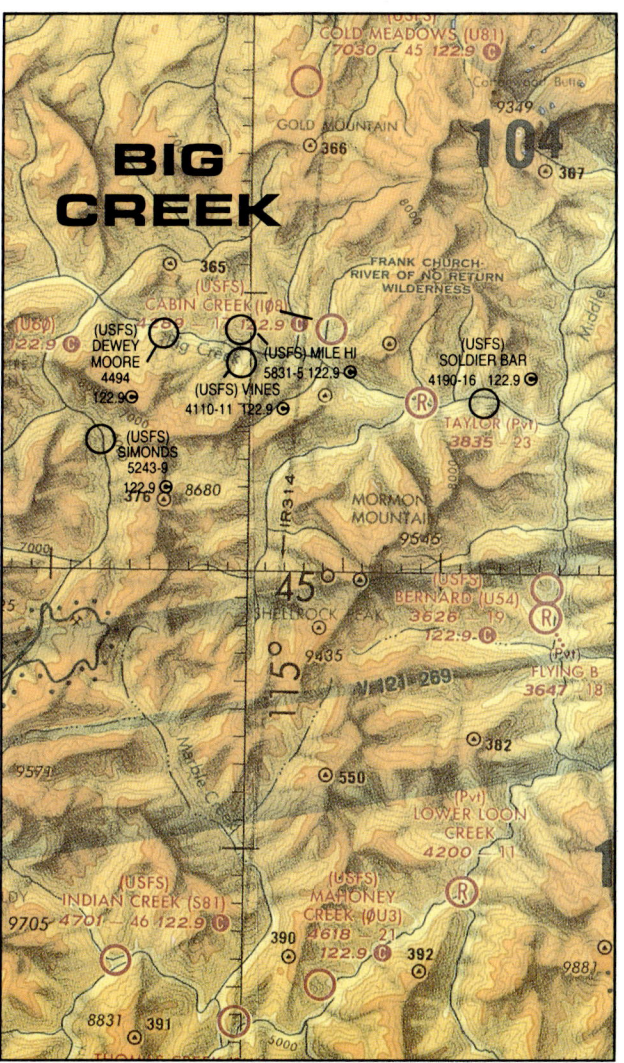

THIS CHART FOR INFORMATION ONLY AND NOT FOR NAVIGATION.

I-33

GOSPEL
HUMP

93

GOSPEL HUMP
WILDERNESS

Elk
City

ELK CITY (S90)
4097 – 26 122

(USFS)
OROGRANDE
4405-29
122.9

DIXIE TOWN
5600-30 122.9

(USFS)
DIXIE (IDØ5)
5148 – 45
122.9

Dixie

ranger station

THIS CHART FOR INFORMATION ONLY AND NOT FOR NAVIGATION.

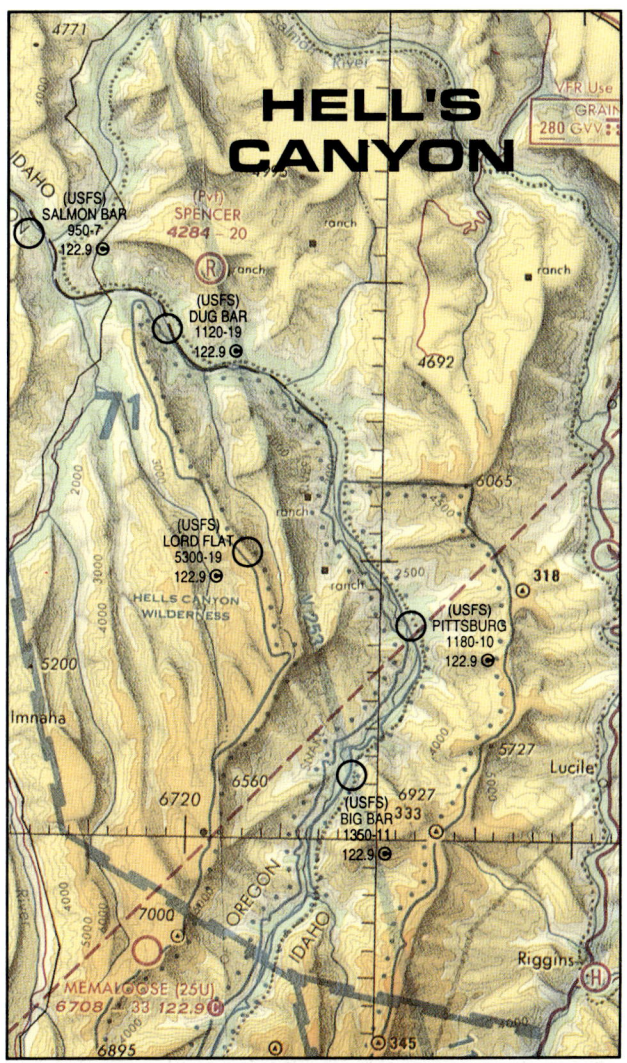

HELL'S CANYON

(USFS)
SALMON BAR
950-7
122.9 Ⓒ

(Pvt)
SPENCER
4284 - 20

Ⓡ

(USFS)
DUG BAR
1120-19
122.9 Ⓒ

(USFS)
LORD FLAT
5300-19
122.9 Ⓒ

HELLS CANYON
WILDERNESS

(USFS)
PITTSBURG
1180-10
122.9 Ⓒ

• 318

(USFS)
BIG BAR
1350-11
122.9 Ⓒ

6927
333

5727

Lucile

Riggins Ⓗ

MEMALOOSE (25U)
6708 33 122.9 Ⓒ

• 345

IDAHO

OREGON

IDAHO

Imnaha

4771

4692

5065

6720

6560

7000

6895

THIS CHART FOR INFORMATION ONLY AND NOT FOR NAVIGATION.

I-35

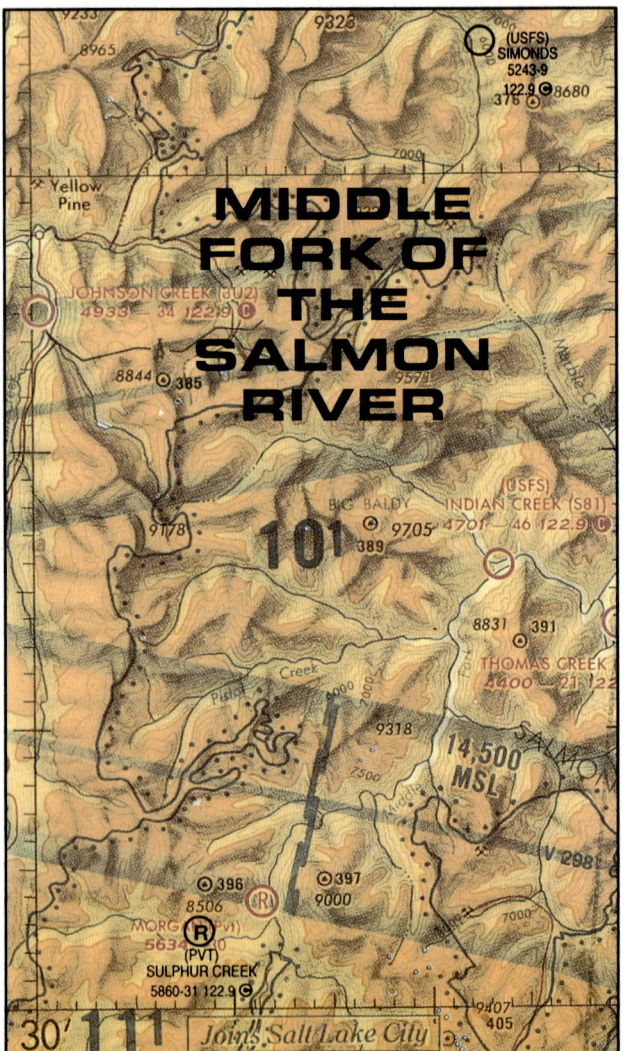

MIDDLE FORK OF THE SALMON RIVER

(USFS)
SIMONDS
5243-9
122.9
376

9233
8965
9323
8680

Yellow Pine

JOHNSON CREEK (3U2)
4933 - 34 1221.9

8844 385

9178

Marble C

9571

BIG BALDY
101 9705 389

(USFS)
INDIAN CREEK (S81)
4701 - 46 122.9

8831 391

THOMAS CREEK
4400 - 21 122

9318

14,500
MSL

SALM

Creek

Pistol

V 298

8506 396

397
9000

R

MORG (PVT)
5634- 0
(PVT)
SULPHUR CREEK
5860-31 122.9

2407
405

30' 111

Join Salt Lake City

BOOK REGISTRATION

   This guide was not designed for annual updates. However, as in any undertaking, errors do occur. A periodic errata update will be issued to correct navigational and airport data errors. (This does not include changes in telephone numbers, address, etc.). Please complete and return this card to receive **FREE** errata updates.

Name: _____

Street: _____

P.O. Box: _____ City: _____

State: _____ Zip: _____

Telephone: _____

Where did you purchase the book? _____

_____

Suggestions for improving *FLY IDAHO!* _____

_____

_____

_____

_____

REPORTING FORM

Please return this form to report any changes, errors, unreported hazards or conditions of the airstrips found in *FLY IDAHO!*

Name: _____

Street: _____

P.O. Box: _____ City: _____

State: _____ Zip: _____

Telephone: _____

Description: _____

_____

_____

_____

_____

THANK YOU!

Q.E.I. Publishing
Box 1236
Hailey, Idaho
83333

Q.E.I. Publishing
Box 1236
Hailey, Idaho
83333

ORDER/GIFT FORM

Please send _____ copies of *FLY IDAHO!* @ $39.95 each. I understand that I may return any books for a full refund-for any reason, no questions asked.

Send book/s to:

Name:_____

Address:_____

City:_____ State:_____ Zip:_____

Additional addresses for gifts:

Name:_____

Address:_____

City:_____ State:_____ Zip:_____

Name:_____

Address:_____

City:_____ State:_____ Zip:_____

Telephone orders: Call 1(800)574-9702 or (208)788-5176
Please have Visa or MasterCard ready. *Fax orders: (208)788-4621

Postal Orders: Q.E.I. Publishing, Box 1236, Hailey, ID 83333

Sales tax: Please add 5% for books shipped to Idaho addresses.

Shipping: Book Rate: $3.00 for the first book and 75 cents for each additional book to the same address. (Surface shipping may take three to four weeks.)
Air Mail: $4.75 per book.

Payment: ☐ Check   ☐ Visa   ☐ MasterCard

Card Number:

___:___:___:___:___:___:___:___:___:___:___:___:___:___:___:___

Name on Card: _____

Experiation Date: _____

Call TOLL FREE and ORDER NOW!